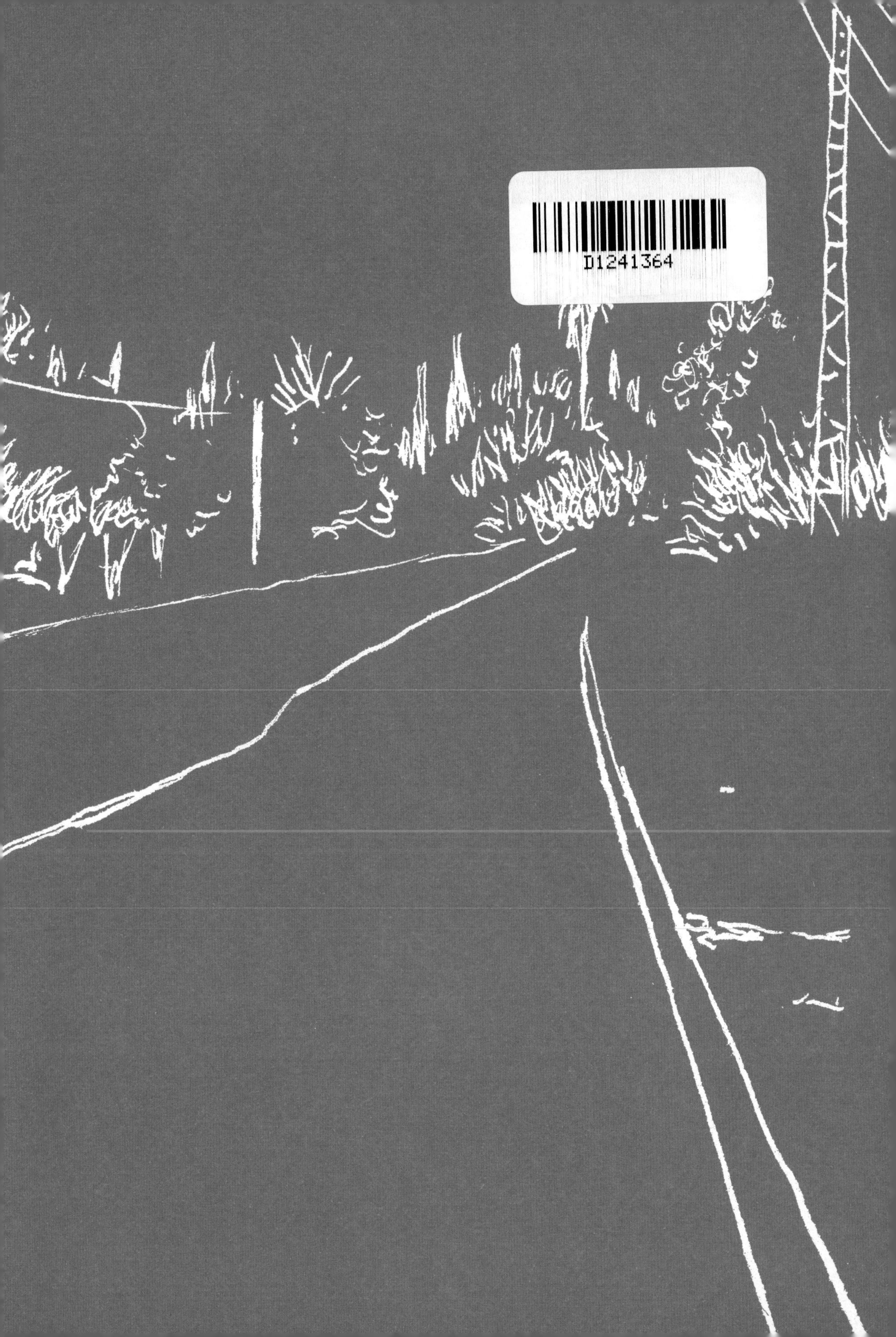

FARM 54

GALIT & GILAD SELIKTAR

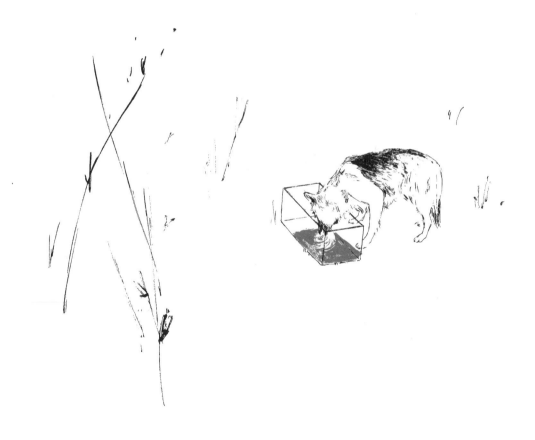

FANFARE · PONENT MON

The story "The Substitute Lifeguard" was first published in *Masmerim Literary Magazine* edited by Amir Rotem, Issue no.5, April 2007

The story "Houses" was first published in *MITA'AM – A Review of Literature and Radical Thought* edited by Yitzhak Laor, Issue no.10, June 2007

Special thank you:

To my wife Adi Seliktar, for believing and supporting me all along; her image and inspiration are inseparable from this book.

To my husband On Barak, for re-visiting *Farm 54* again and again with unlimited patience and love.

To Serge Ewenczyk, for believing in our vision and for helping bring our memories and dreams into *Ferme 54*.

Thank you to:

Dr. Dana Amir, Adi Assis, James Baldwin, Chen Barak, Dvora & Moshe Barak, Ayelet Barak & Ofir Nahum, Edna & Avi Bar-Or, Shely Bar-Or, Ben Bar-Or, Anne Beauchard, Dror Burstein, Joyce Camm, Helena Clare Wright, Anat Curiel, Seth Fishman, Liran Golod, Susan Harris, Anat Levin, Susan Lurie, Roni Mahadav, Susan Mahler, Gail Marcus, Mei-Tal Nadler, Ziv Nevo-Kulman, Yirmi Pinkus, Shirley & Lenny Queen, Marilyn Reader, Nina Schwartz, Rabbi Jeffrey Segelman, Oren Seliktar, Rani Shachar, Sharon, Roni & Tal Shachar, Sahar Shalev, Robin Shulman, Andrea Siegel, Colby Cedar Smith, Dr. Shira Stav, Nancy Thaul, Dr. Alan Tipermas, Moshe Tzadok, Rhona & Arthur Wexler, Arlene Wexler, Ortal Yaffe, Noa Yedlin

Translated from the Hebrew by **Ronen Altman Kaydar**

© **Farm 54**, 2011 – Galit Seliktar and Gilad Seliktar
Original title: Meshek 54
Design by Gilad Seliktar
Published 2011 by Ponent Mon Ltd.
Edited by Fanfare
Graphic adaptation by Ill Wind Tidings
ISBN : 978-1-908007-00-1
D.L.: B-13.316-2011
Printed and bound in Spain

To our parents, Hannah and Moni Seliktar

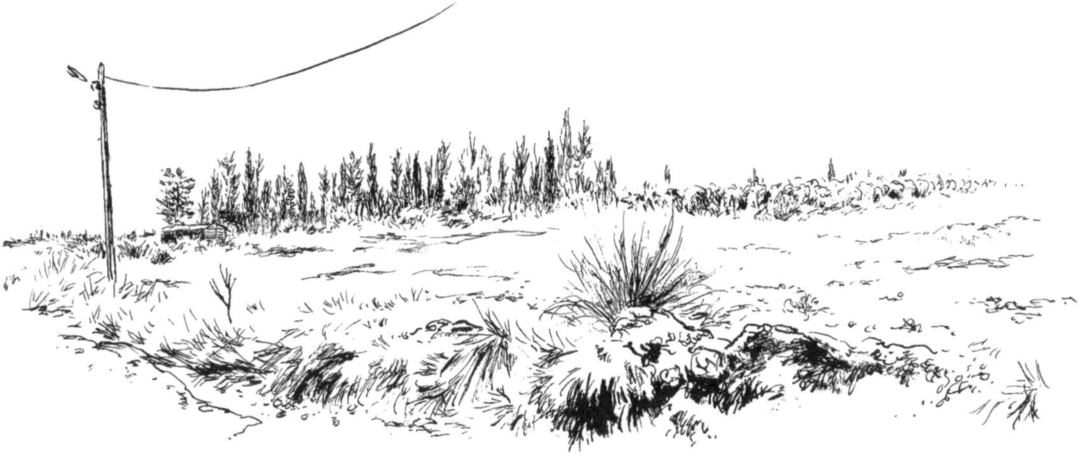

What day is it anyway?

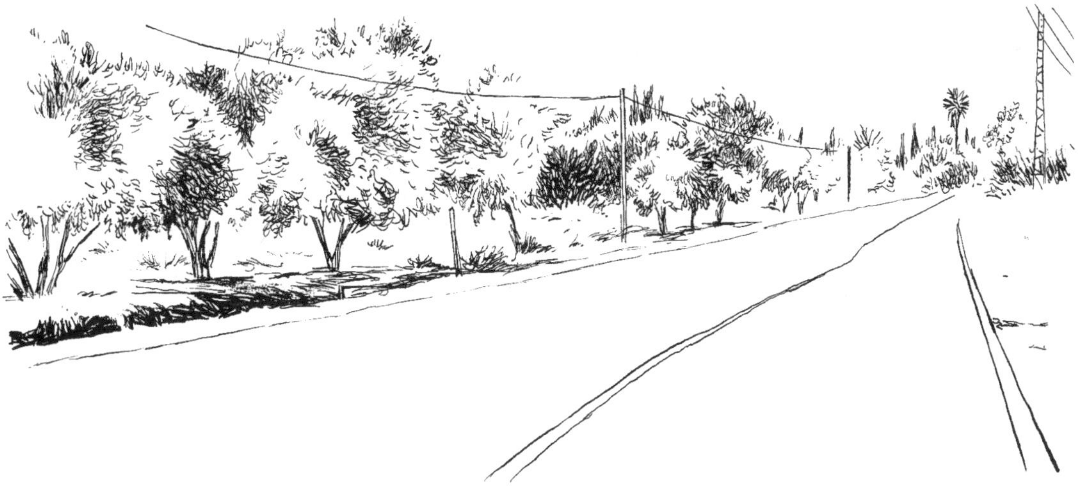

Amnon would always ask what day is it today.

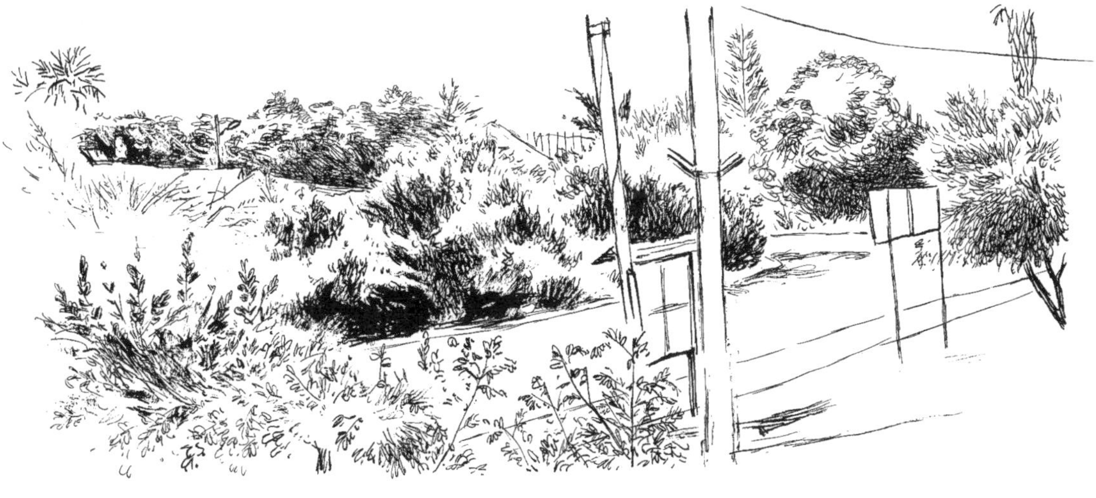

Mom would tell him today's Sunday Amnon, or Monday and so on.

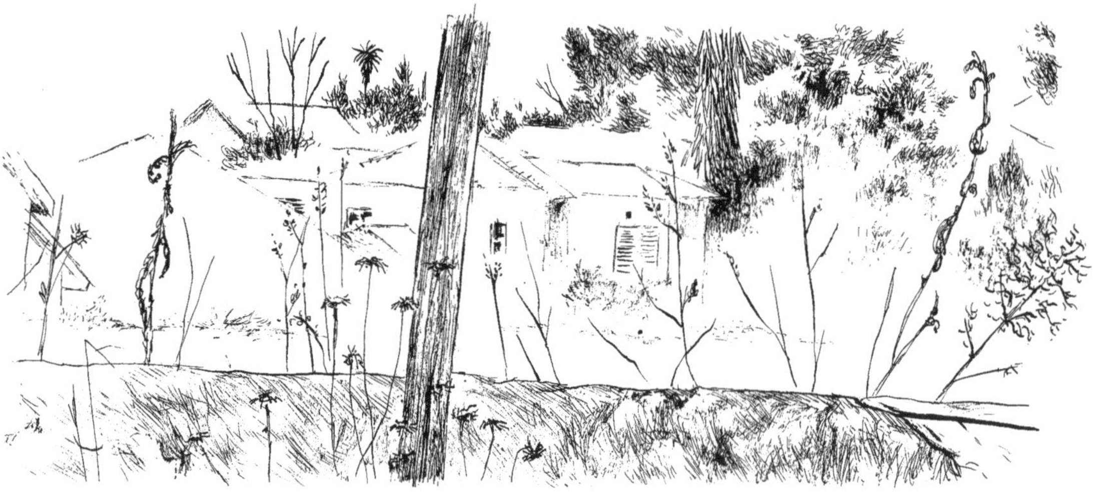

On Tuesdays Mom would say it's Tuesday, twice blessed.*

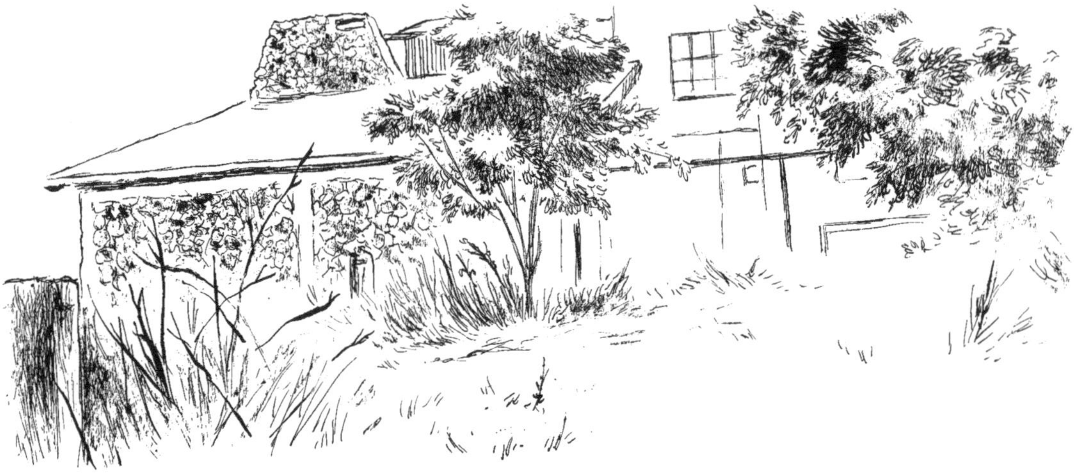

Amnon would laugh at the "twice blessed"

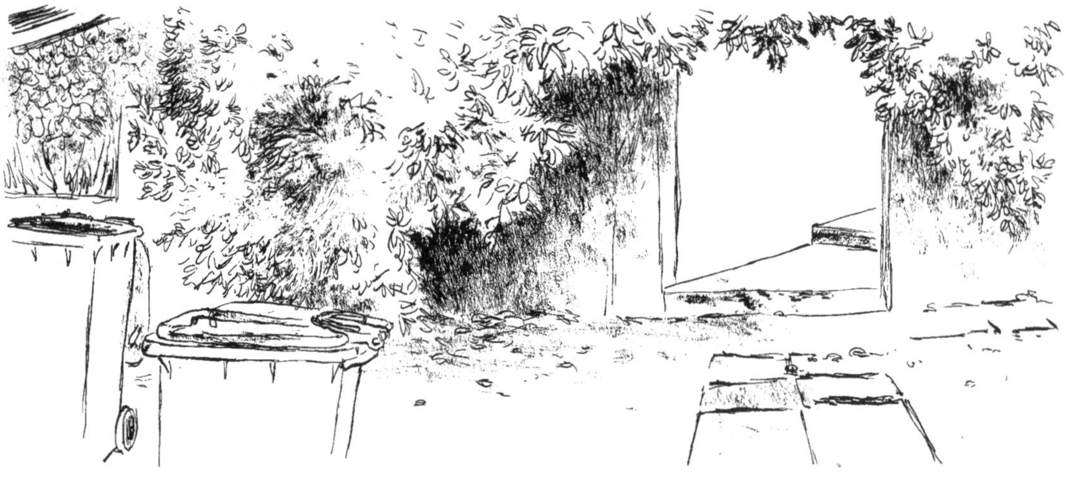

* According to Jewish tradition, on the third day God separated the seas to create land and then caused the land to produce vegetation and each time "God saw that this was good". Genesis I, 9-13.

and repeat to himself before bedtime, 'It's Tuesday, twice blessed'.

On Wednesdays Amnon would ask Mom to say it's Wednesday, twice blessed,

but Mom would only make Amnon laugh on Tuesdays.

THE SUBSTITUTE LIFEGUARD
1981

That hot Saturday the yard was full of guests.

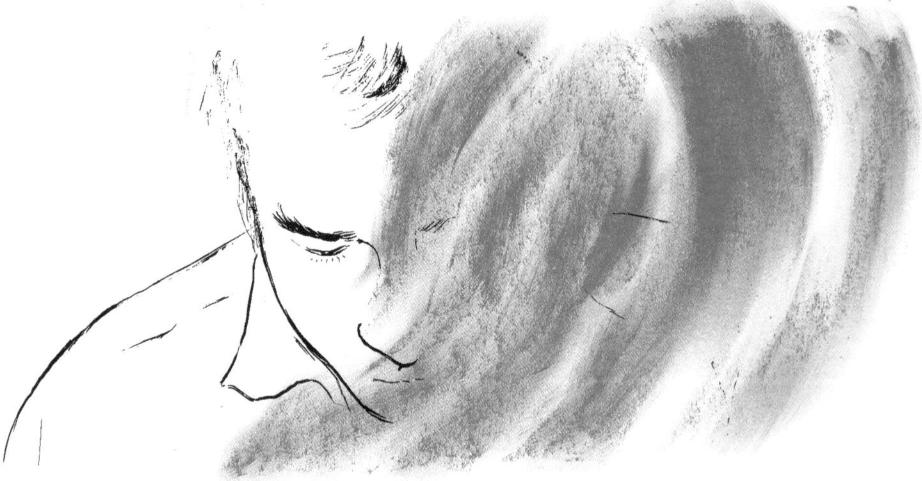

When we got our parents' permission, we jumped in the pool that used to be a manure pit.

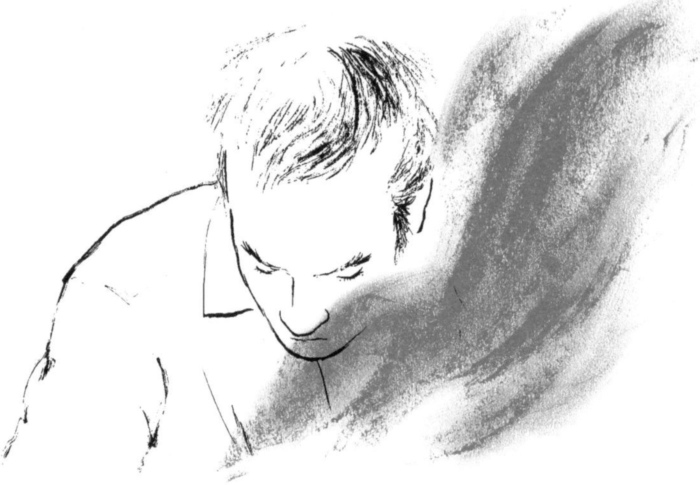

Though we were sad every time Dad told the story of the calf that died in the big frost of '73, we were a little happy too

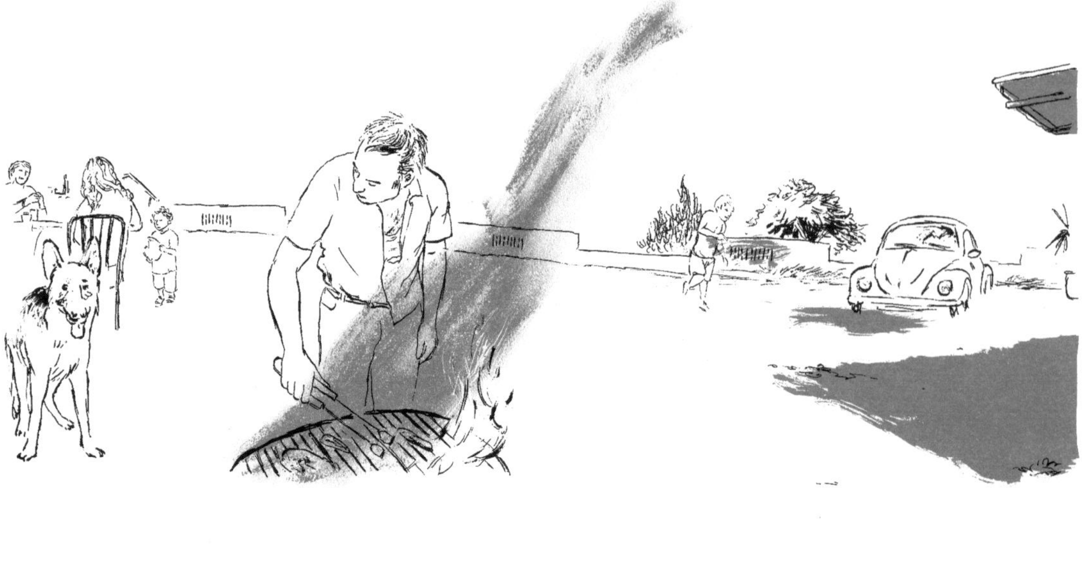

'cause if that calf had lived and kept shitting in that pit, we'd have had to go to the public pool, which was crowded and full of warm kiddy pee.

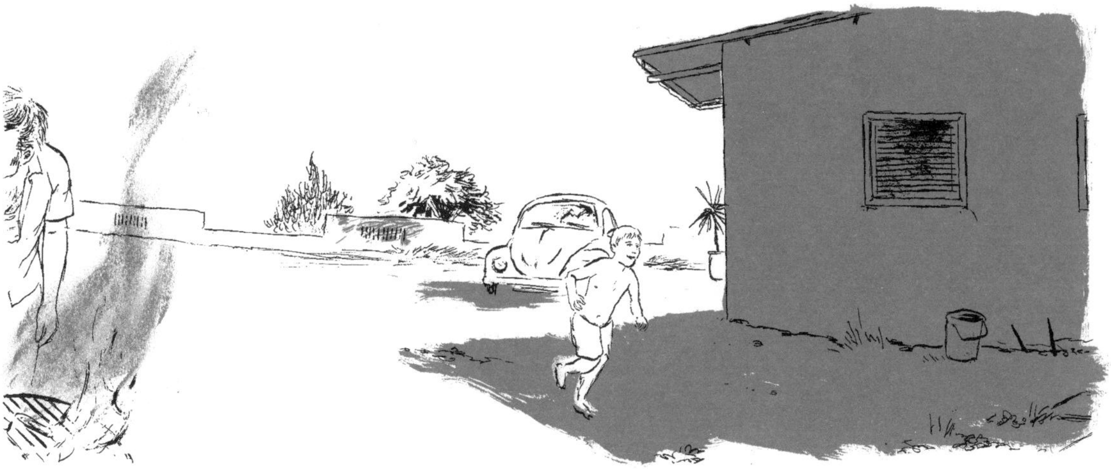

But I went there with Smadar from time to time anyway

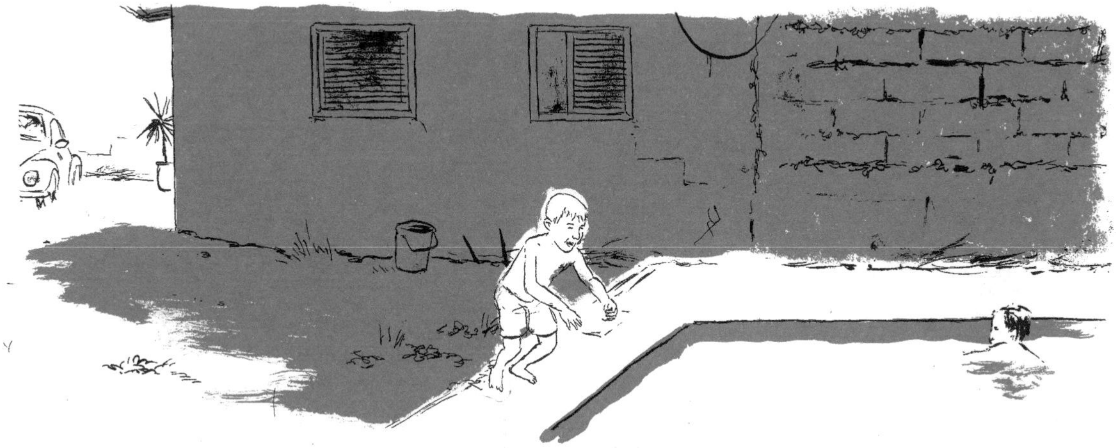

because of the substitute lifeguard.

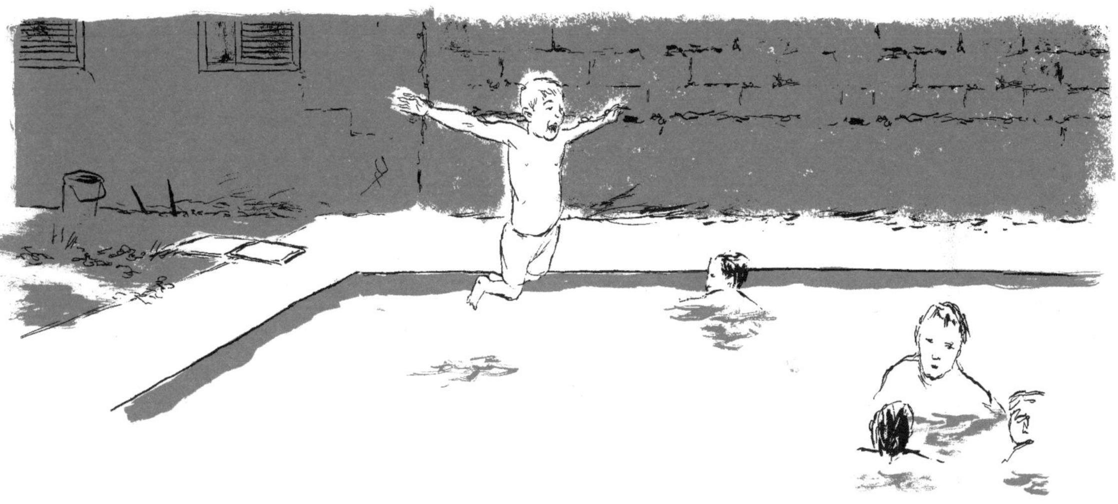

At noon, Dror came by and asked me once again to be his girlfriend.

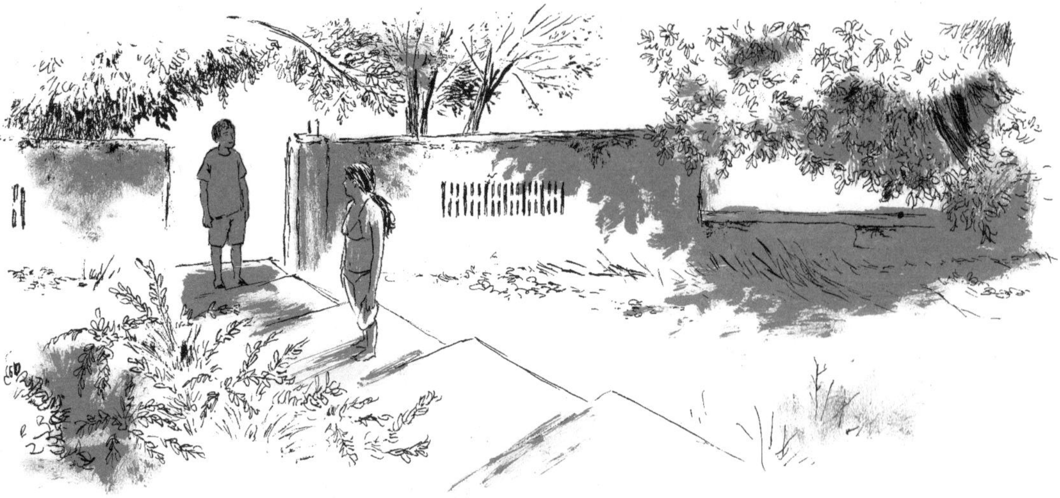

He wore an orange shirt and his green eyes shone

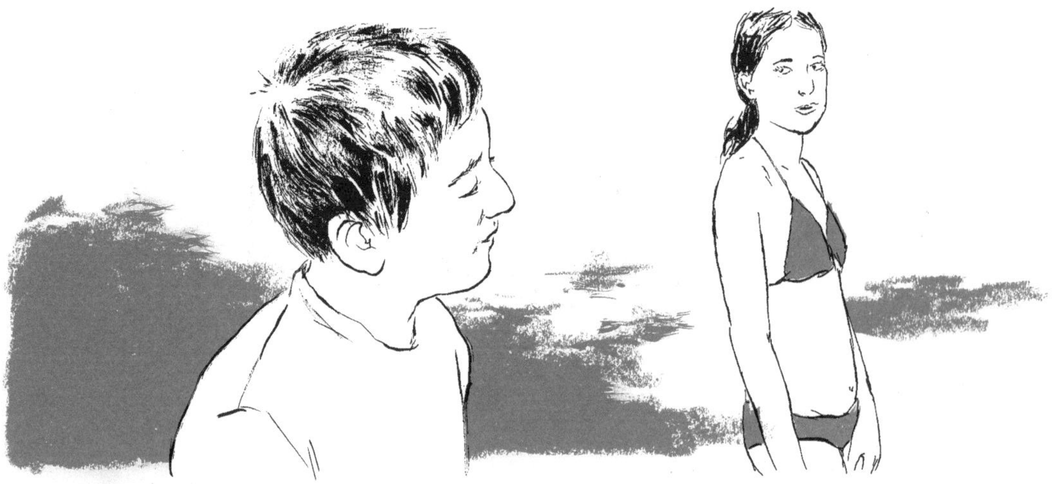

like new marbles that nobody's ever rolled in the sand.

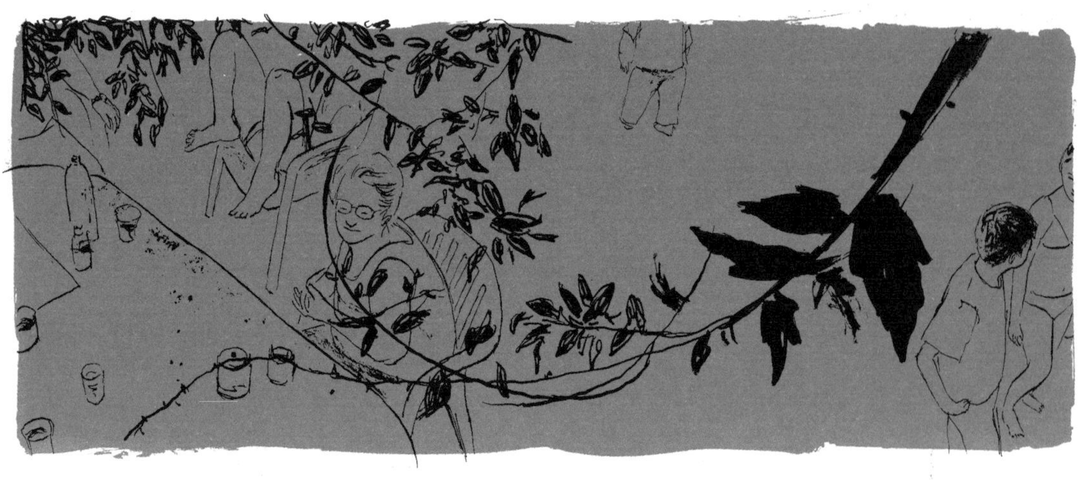

I told him that if he wants to stay, he'd have to be my own personal lifeguard, and stay out of the pool, even if it gets really hot.

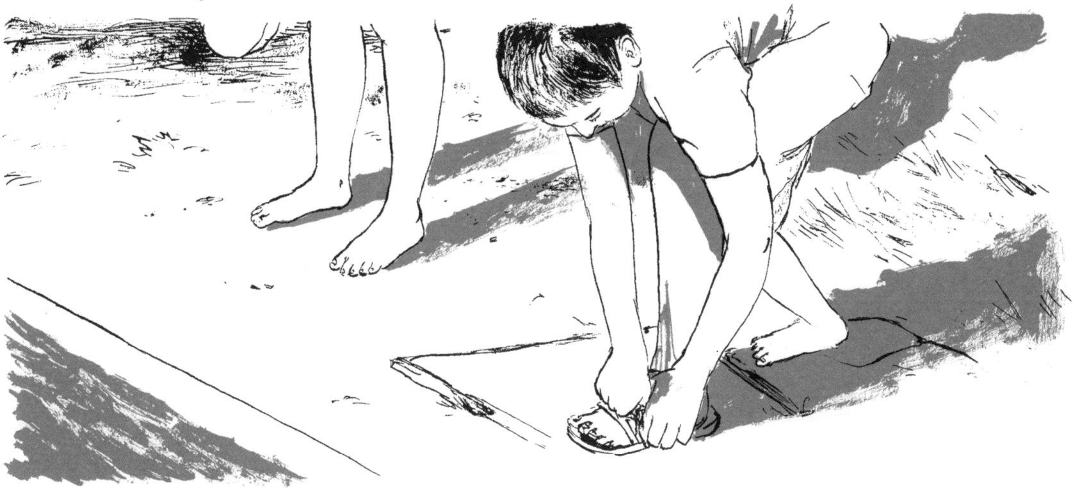

I told him, I don't care if you don't have a bathing suit,

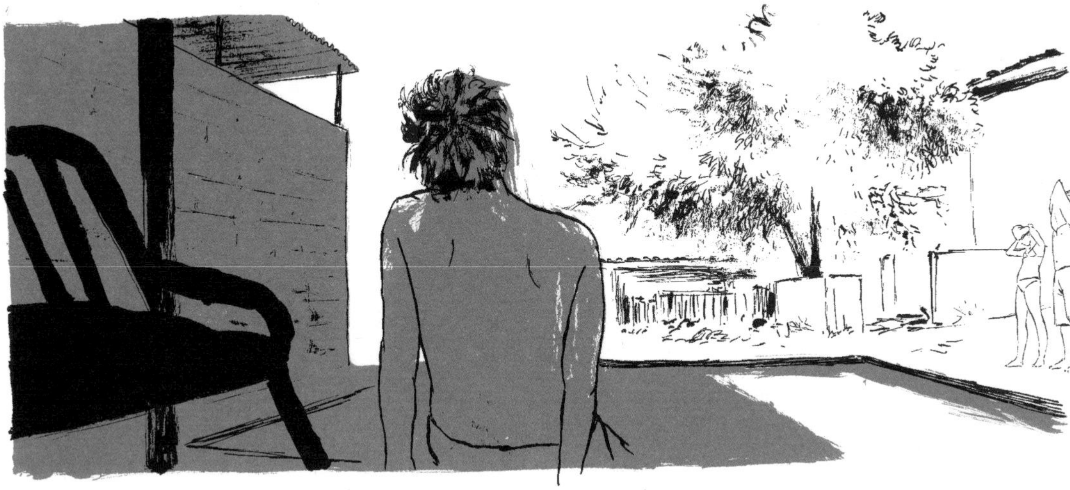

you can wear your underpants for all I care.

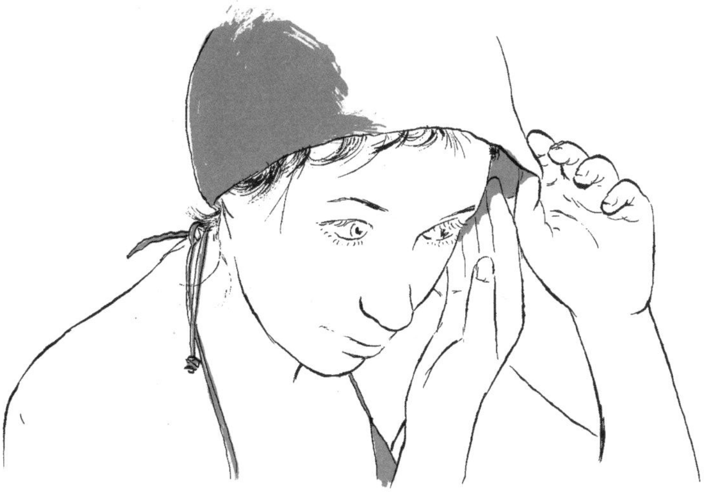

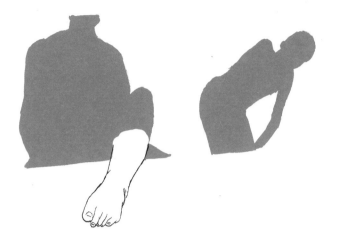

I explained that first he has to be a substitute lifeguard and if he proves himself I'll let him be my regular lifeguard.

Dror watched my straight, flat body plowing through the water

seeing only me,

alone among all those bobbing heads.

When Dad called everybody to eat I screamed, "I'm coming already! Save me a pita and some kebab for later."

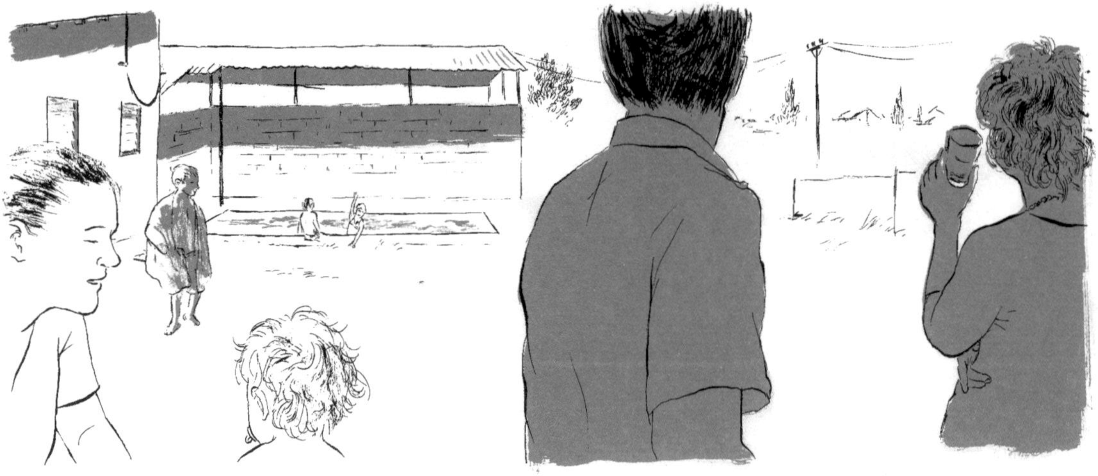

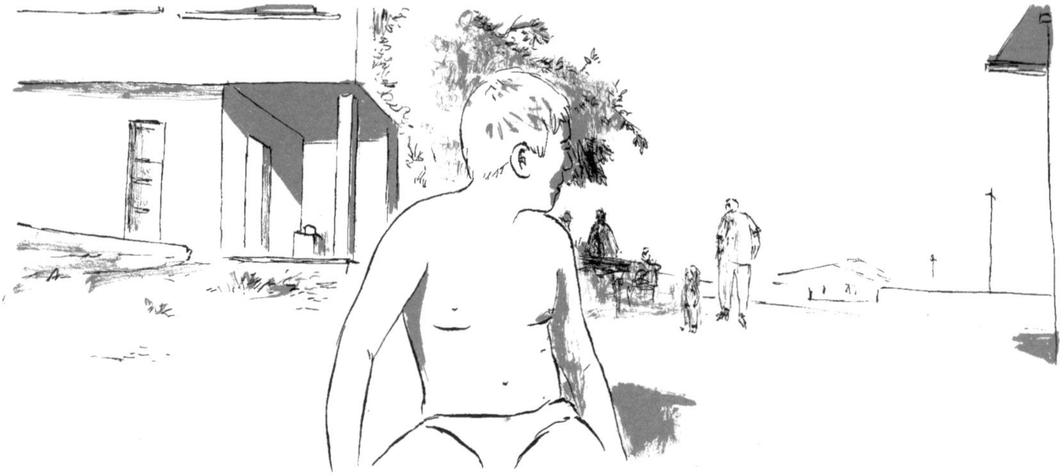

The pool emptied.

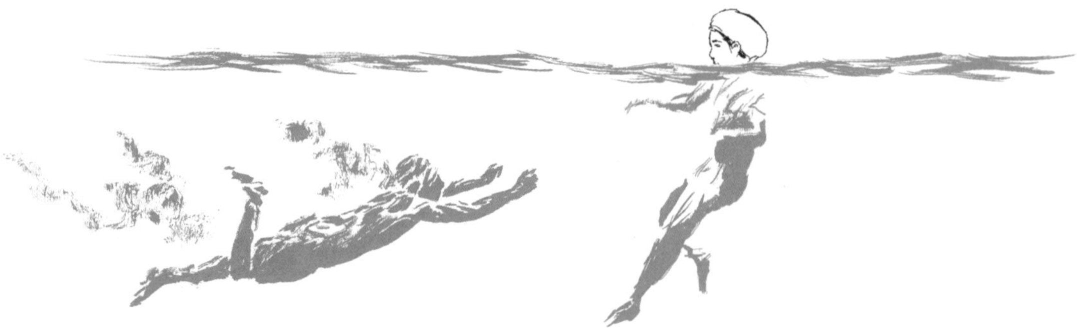

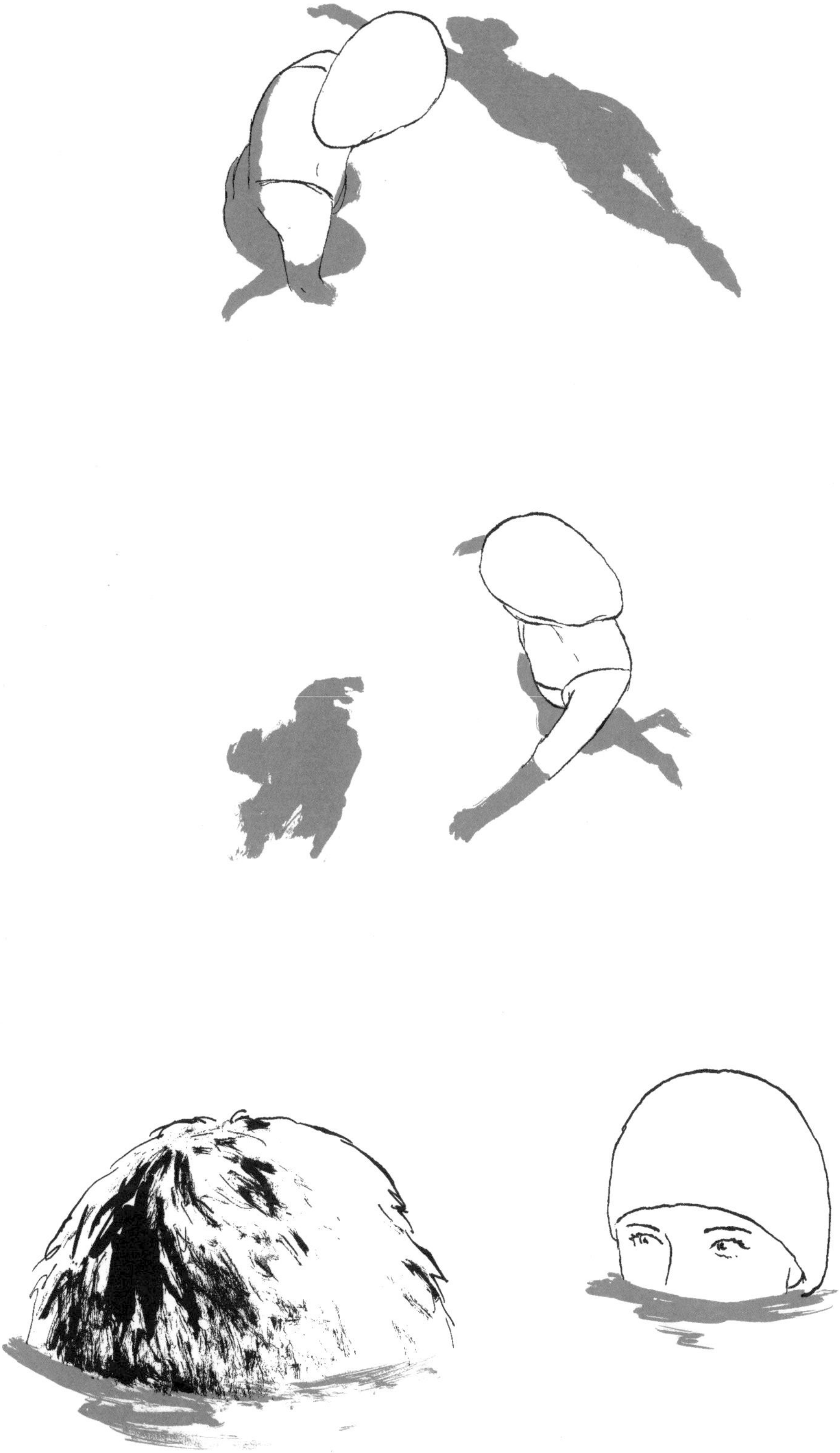

All of a sudden I really wanted to see if Dror's underpants would get tight like the sub's.

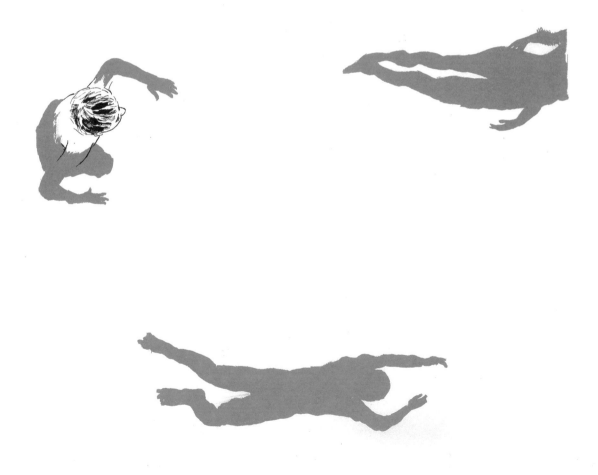

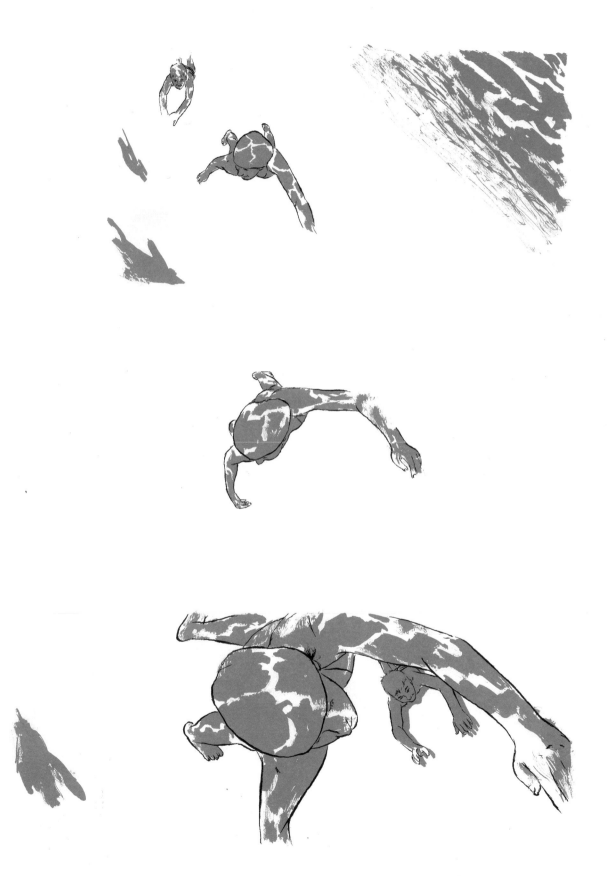

He asked if he can be my regular lifeguard now.

I told him a substitute lifeguard is way cooler then a regular one.

It was getting cold.

Dror touched my face with one hand and held the side of the pool with the other.

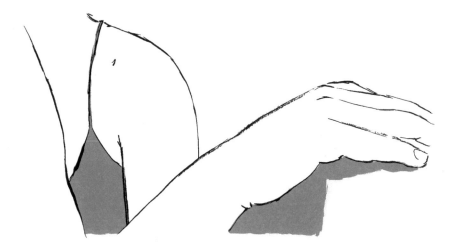

He whispered in my ear that he loved me.

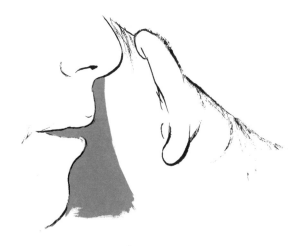

His underpants got really tight like the sub's and, when he came close to me, I almost drowned from all the pleasantness and dizziness.

A strange hunger overcame me.

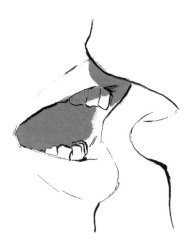

I bit Dror on the lips and couldn't stop till I heard Mom screaming.

We were so startled, Dror bumped into me with his teeth and hurt my lower lip

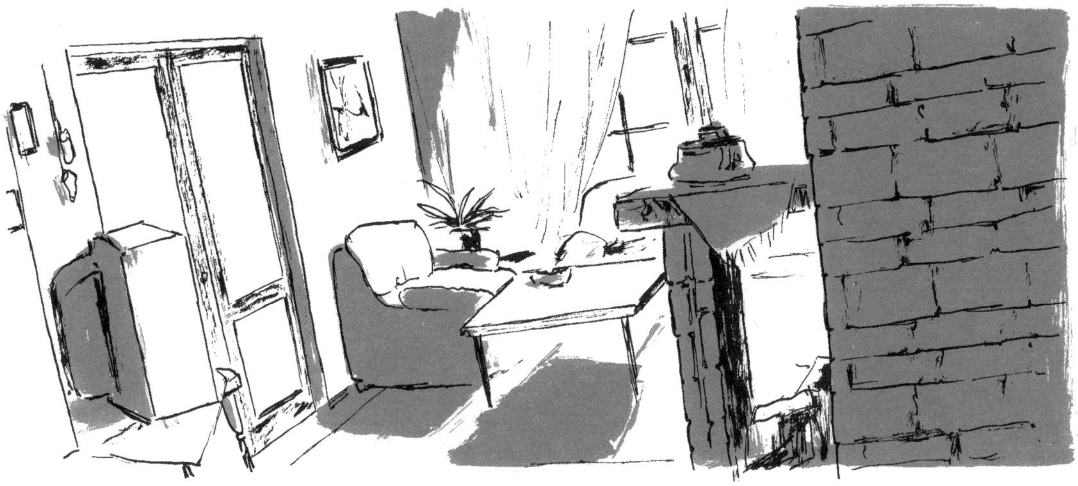

and Mom kept screaming, "Where's Amnon? Where's Amnon?"

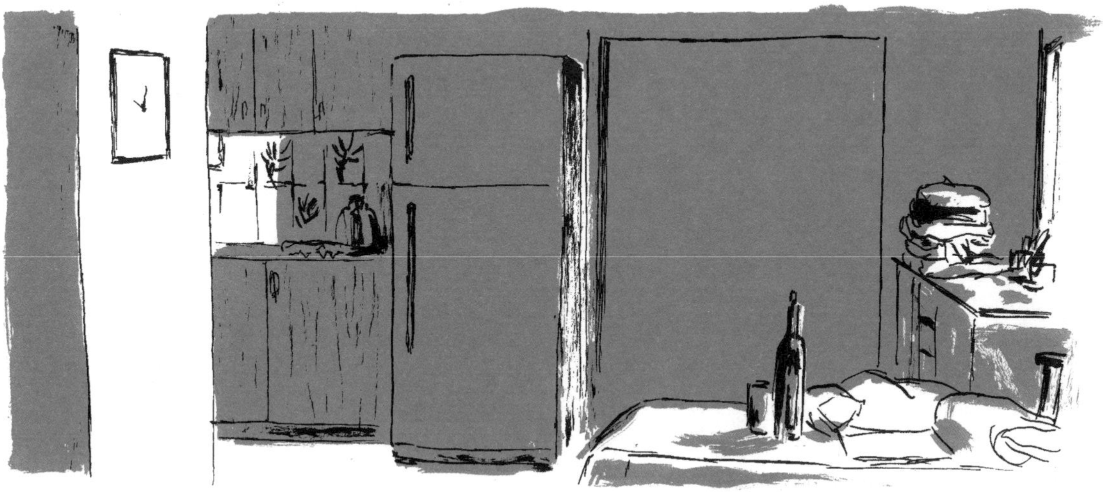

At first I didn't really understand what she was shouting because it sounded so much like her morning rant, "Where are my glasses?"

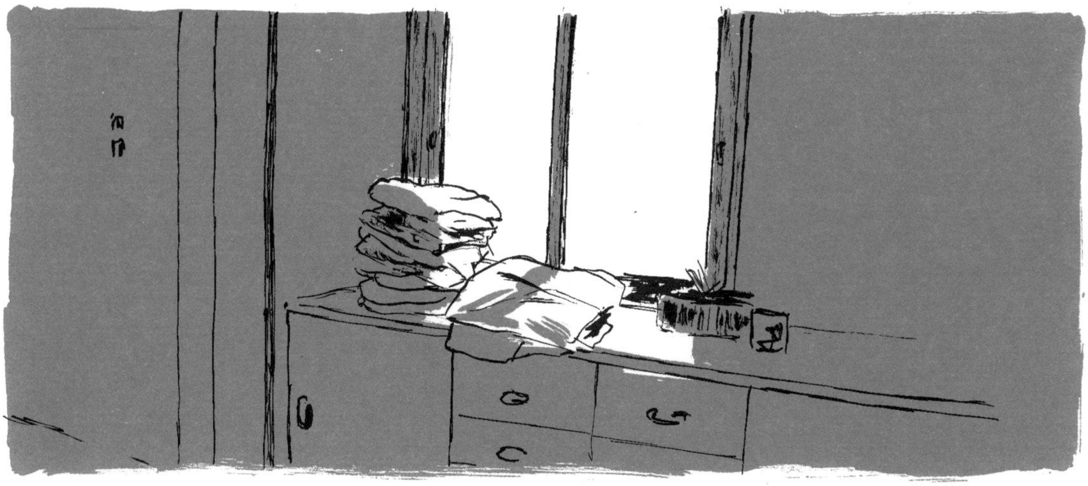

"Where are the car keys?"

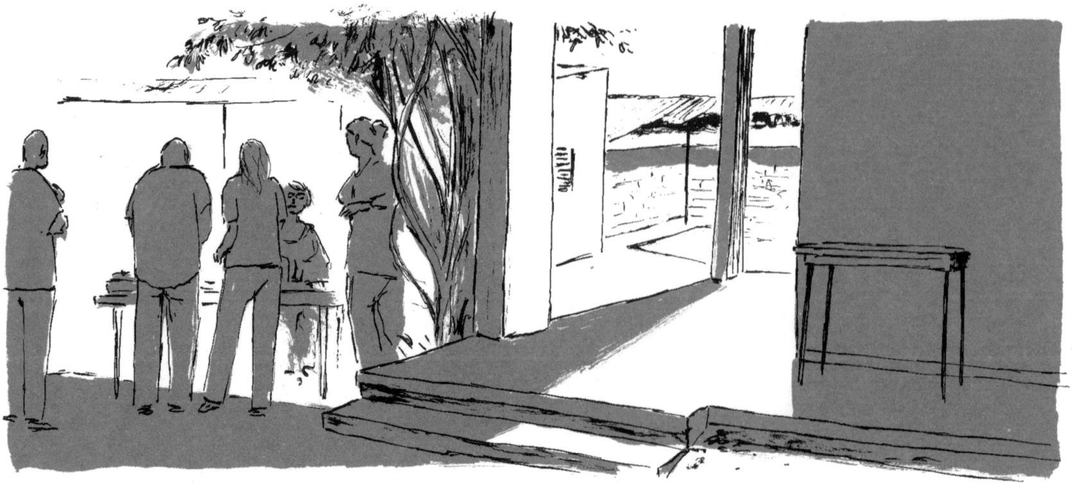

Then Dad started screaming with her, "Where's Amnon? Where's Amnon?"

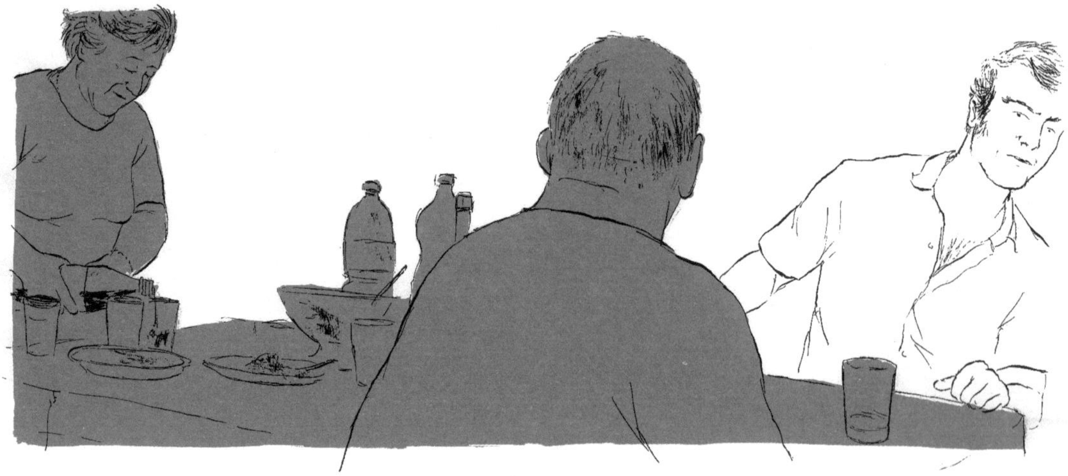

and suddenly it hit me that one word didn't fit in.

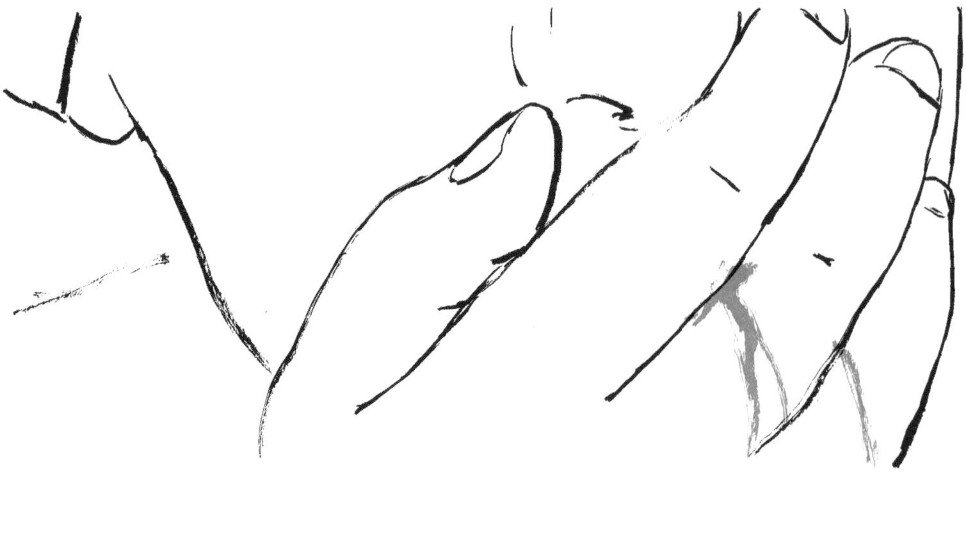

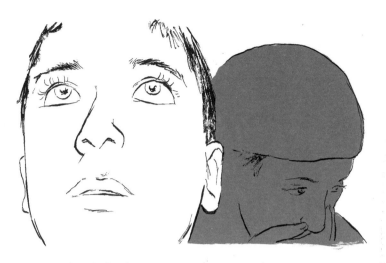

Dad ran to the edge of the pool and, just before he jumped, we saw Amnon right next to us

floating in the calm water.

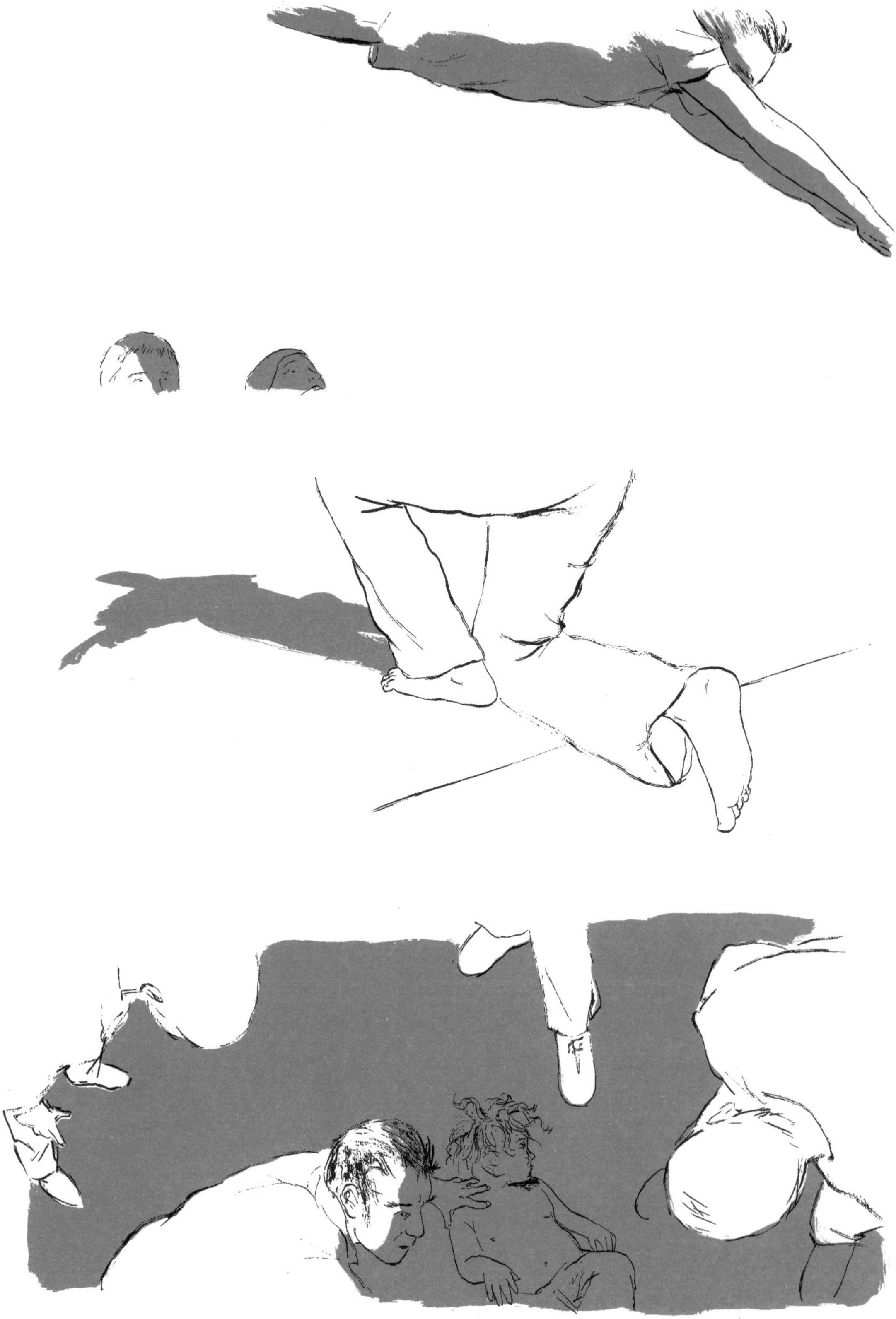

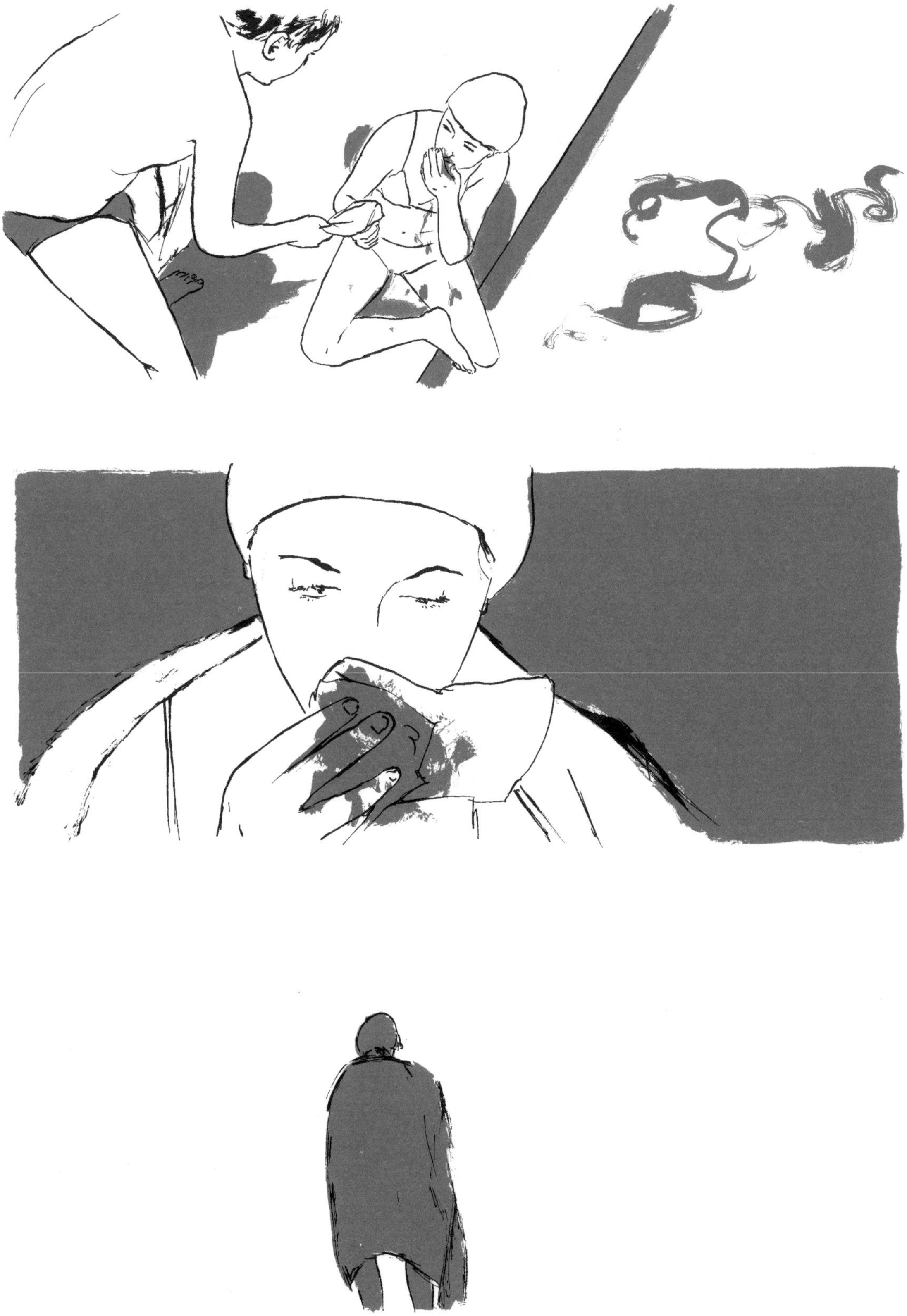

They covered Amnon's body, even his face, with an ambulance blanket and carried him on a stretcher.

That night, Mom and Dad didn't come home from the hospital.

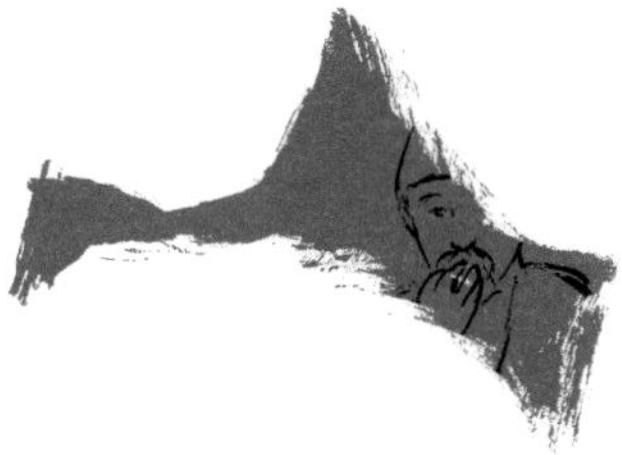

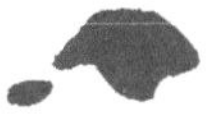

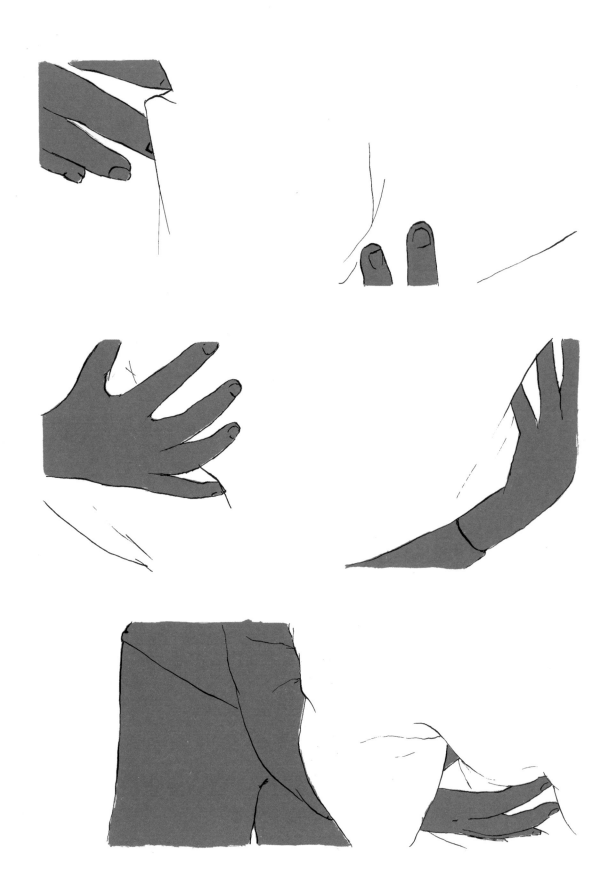

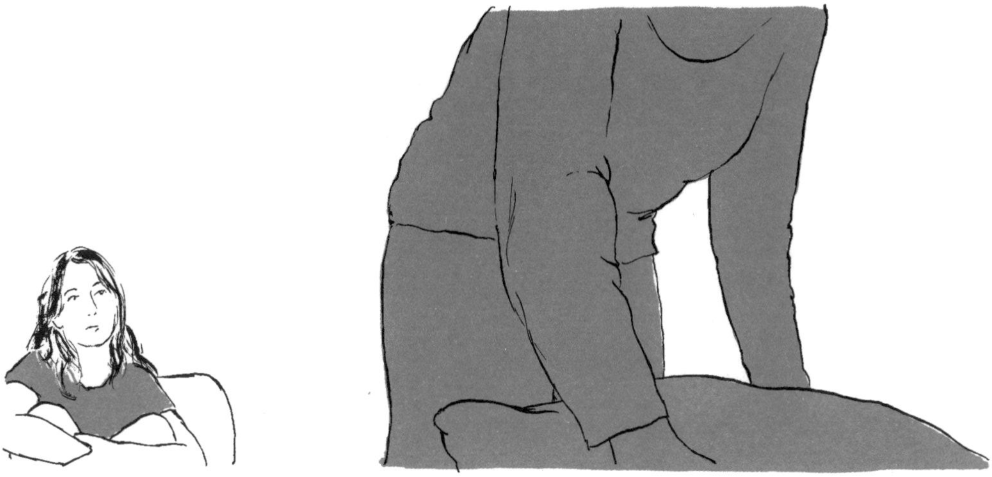

When Mom had the living room all ready for Shiva*, and all the mattresses and the pillows from the green armchairs were laid out on the floor,

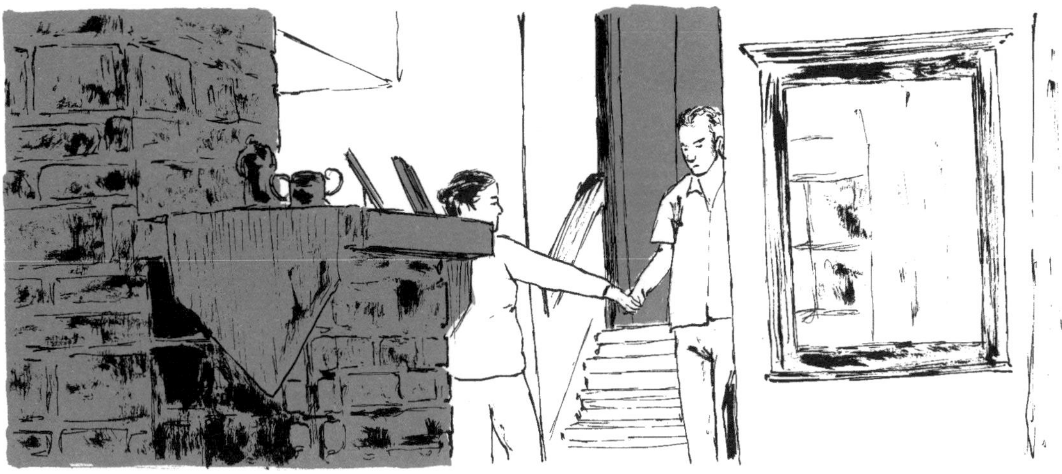

she went to the kitchen and asked Dad to follow her.

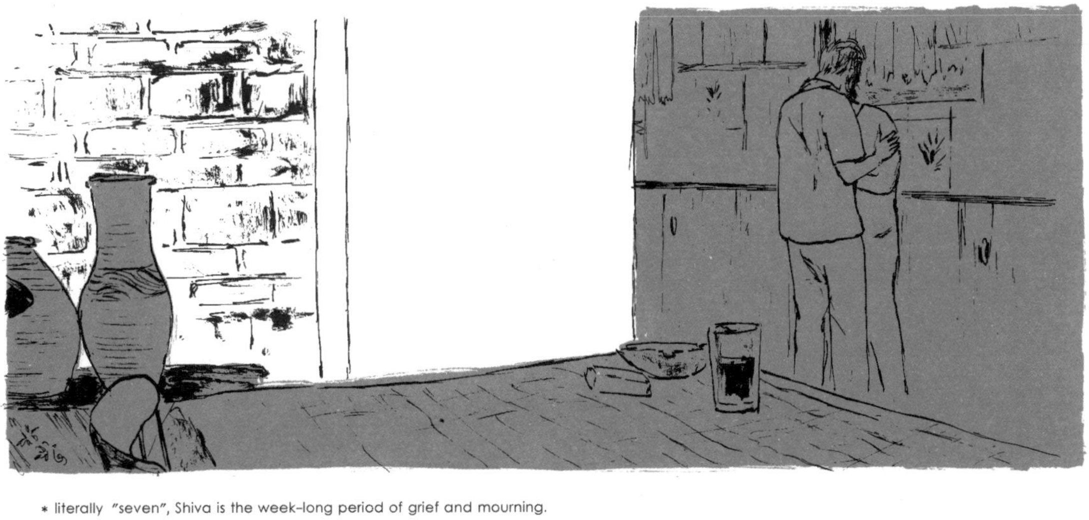

* literally "seven", Shiva is the week-long period of grief and mourning.

She told him

I have a new Amnon in my belly.

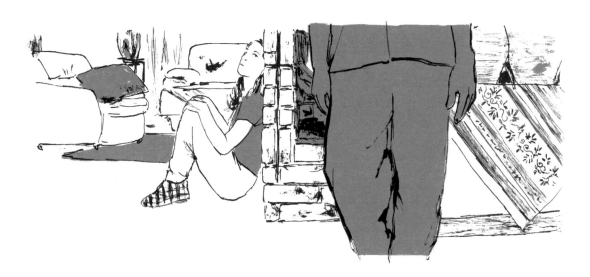

I peeked into the kitchen and saw Mom crying and holding her belly, which looked small and flat as always.

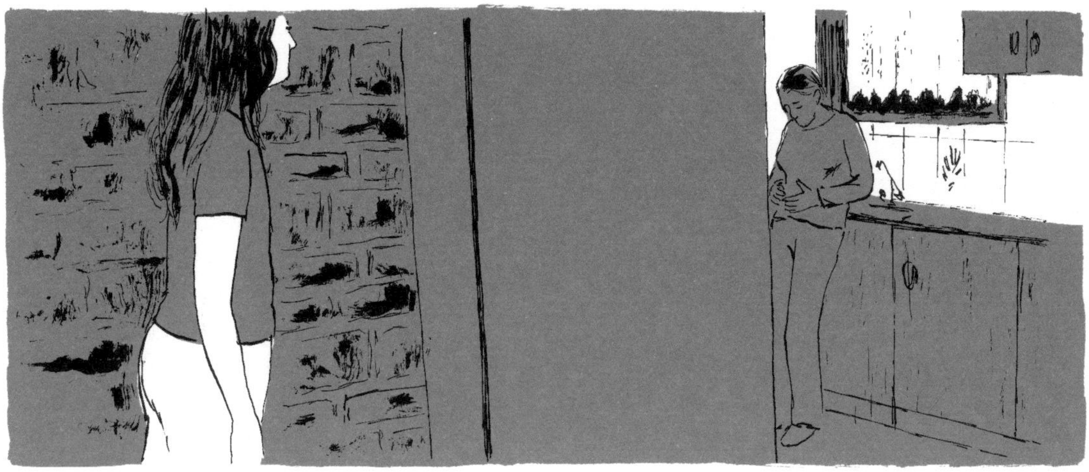

I imagined the new Amnon swimming in Mom's little belly

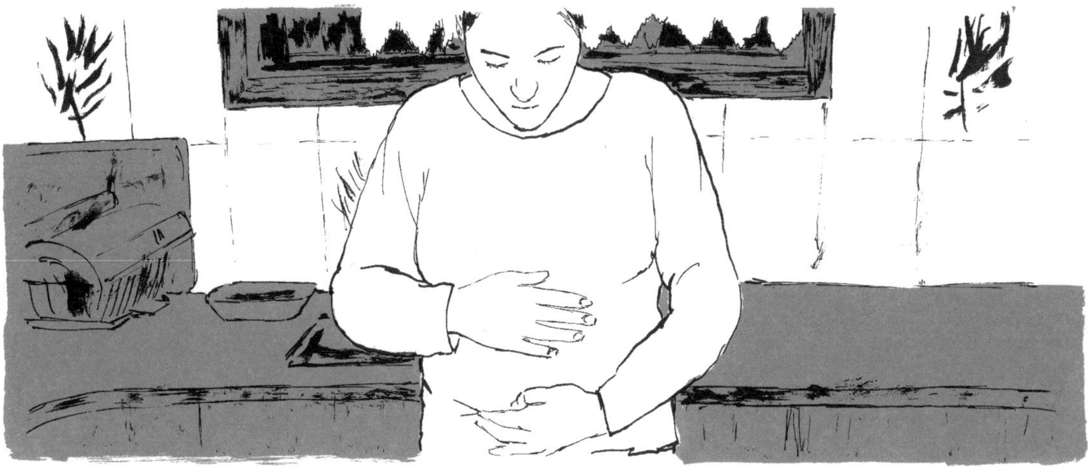

and got scared that, with all those tears, Mom wouldn't have any water left in her body, and then the new Amnon would jump out

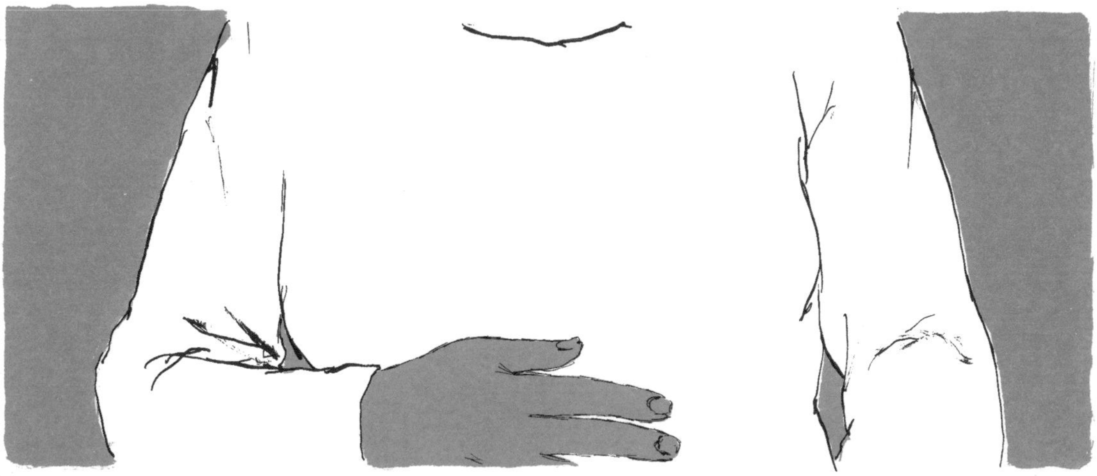

like the guppies that jumped out of the aquarium because we forgot to feed them, and Mom tossed the aquarium into the yard

and replaced it with the basket that held Amnon's baby creams and the small, pale-blue scissors,

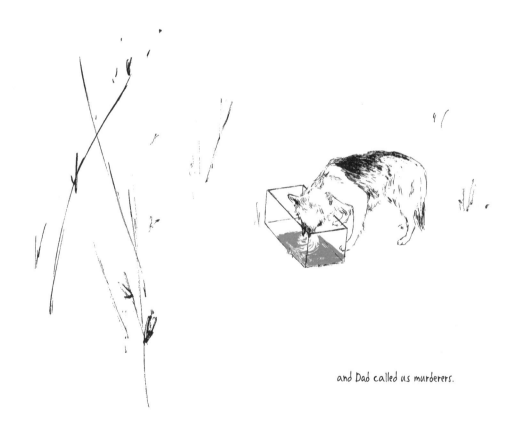

and Dad called us murderers.

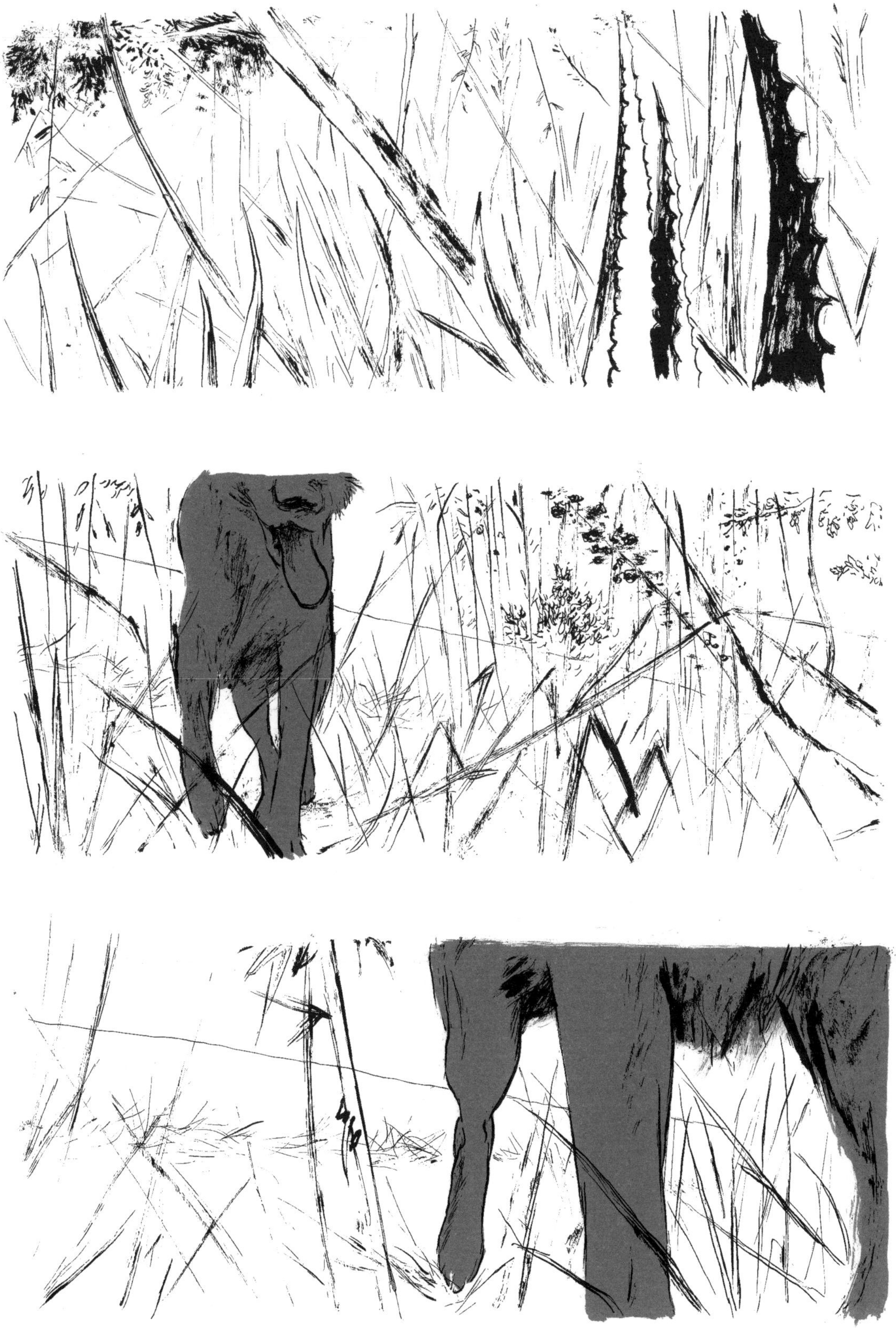

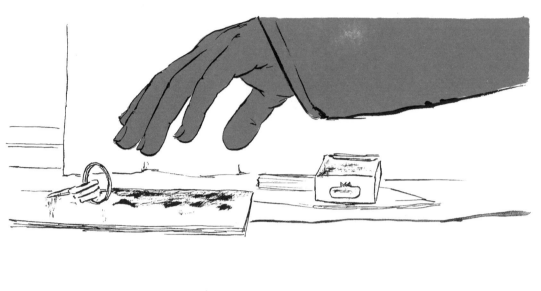

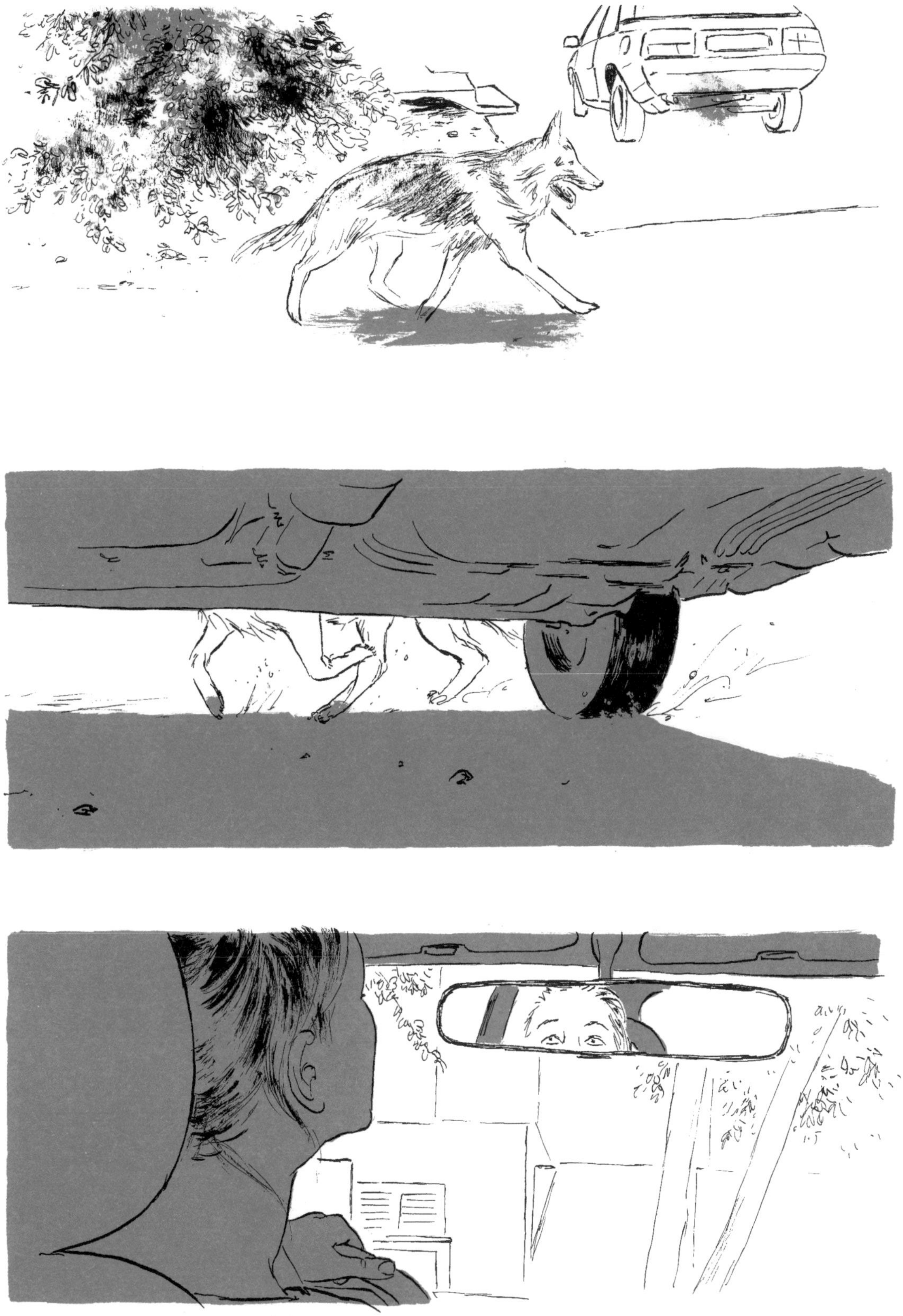

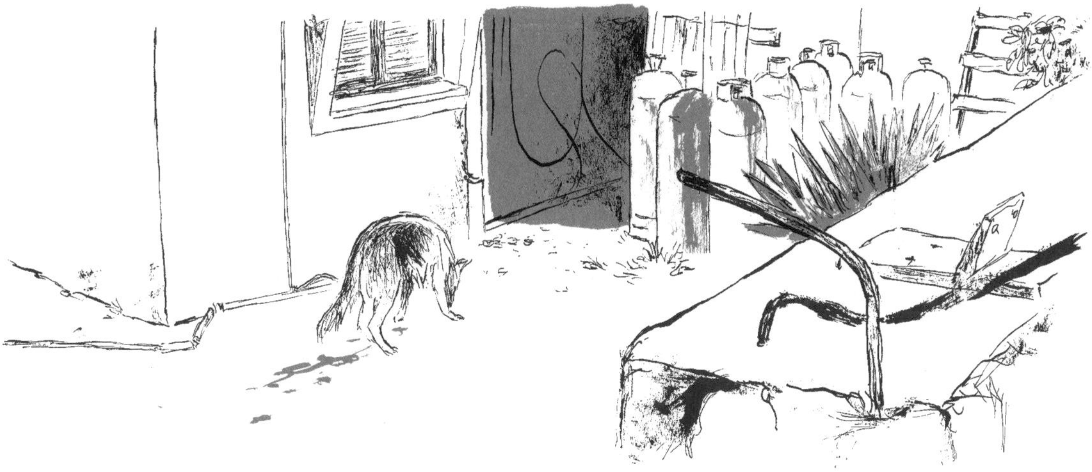

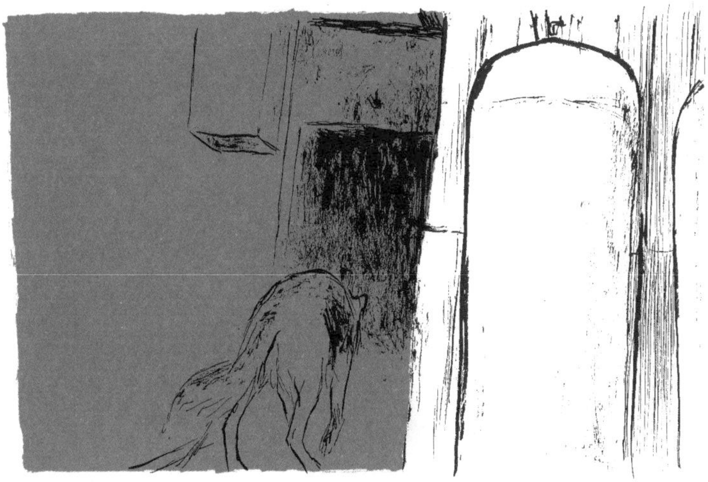

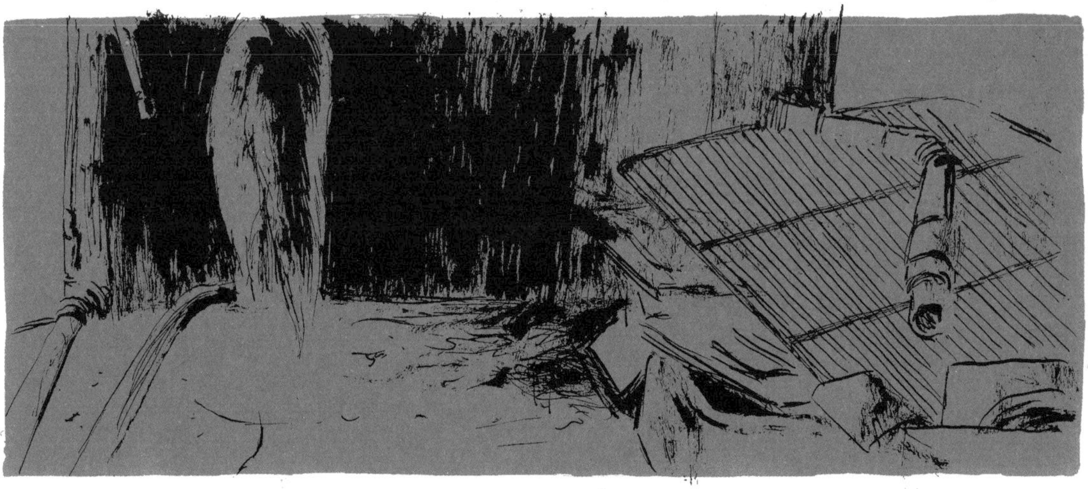

That evening was my birthday.

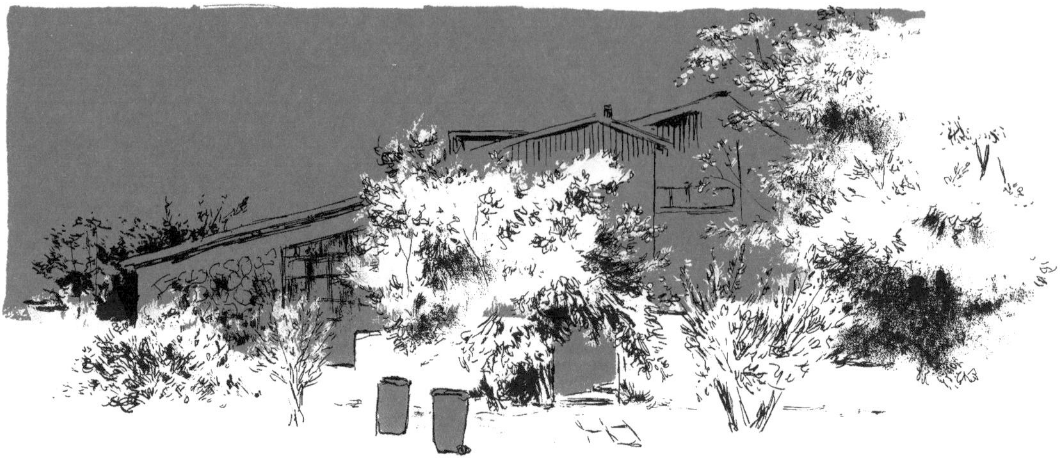

The kids from my class dressed up nice and brought presents.

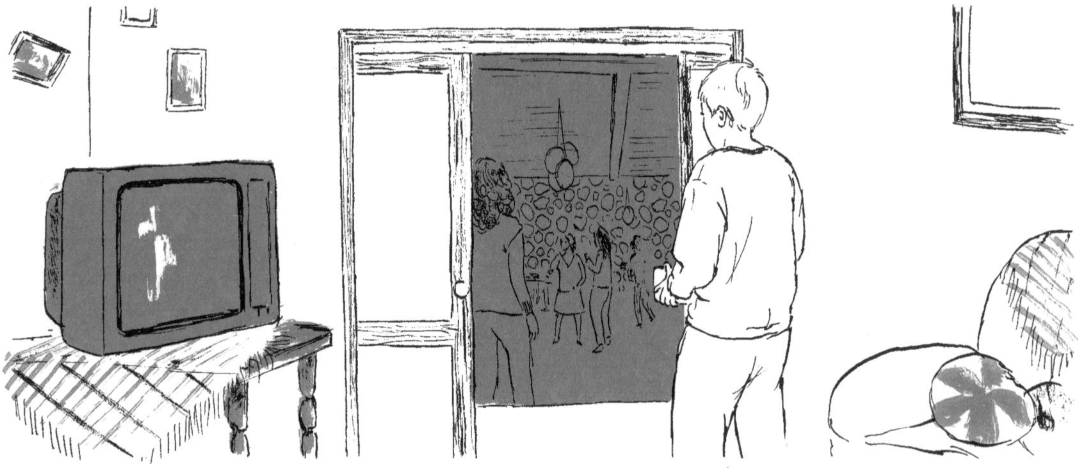

They ate chocolate treats and played a game, trying to insert a candle, which I tied to their pants with yarn, into the neck of a glass bottle.

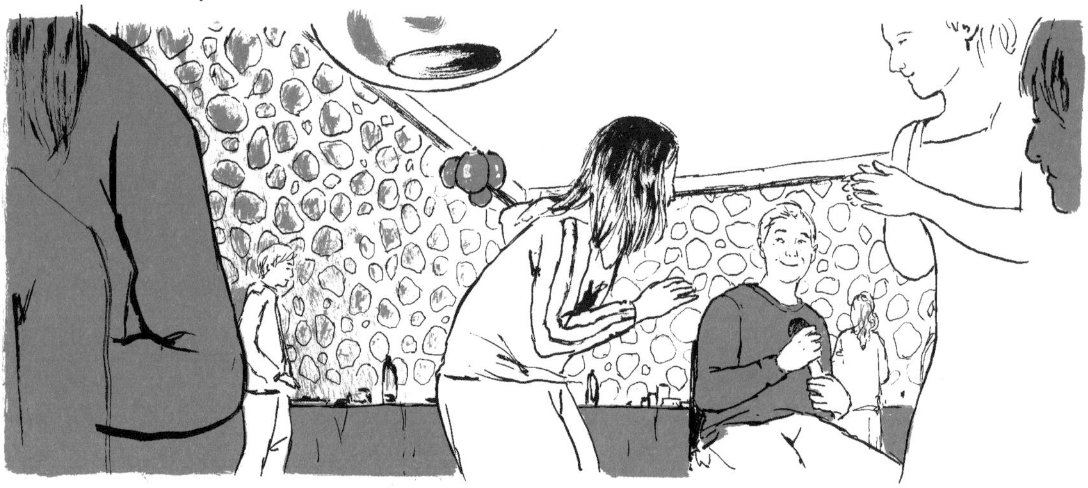

When Mom served the swan-shaped cream puffs, everyone ate and licked their lips and asked for more,

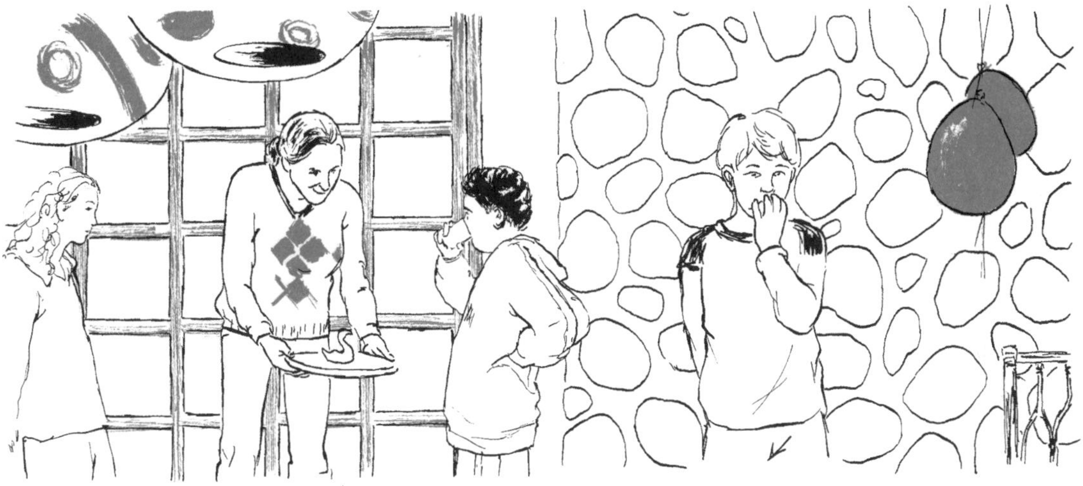

but Mom had only made one swan for every child.

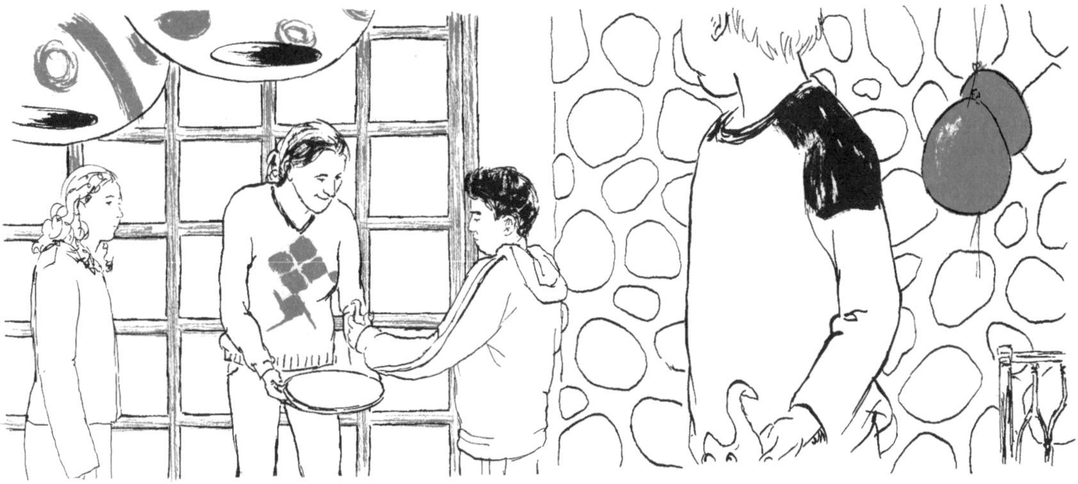

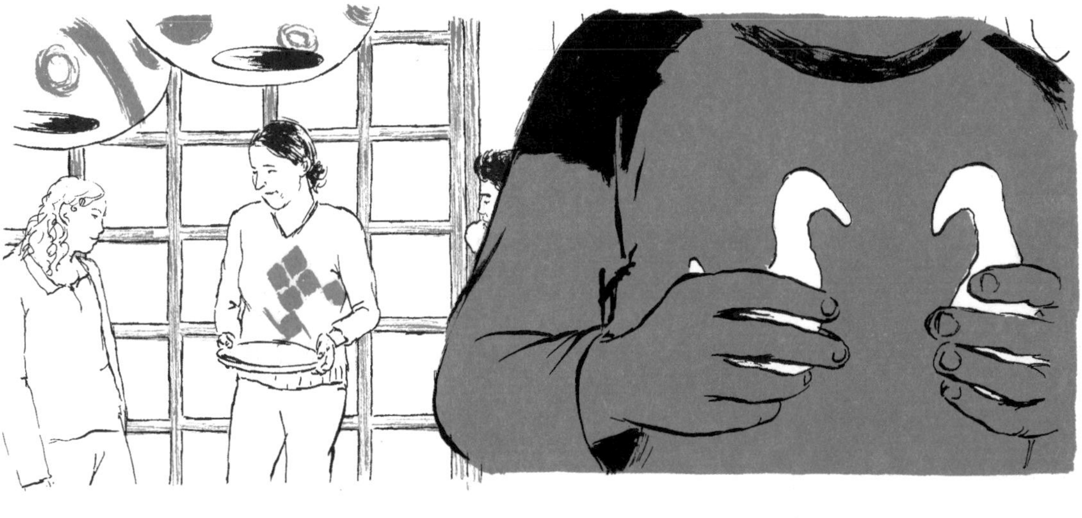

The kids departed, their presents left behind.

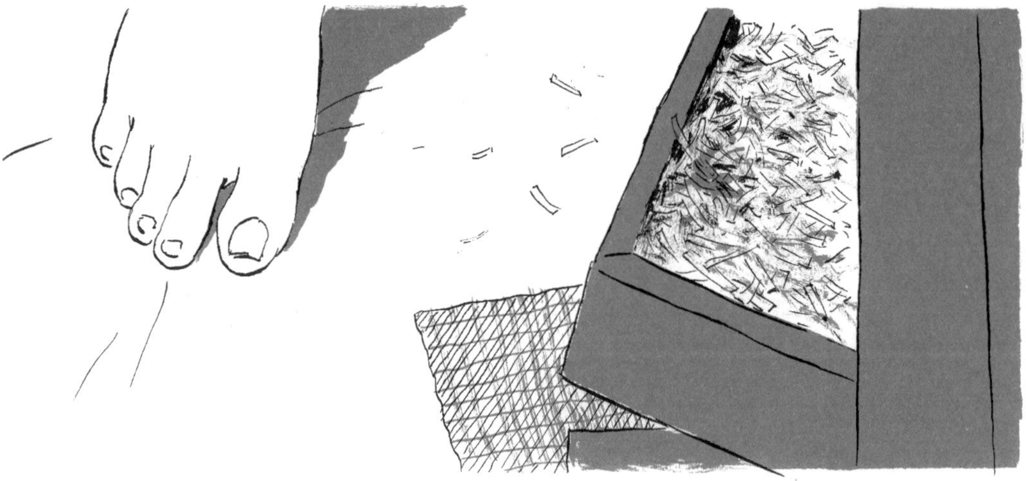

Over my bed, that was still wet from the kids' coats, I arranged ceramic dolls and some perfume bottles onto a wooden shelf.

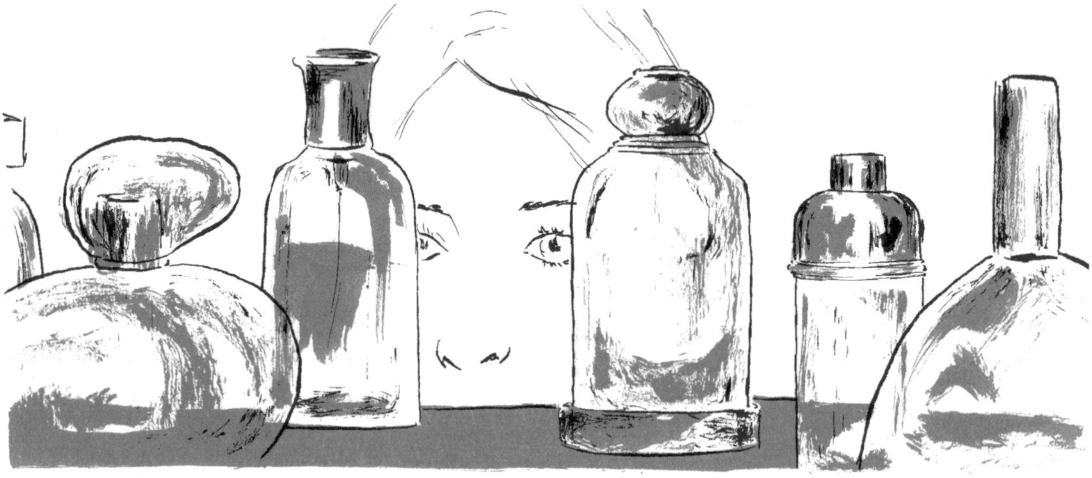

The perfumes in the bottles had a deep, sweet scent, and the one in the big bottle had another scent, a flat one, like the colorful tapestry in Grandma's underwear drawer.

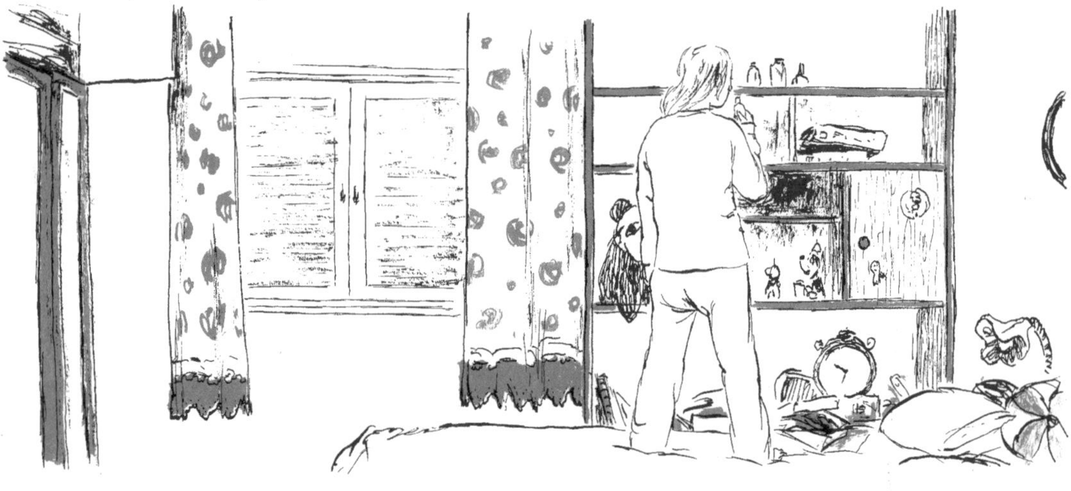

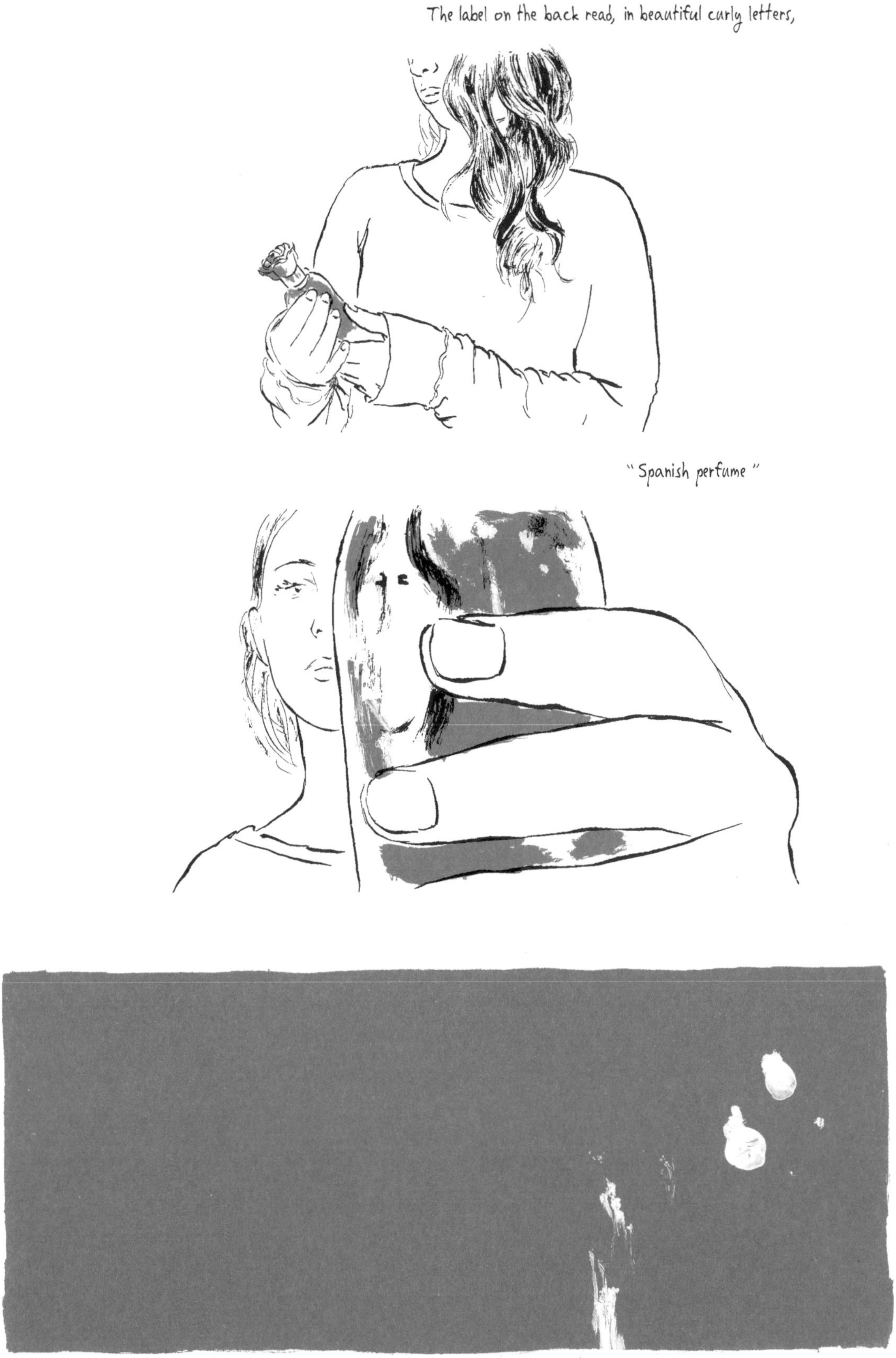
The label on the back read, in beautiful curly letters,
"Spanish perfume"

SPANISH PERFUME
1983

When Dad called from the war, Mom was already out playing cards.

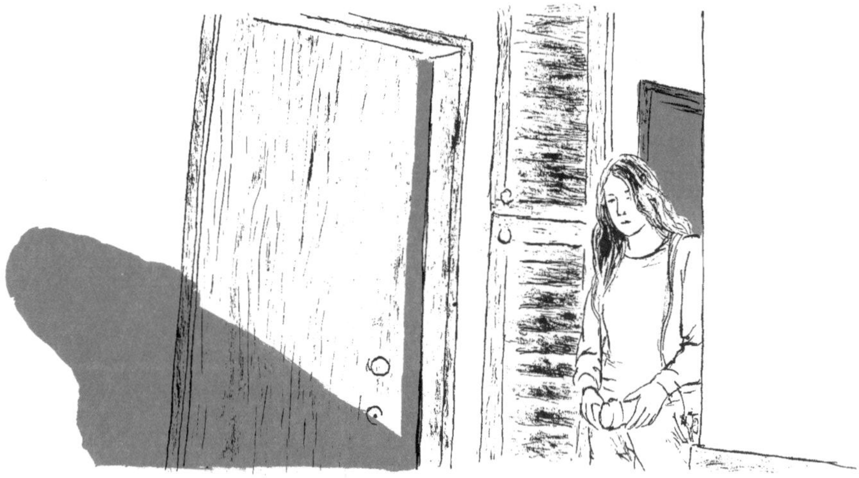

I told him that the dog got killed, and he said, "Dead dogs spread disease, have someone bury him."

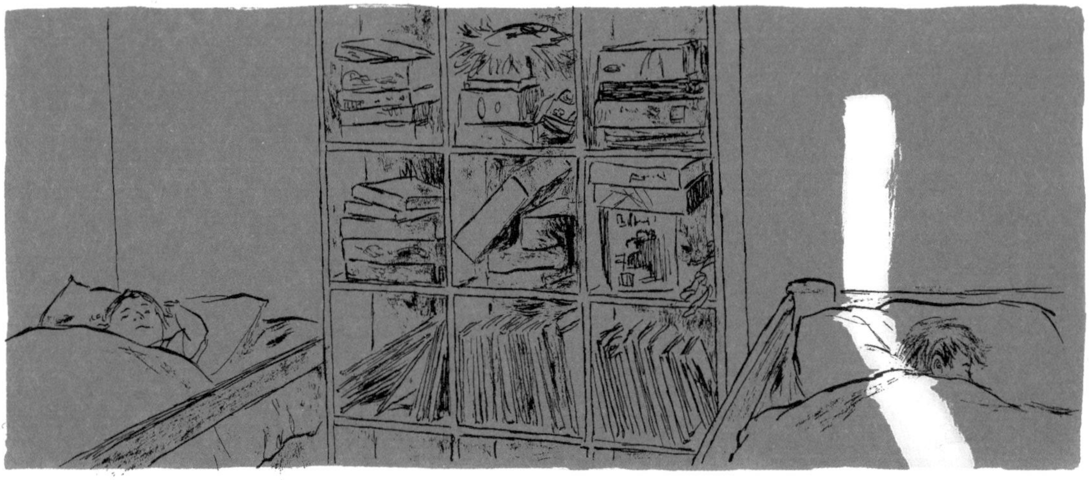

I promised to tell Mom he called and to kiss my brothers for him,

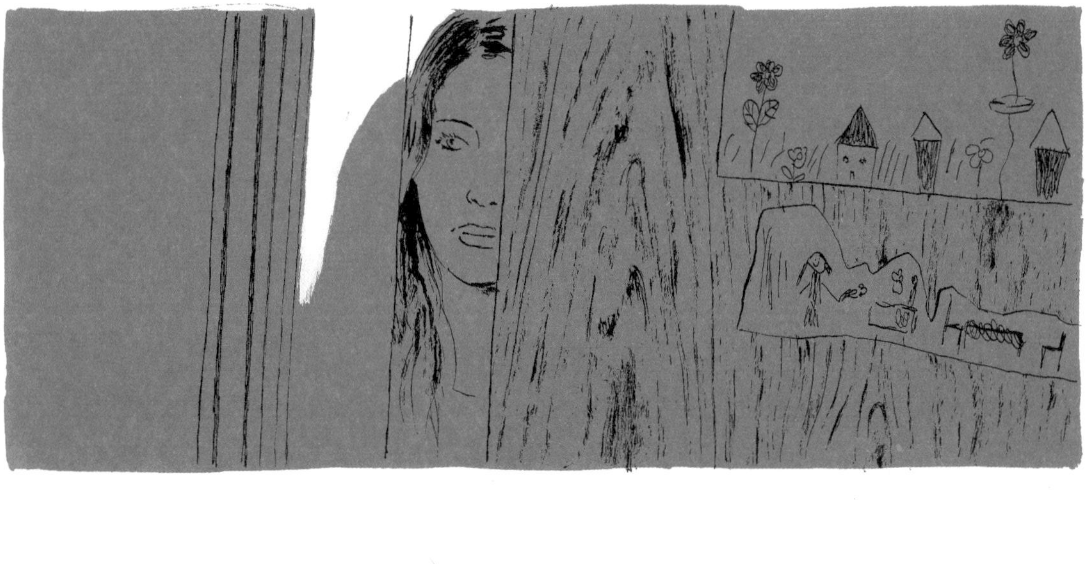

then I called Dror and Omri.

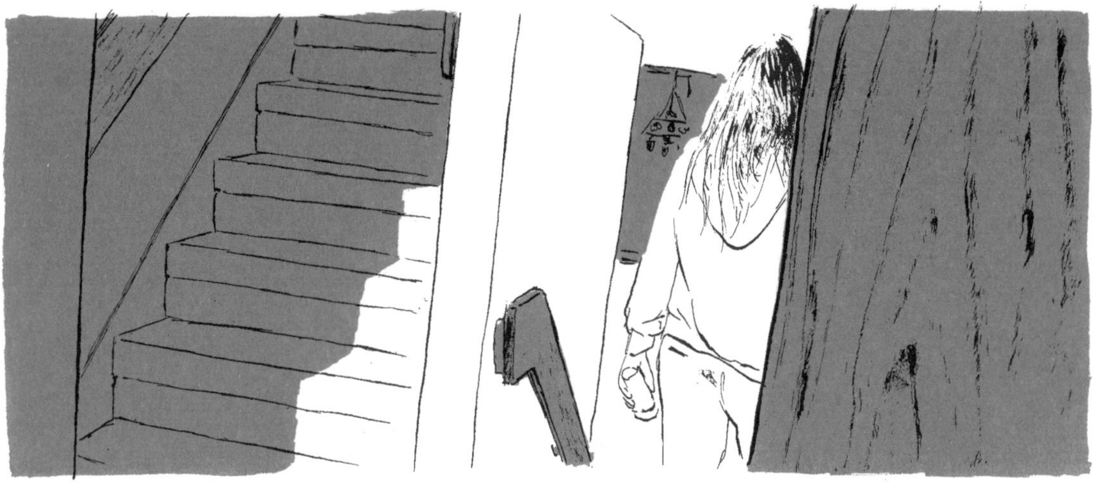

I didn't tell Dad that I found the dog in the basement,

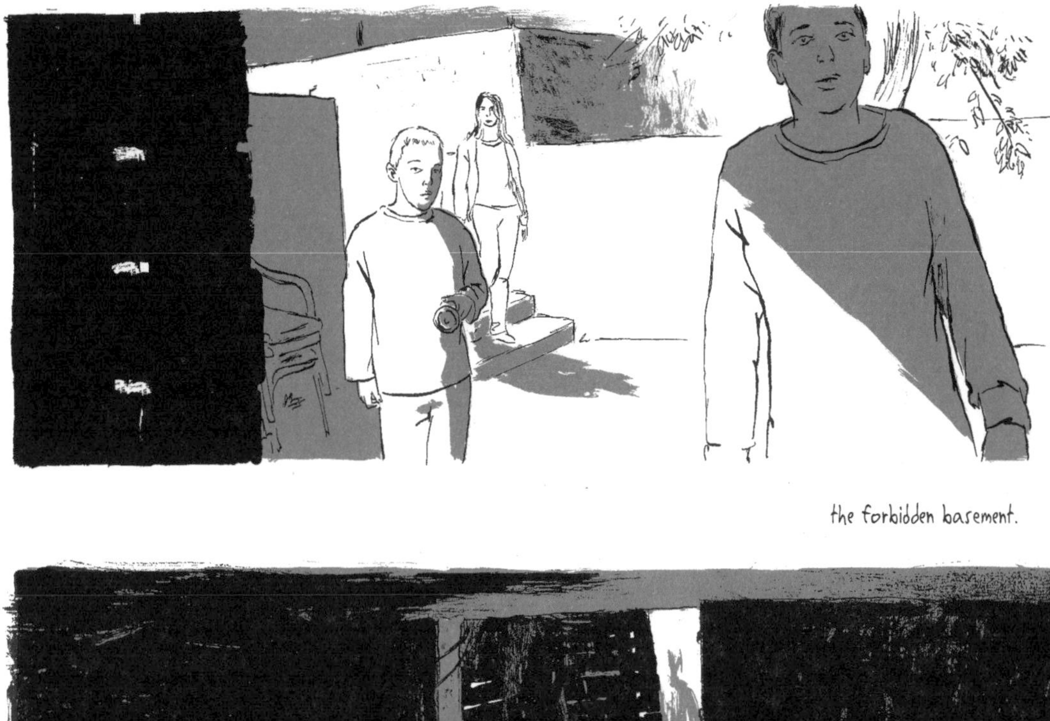

the forbidden basement.

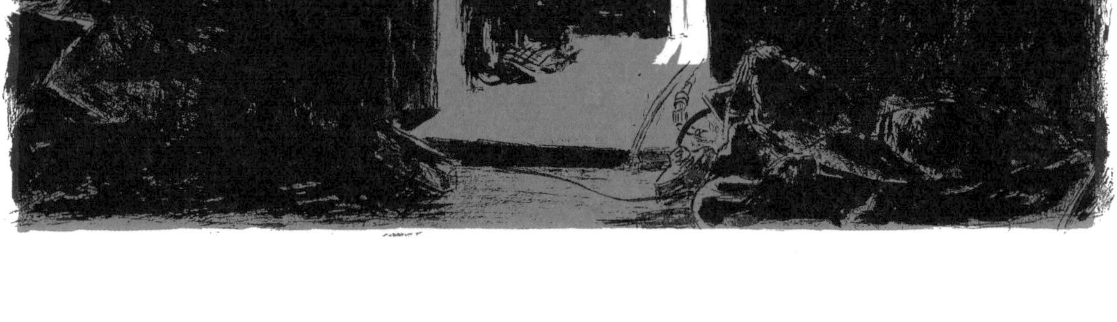

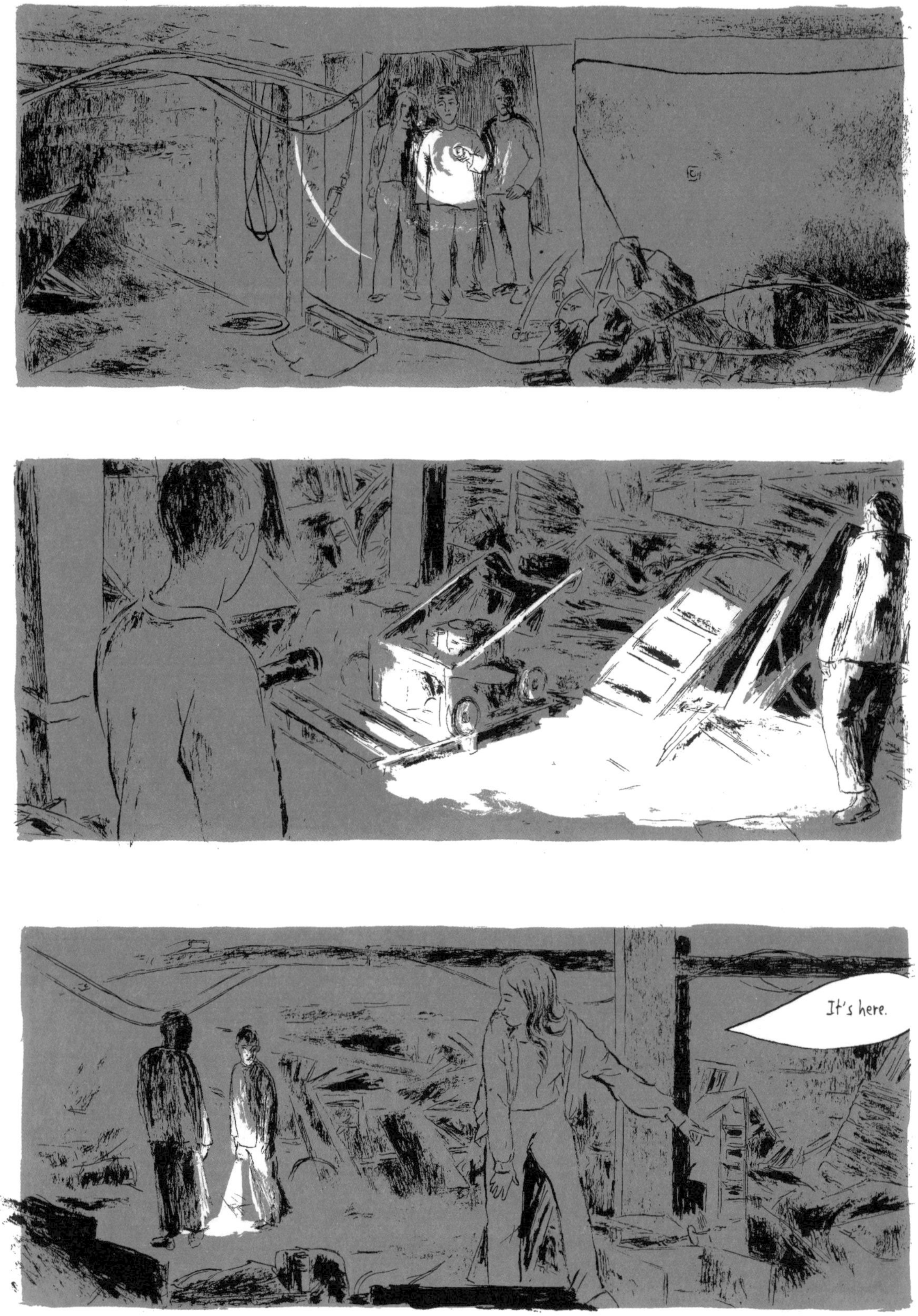
It's here.

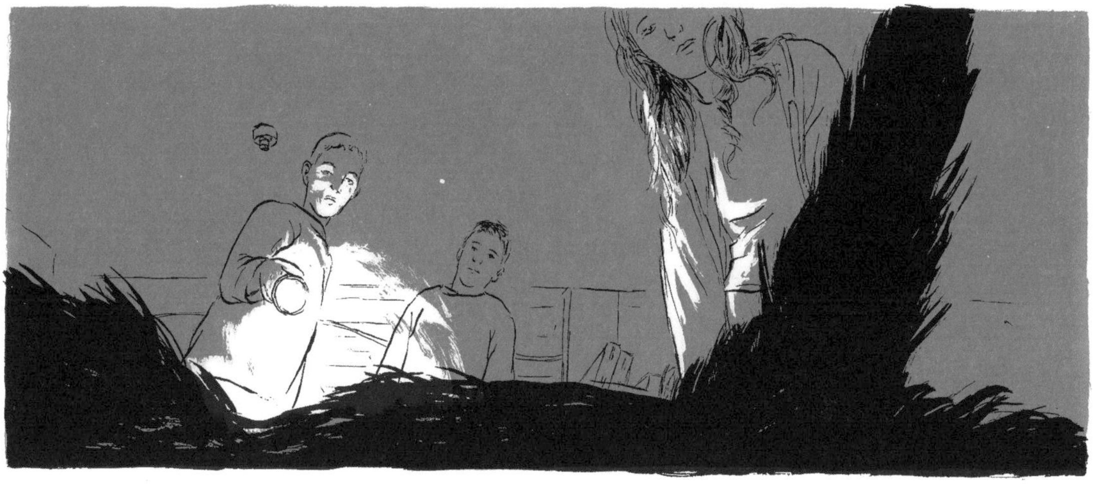

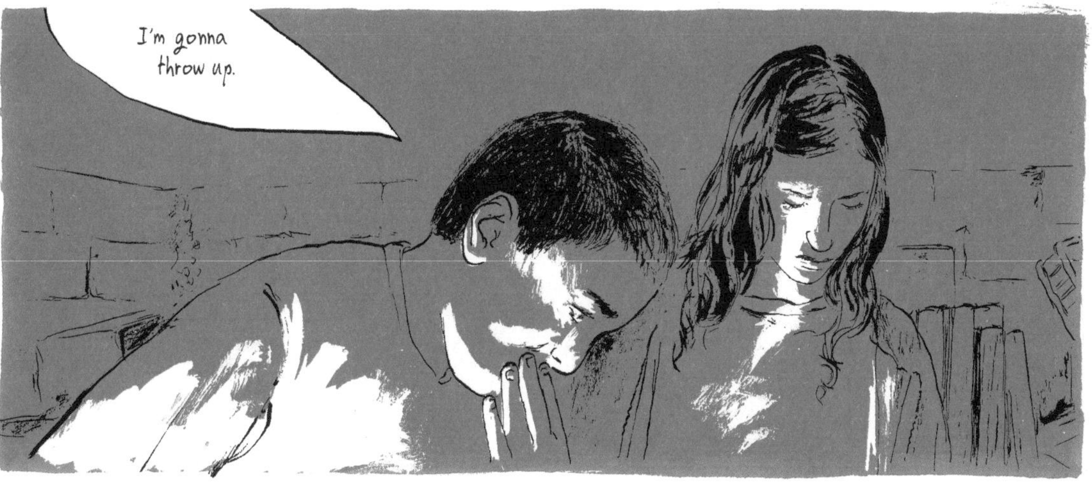
I'm gonna throw up.

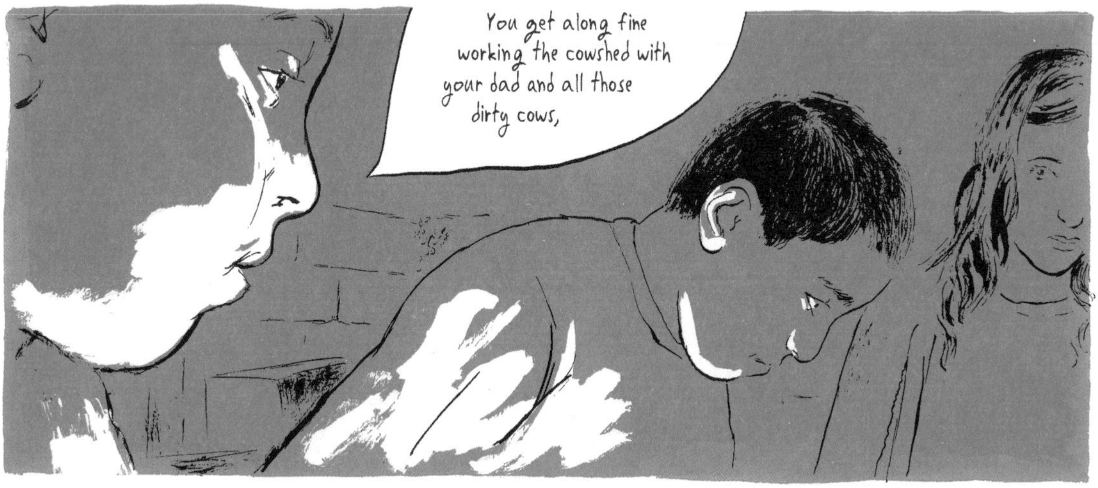
You get along fine working the cowshed with your dad and all those dirty cows,

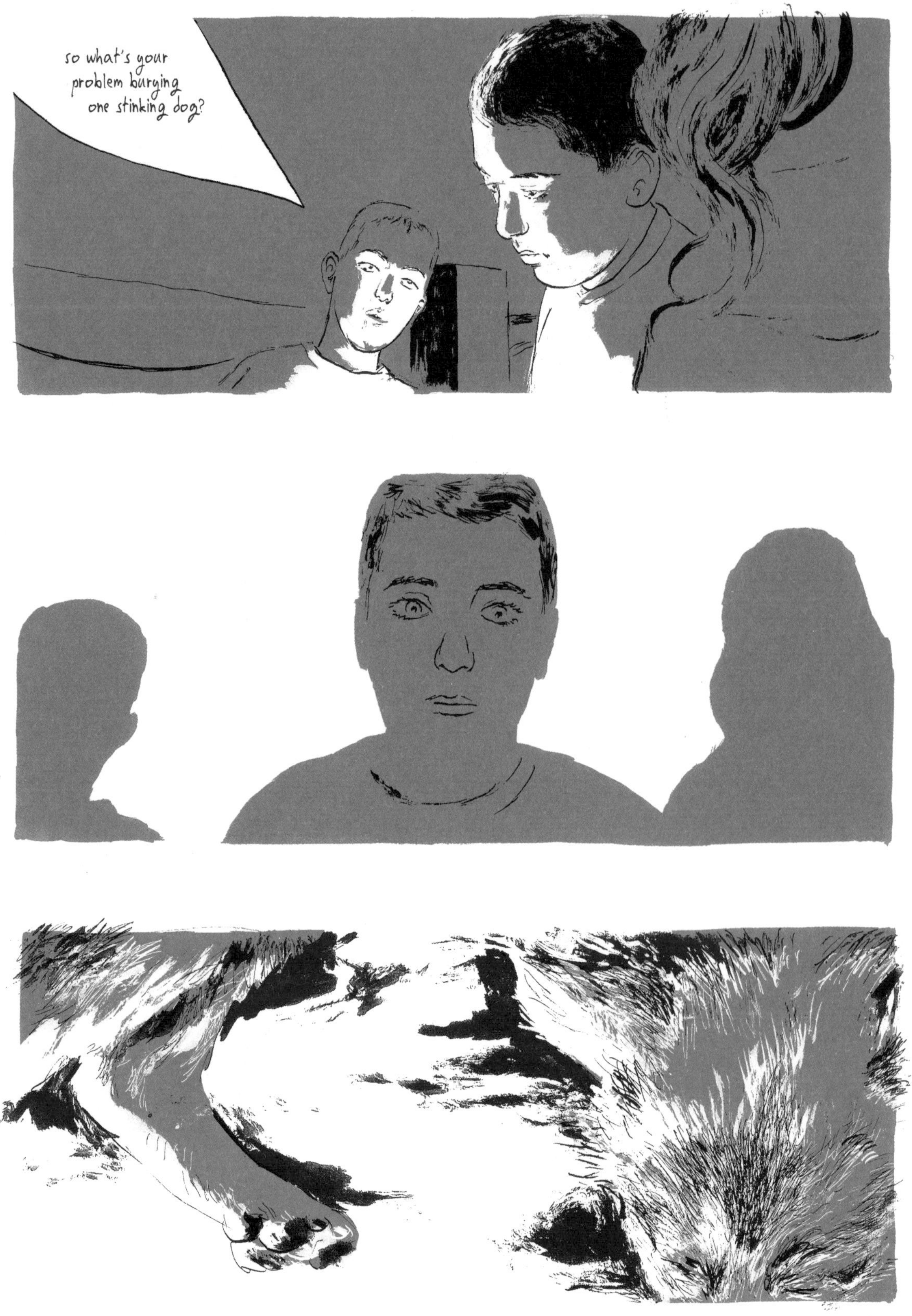
so what's your problem burying one stinking dog?

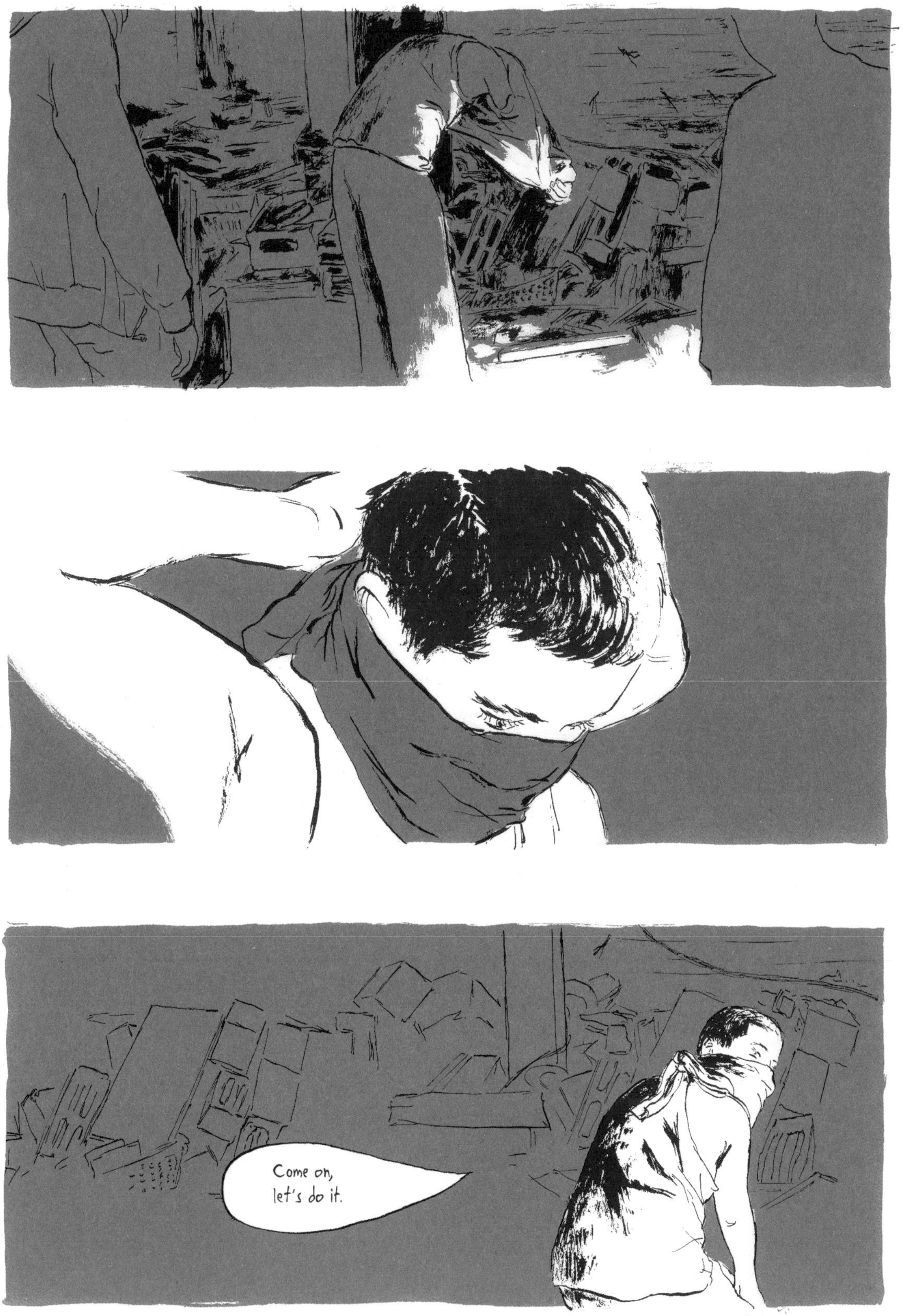
Come on,
let's do it.

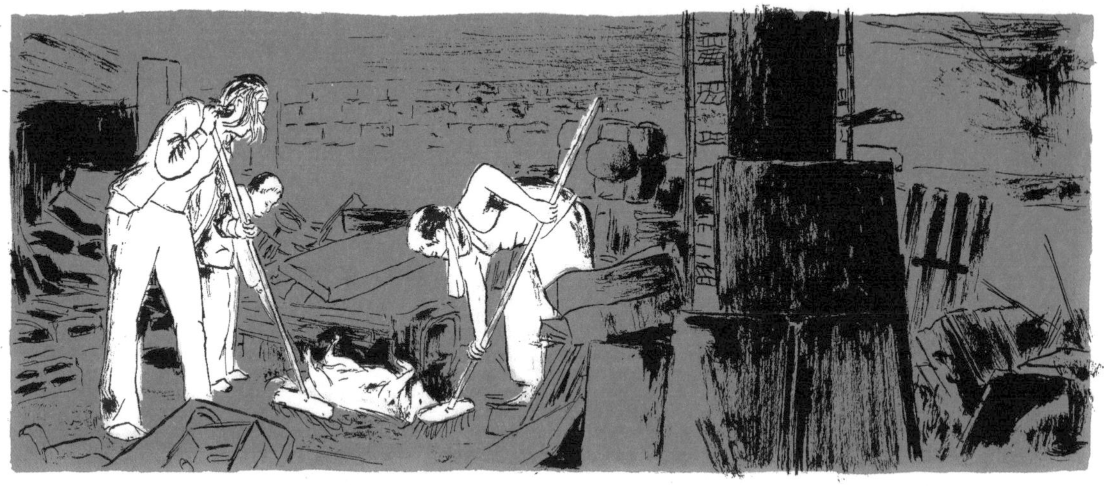

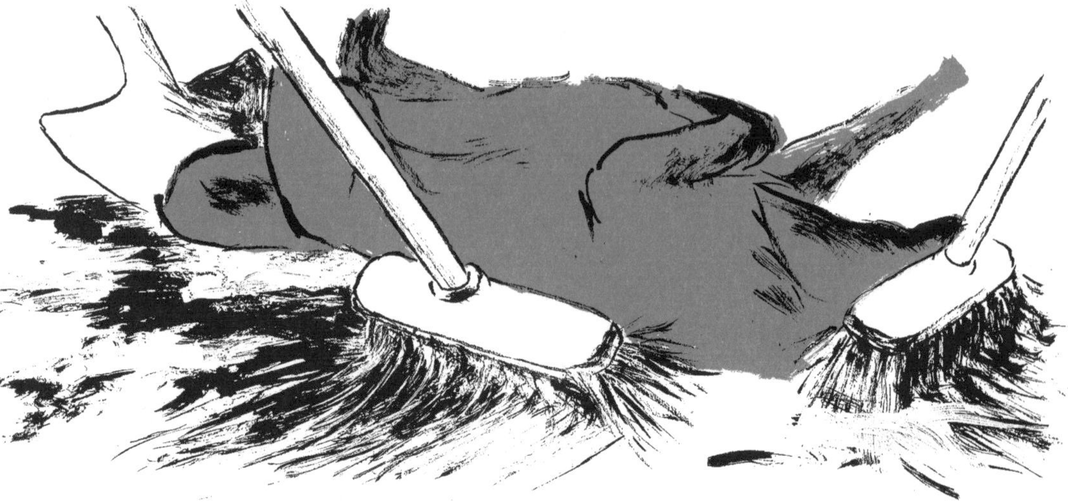

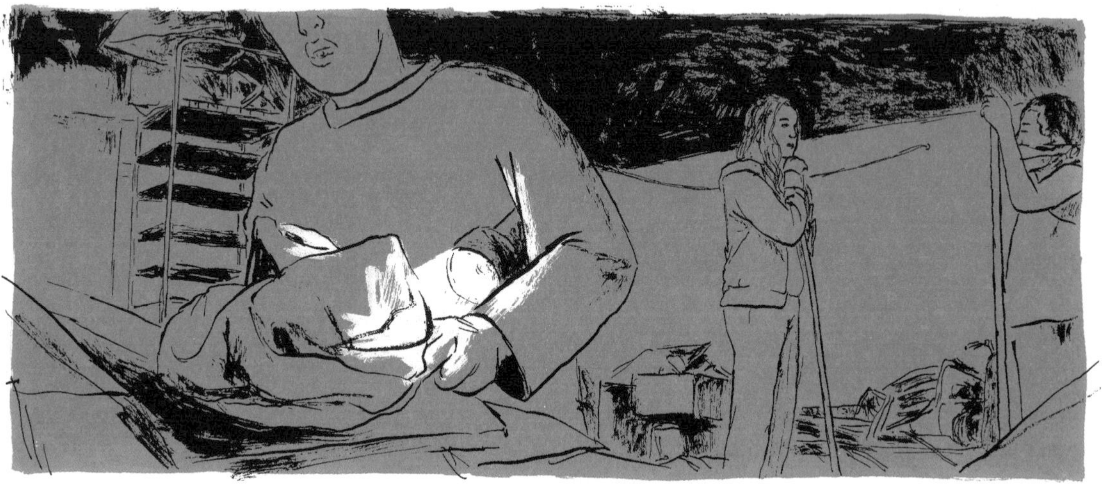

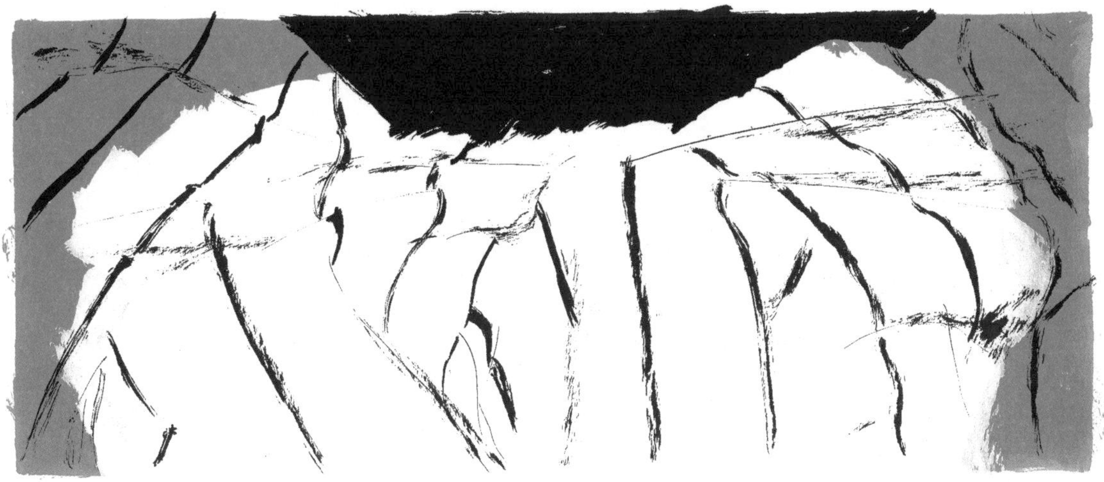

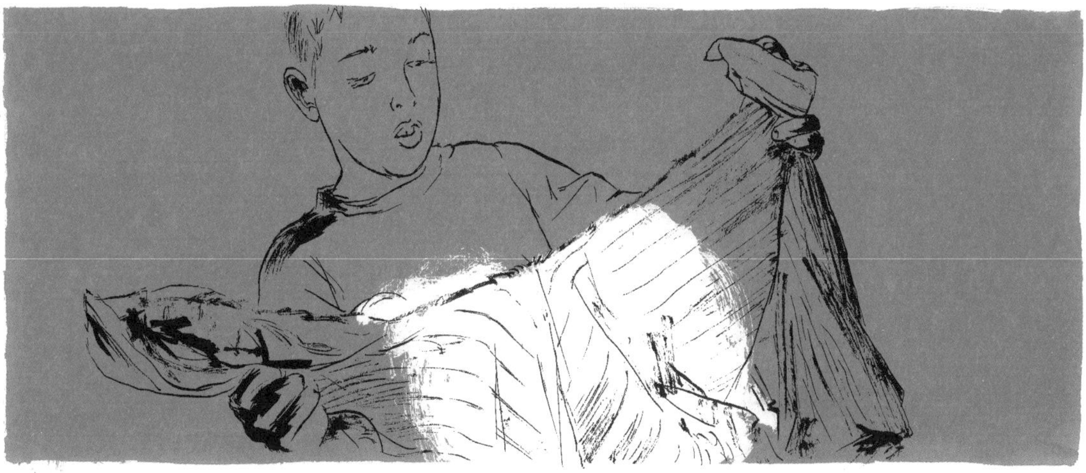

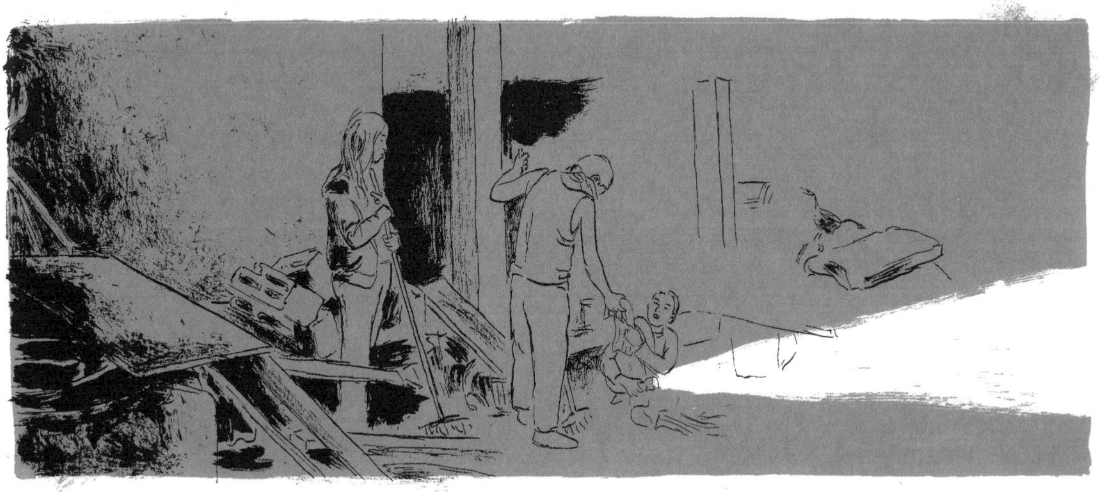

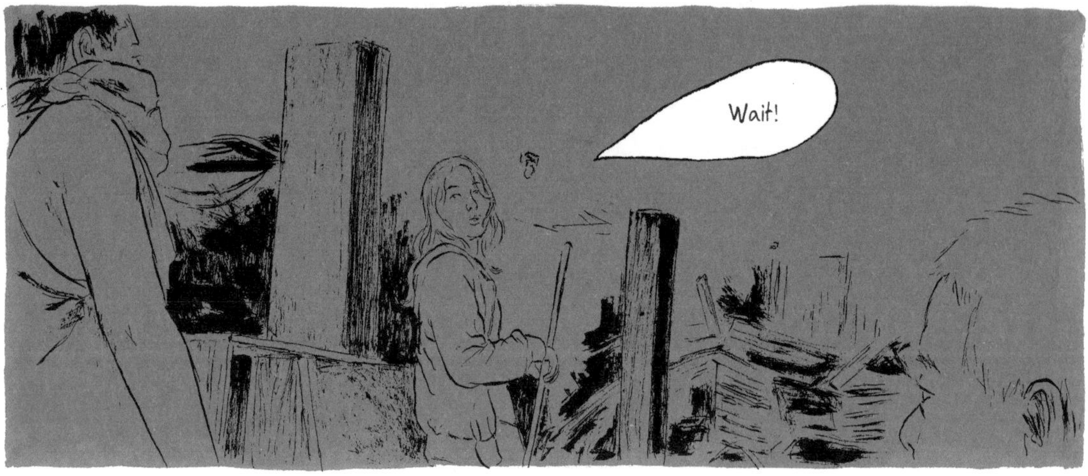
Wait!

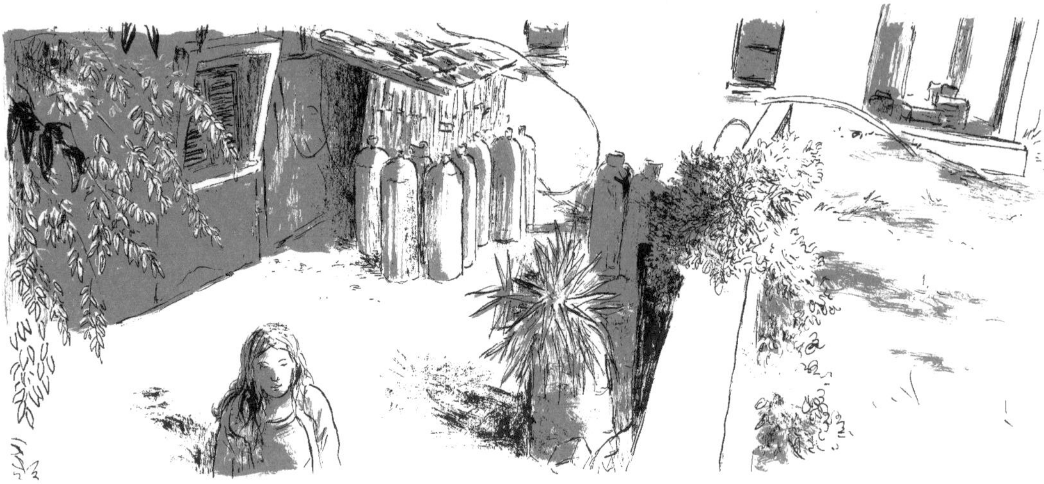

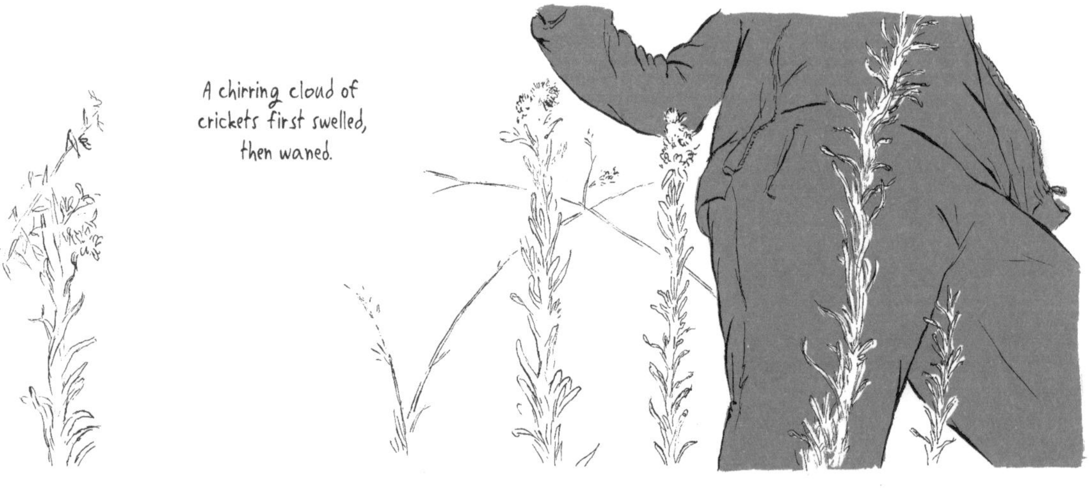
A chirring cloud of crickets first swelled, then waned.

I crept in quietly, careful not to wake my brothers.

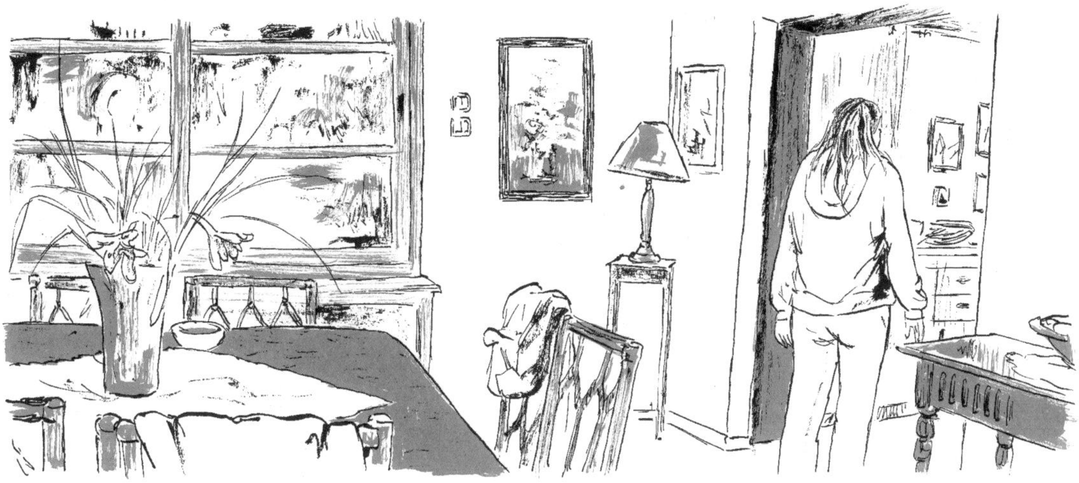

Mom was still playing cards at Levia's with Rachel and Tanya, Fat Nachum and Limping Shimshon,

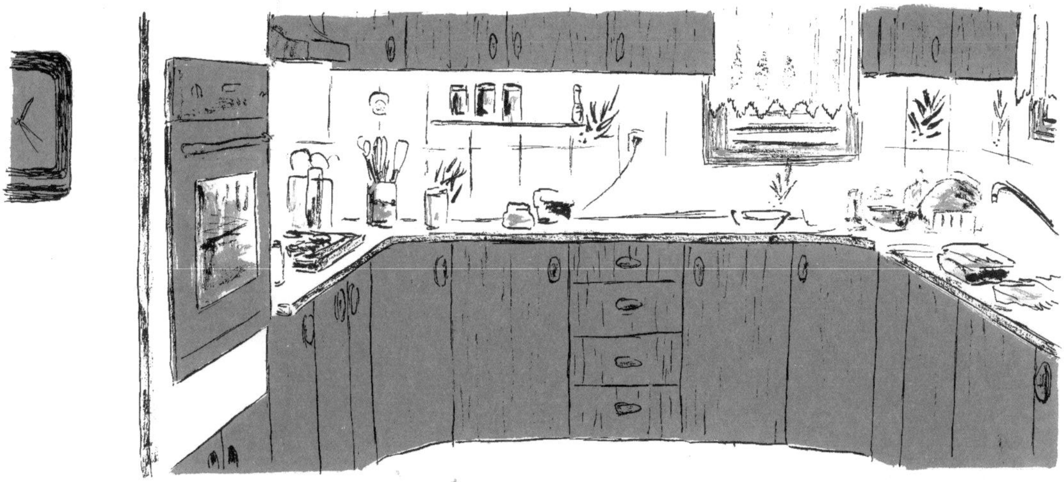

men that no one wanted in the war.

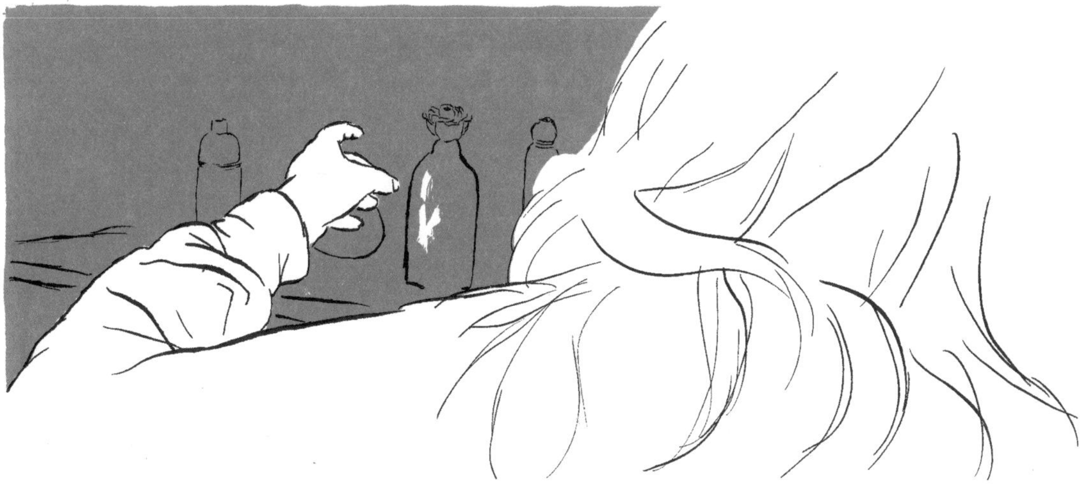

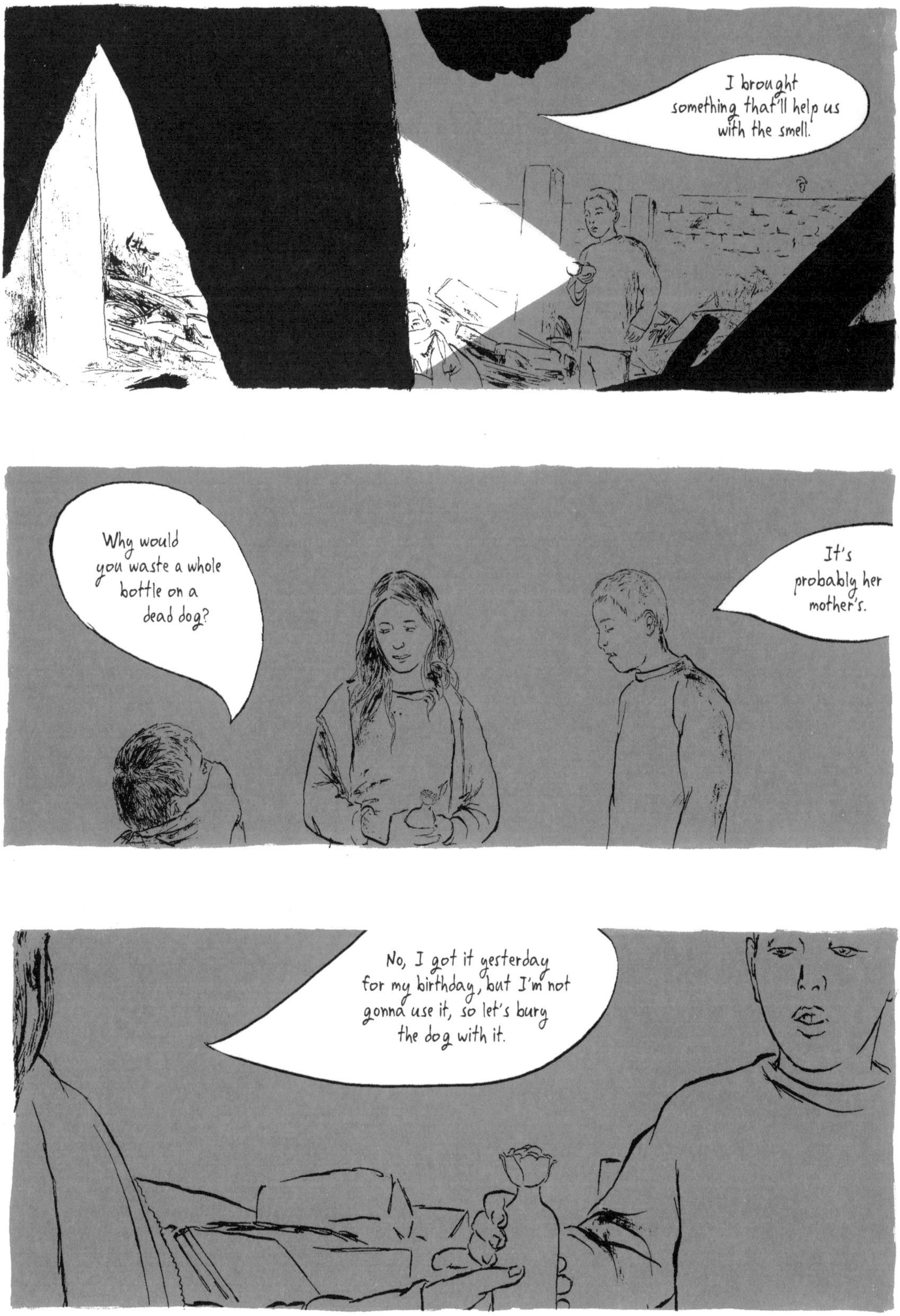
I brought something that'll help us with the smell.
Why would you waste a whole bottle on a dead dog?
It's probably her mother's.
No, I got it yesterday for my birthday, but I'm not gonna use it, so let's bury the dog with it.

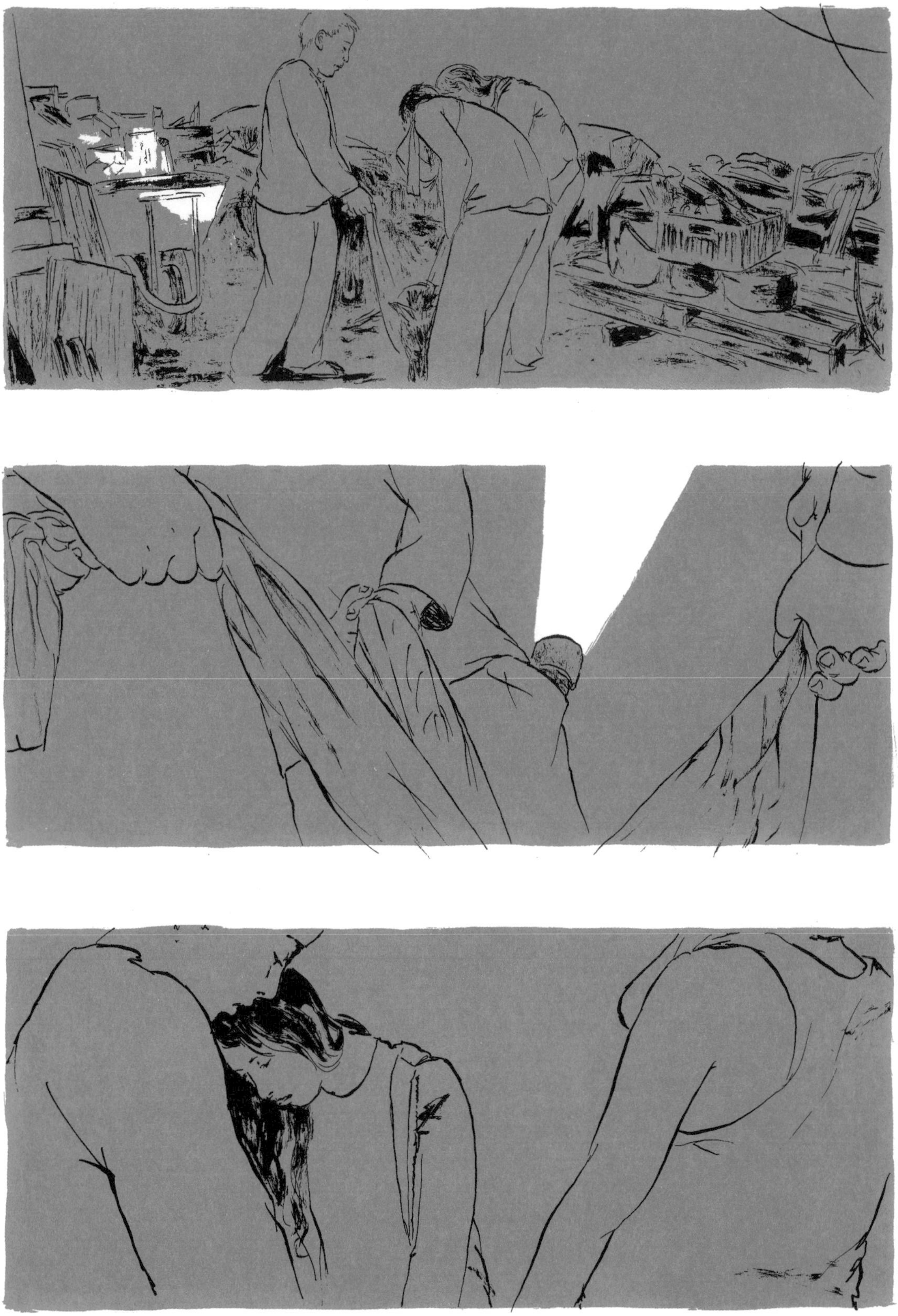

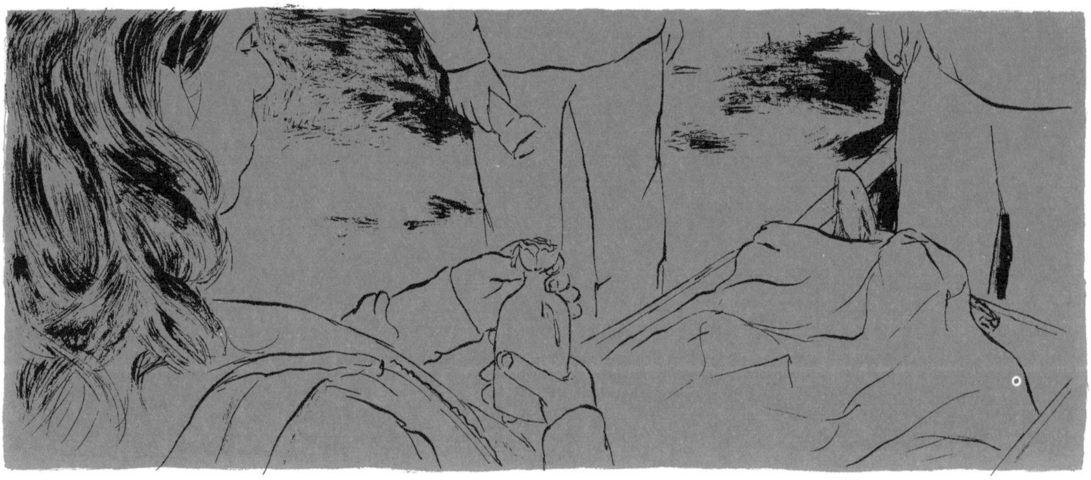

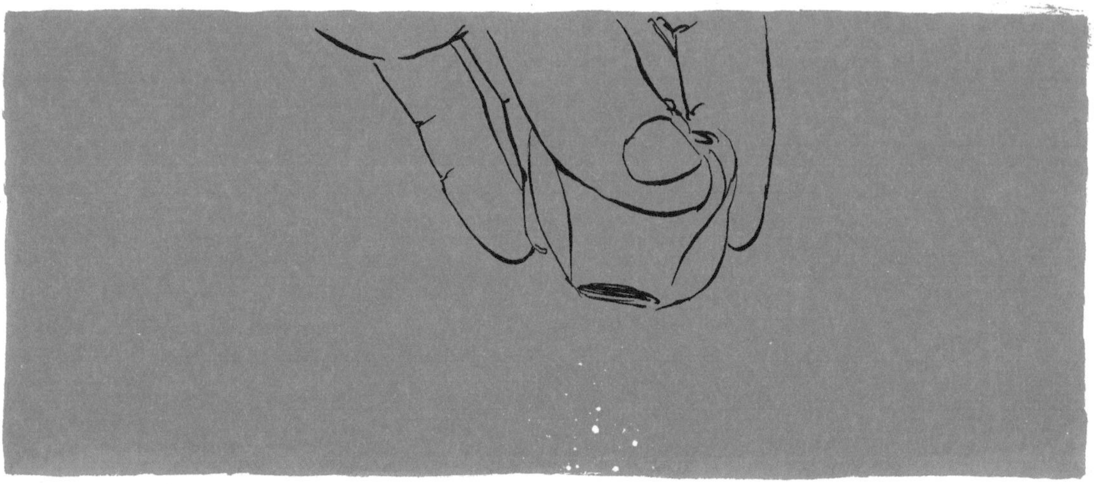

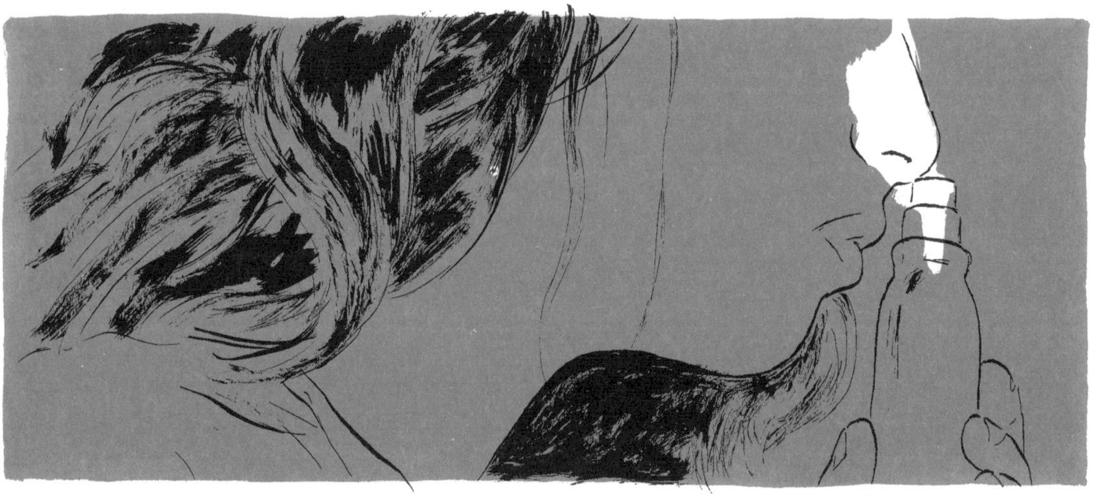

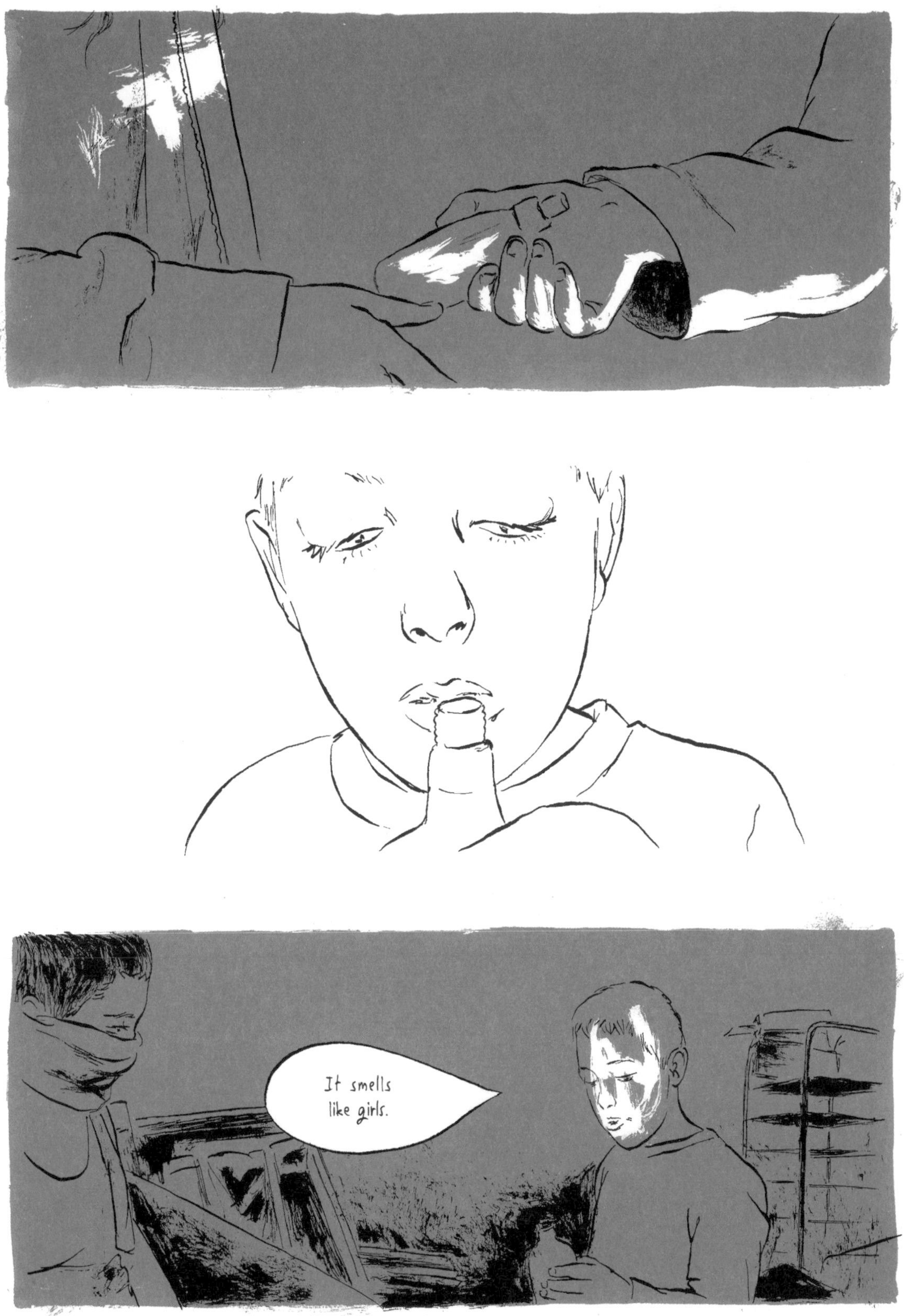
It smells like girls.

Smells like girls.

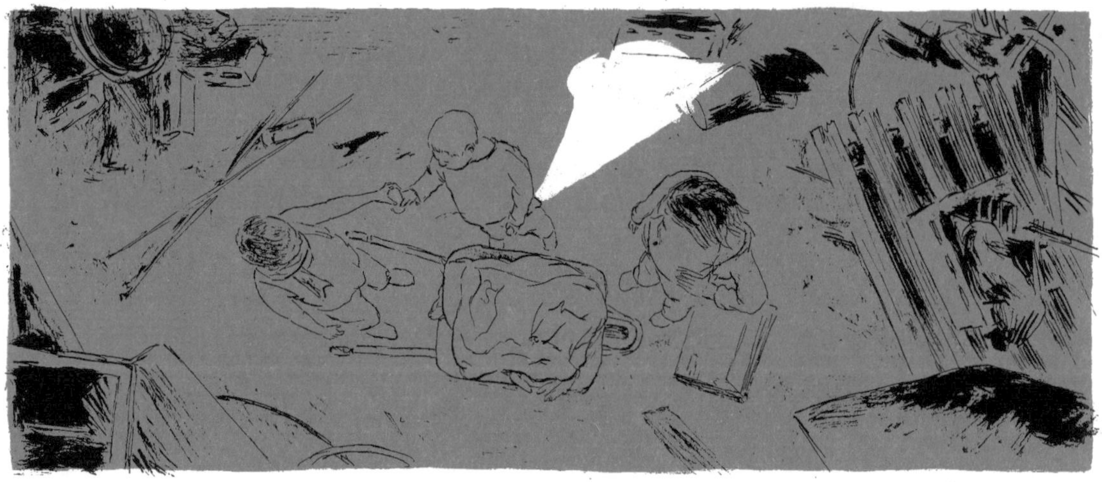

The words slid out of Omri's throat too fast, like a confession.

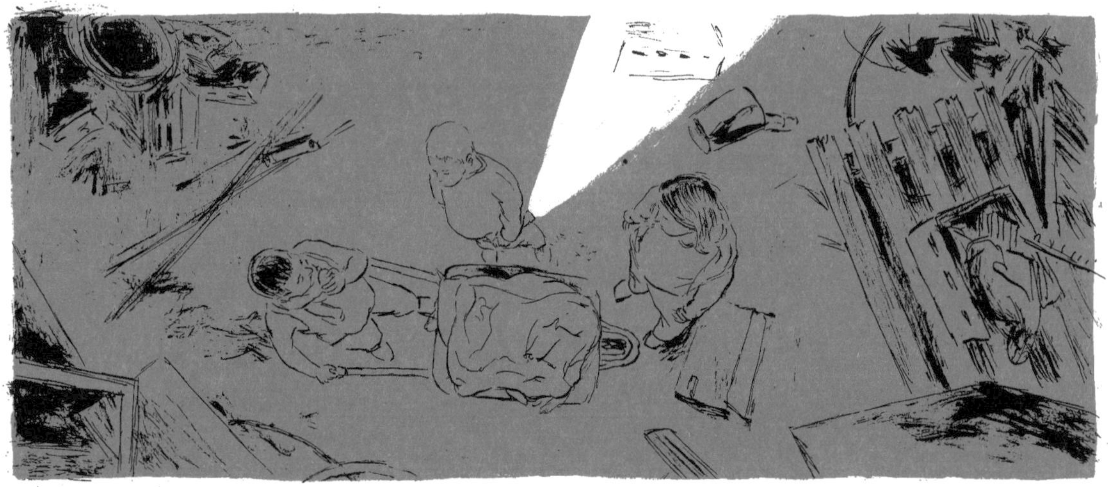

What is this girls' smell that Omri's talking about, here in the damp basement, over the swollen corpse of a German Shepherd?

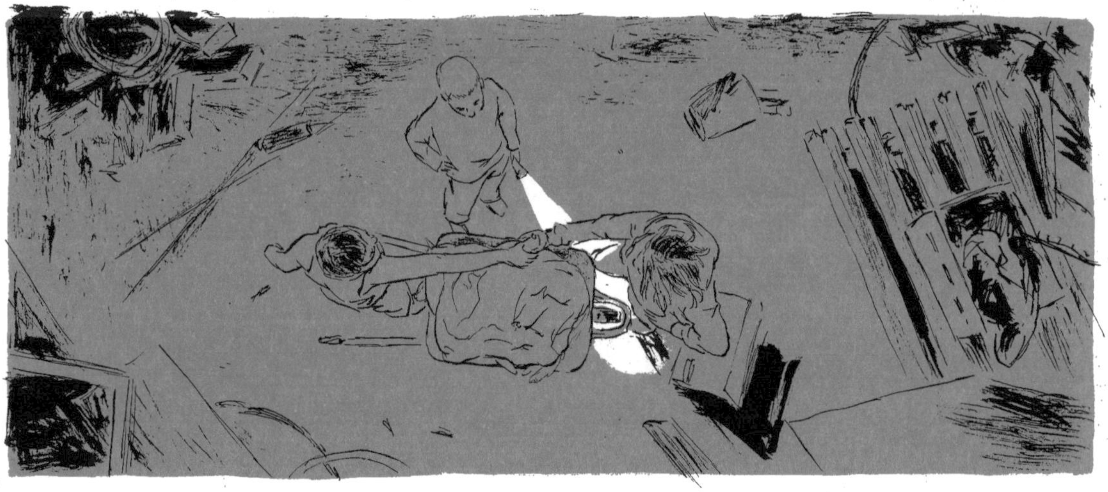

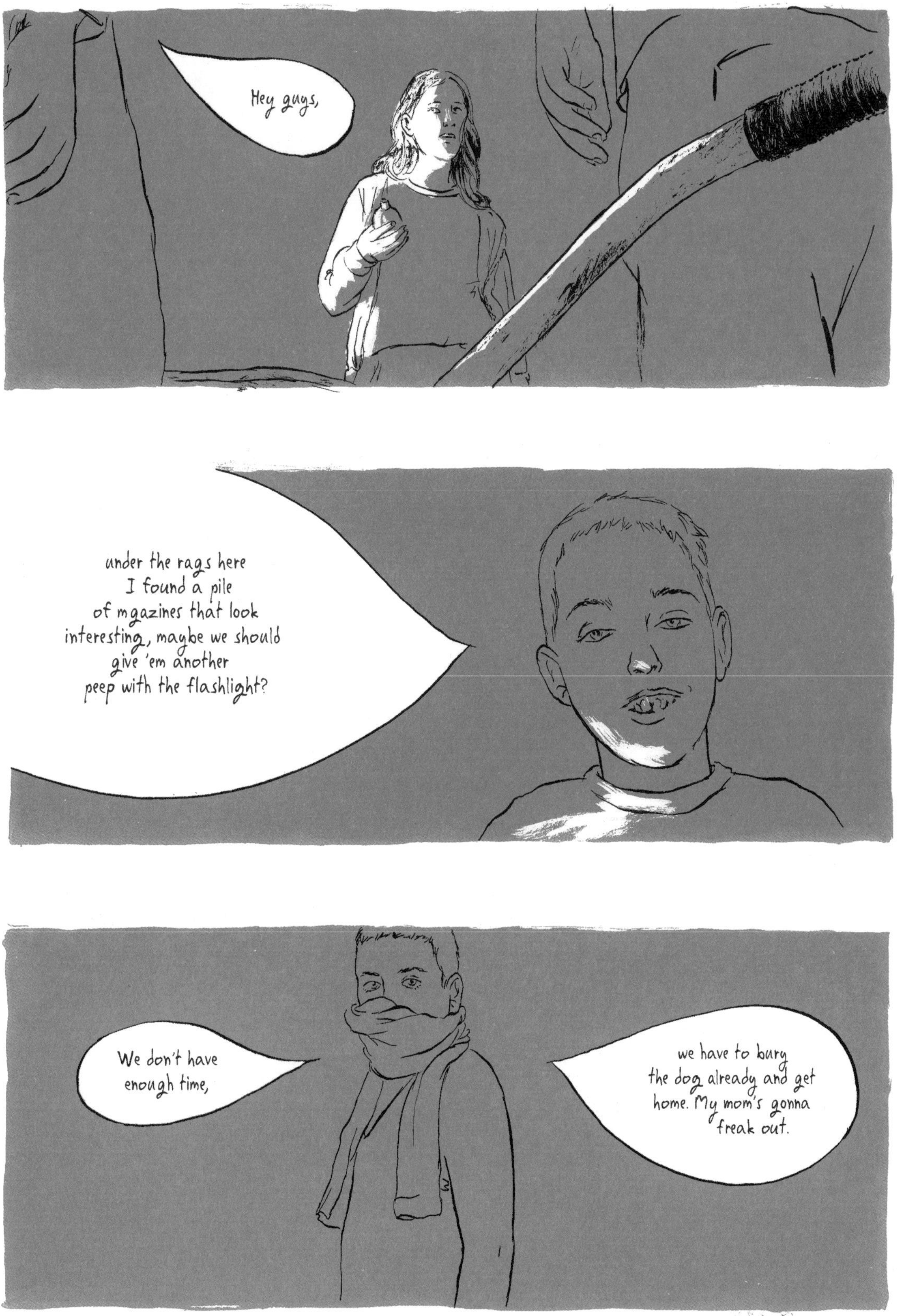
Hey guys,
under the rags here I found a pile of mgazines that look interesting, maybe we should give 'em another peep with the flashlight?
We don't have enough time,
we have to bury the dog already and get home. My mom's gonna freak out.

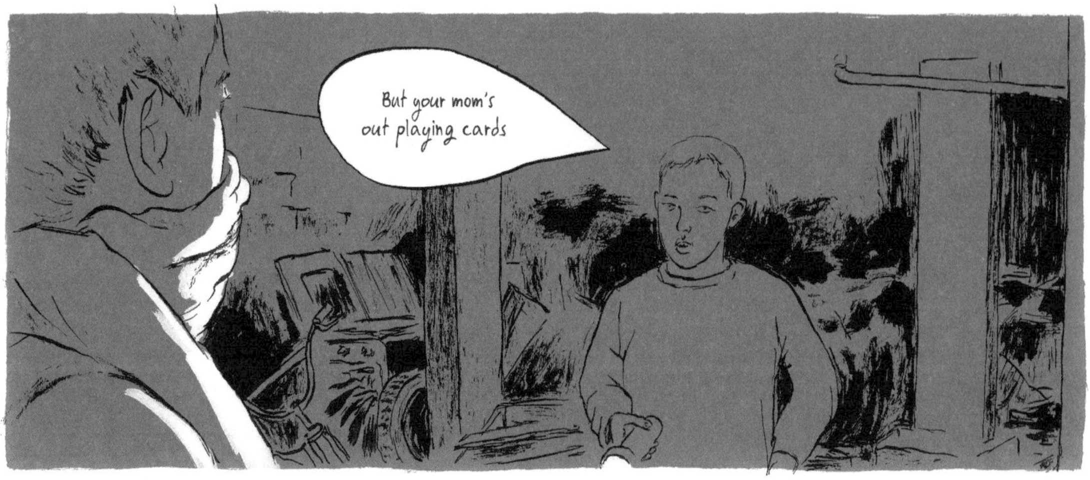
But your mom's out playing cards

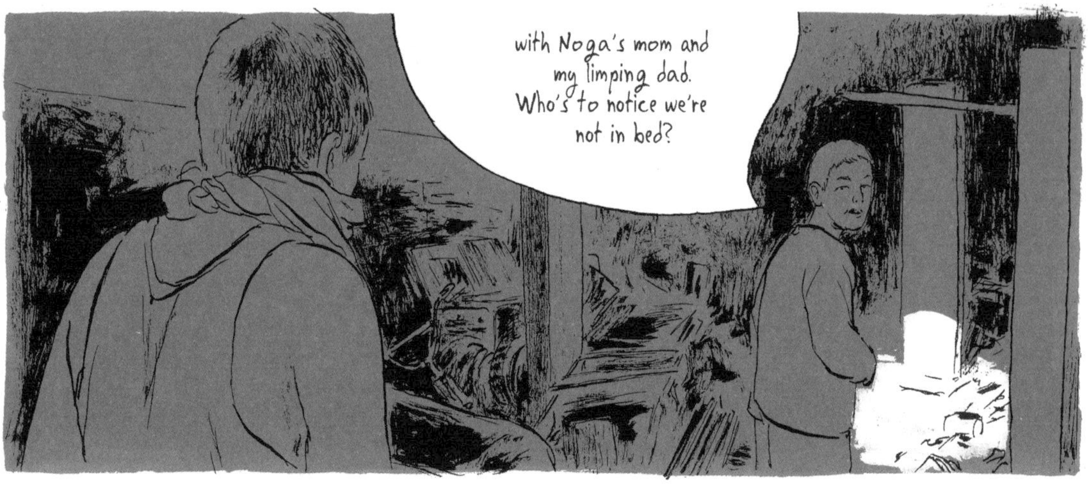
with Noga's mom and my limping dad. Who's to notice we're not in bed?

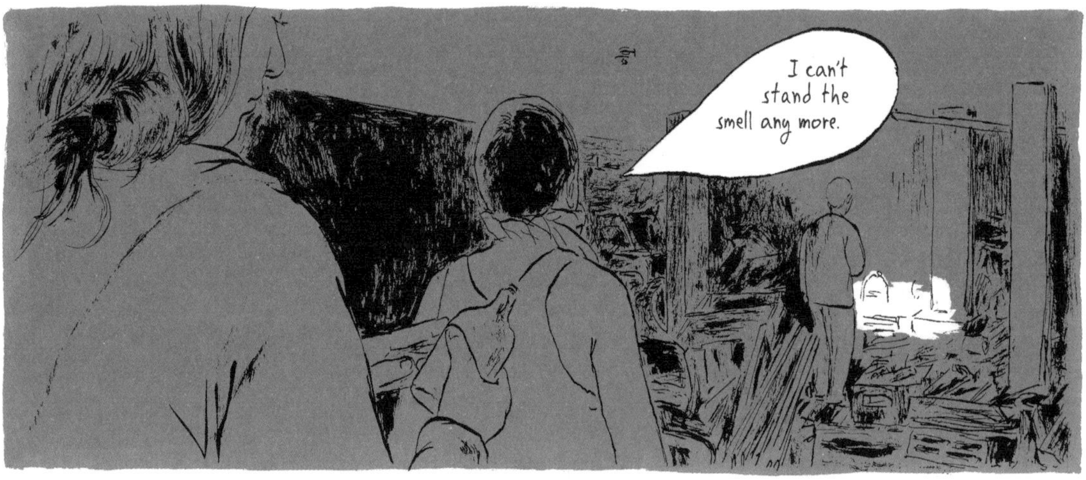
I can't stand the smell any more.

But me, I was curious to see what's hiding in Dad's secret basement.

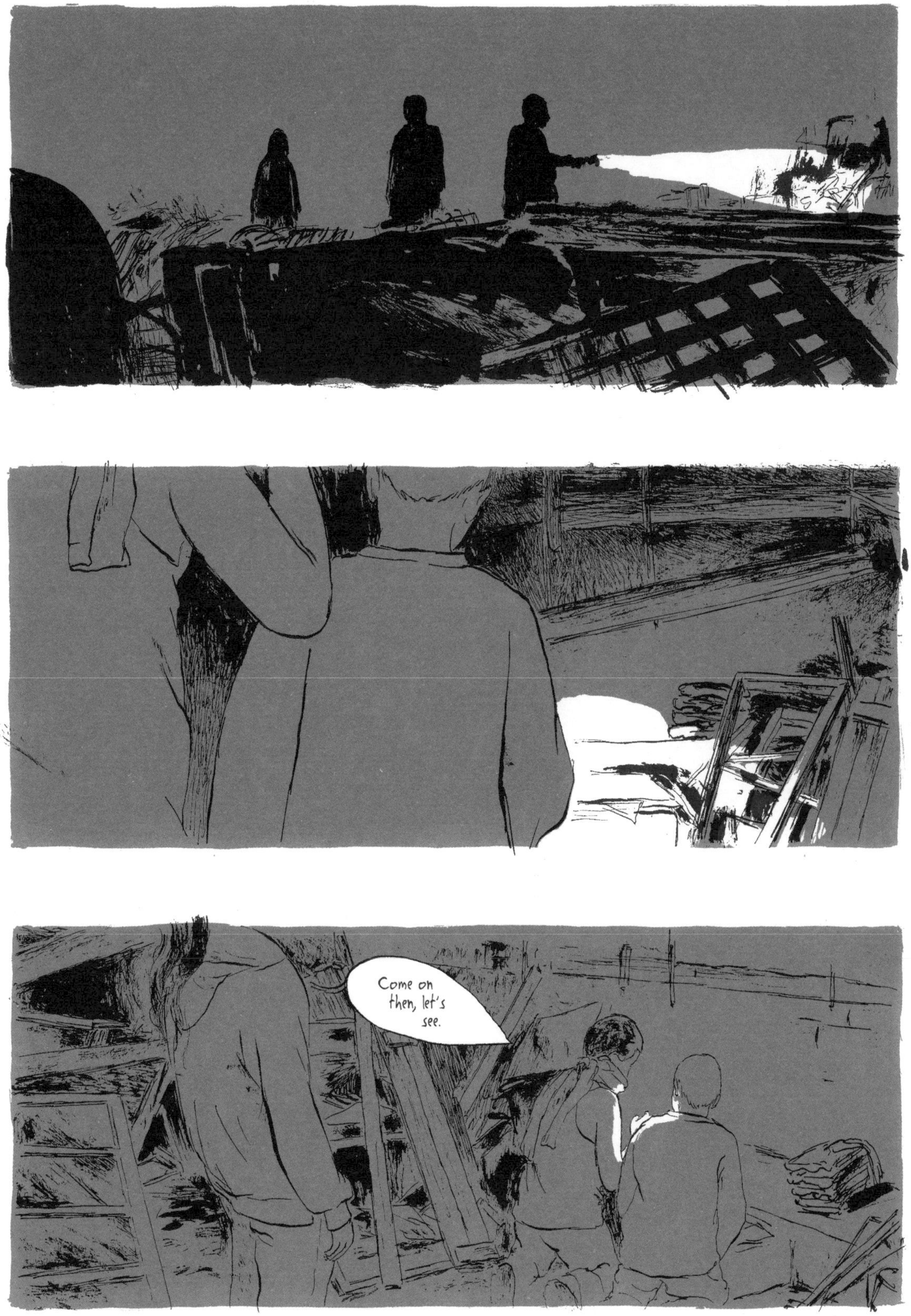
Come on then, let's see.

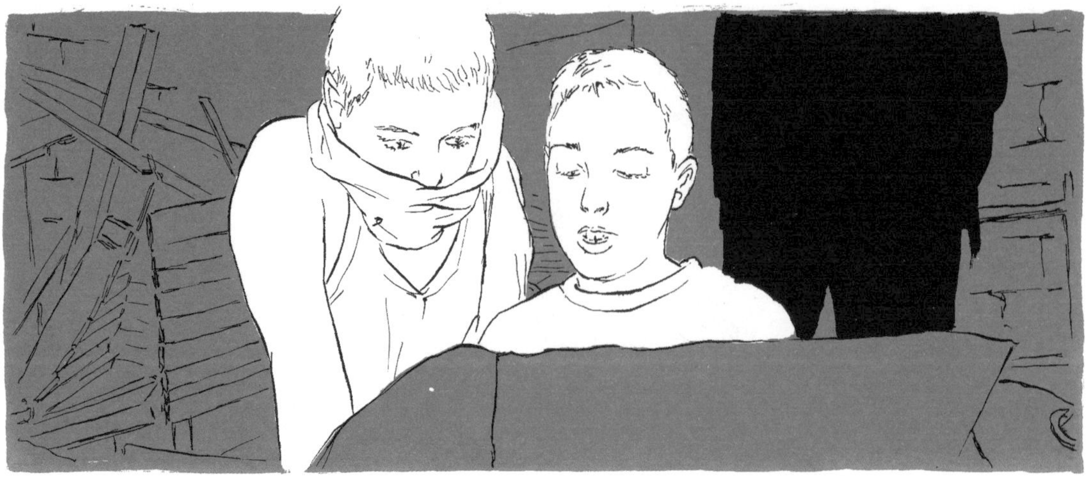

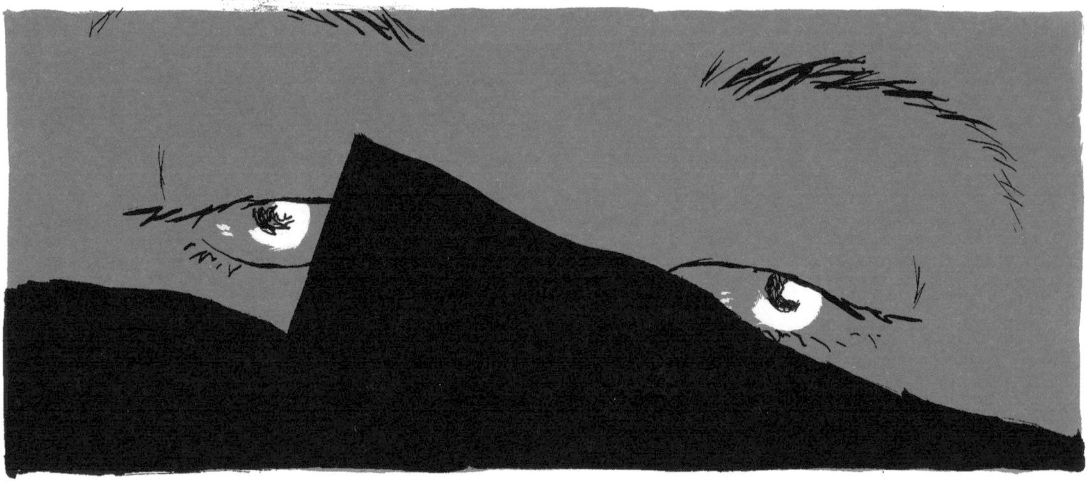

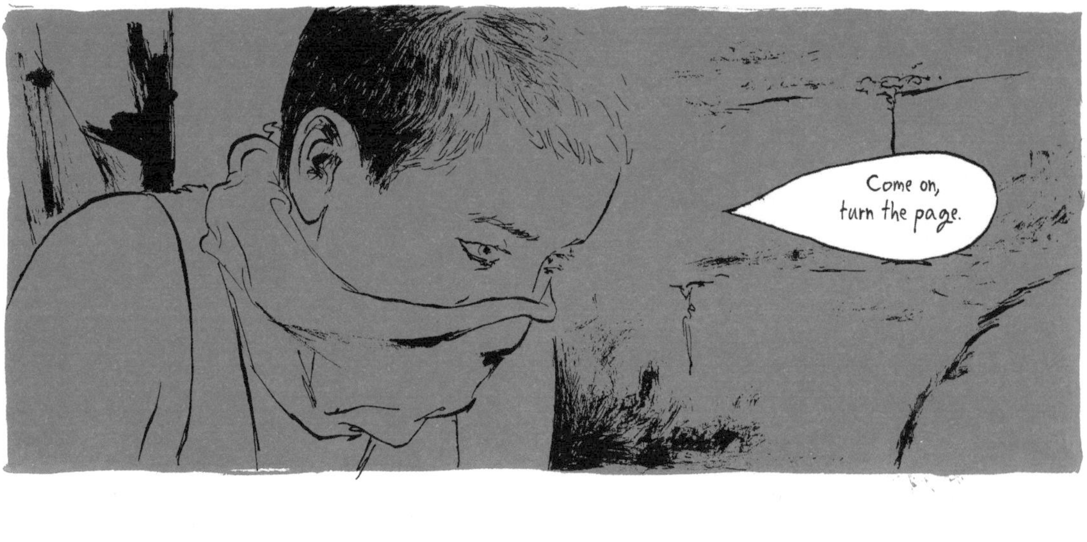
Come on, turn the page.

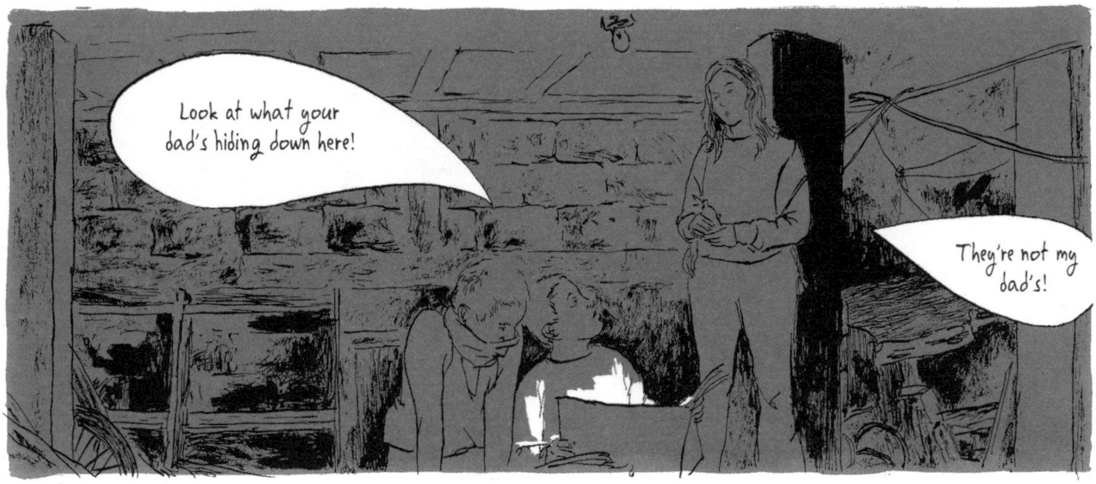
Look at what your dad's hiding down here!
They're not my dad's!

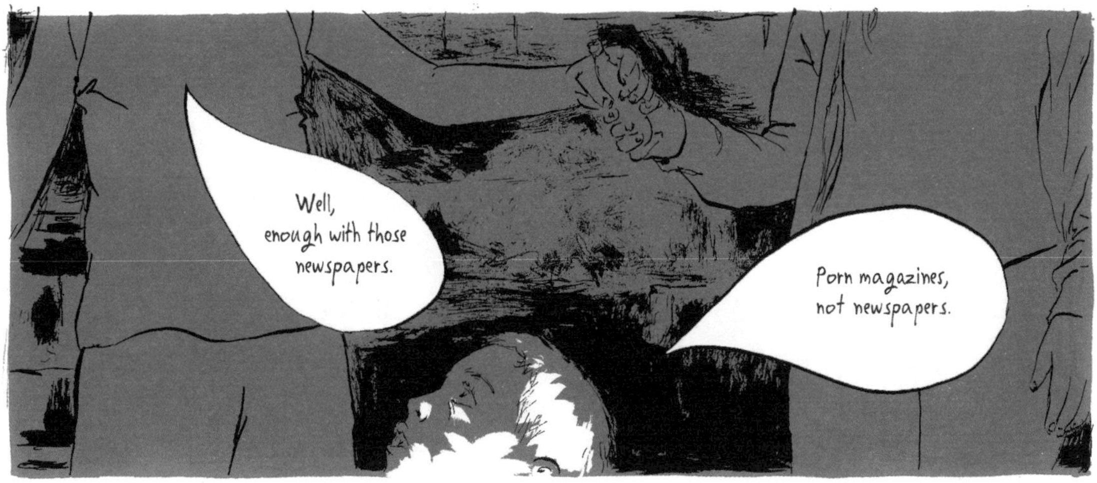
Well, enough with those newspapers.
Porn magazines, not newspapers.

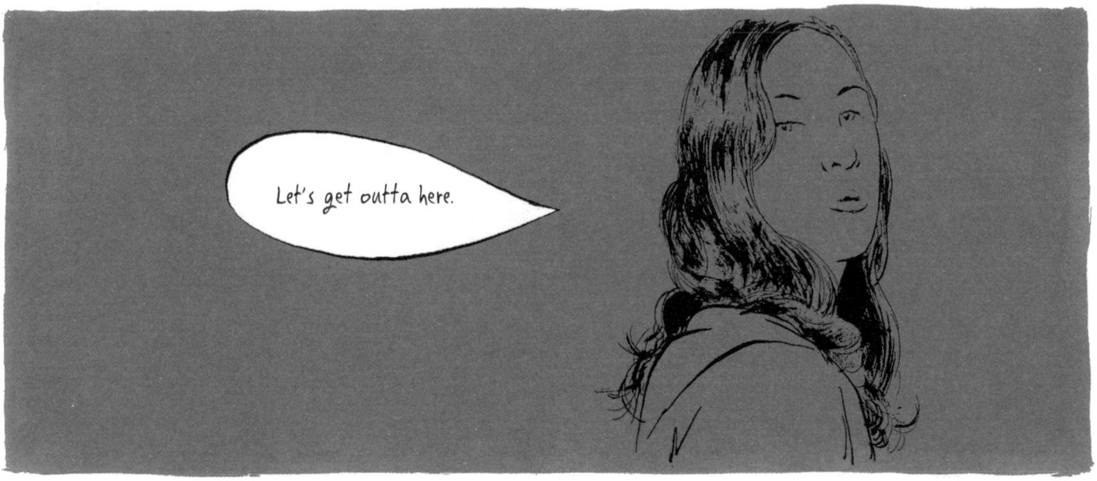
Let's get outta here.

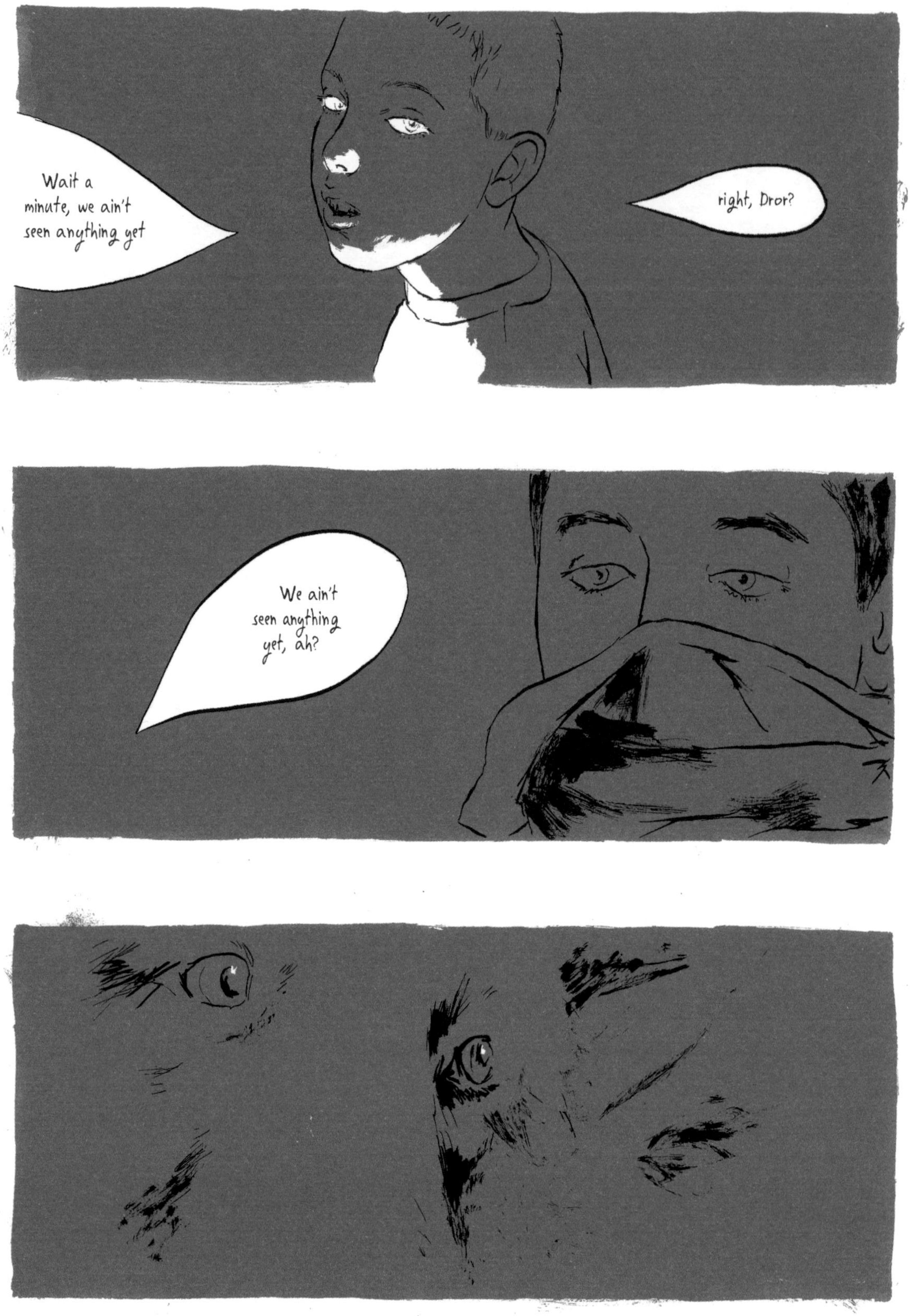
Wait a minute, we ain't seen anything yet
right, Dror?
We ain't seen anything yet, ah?

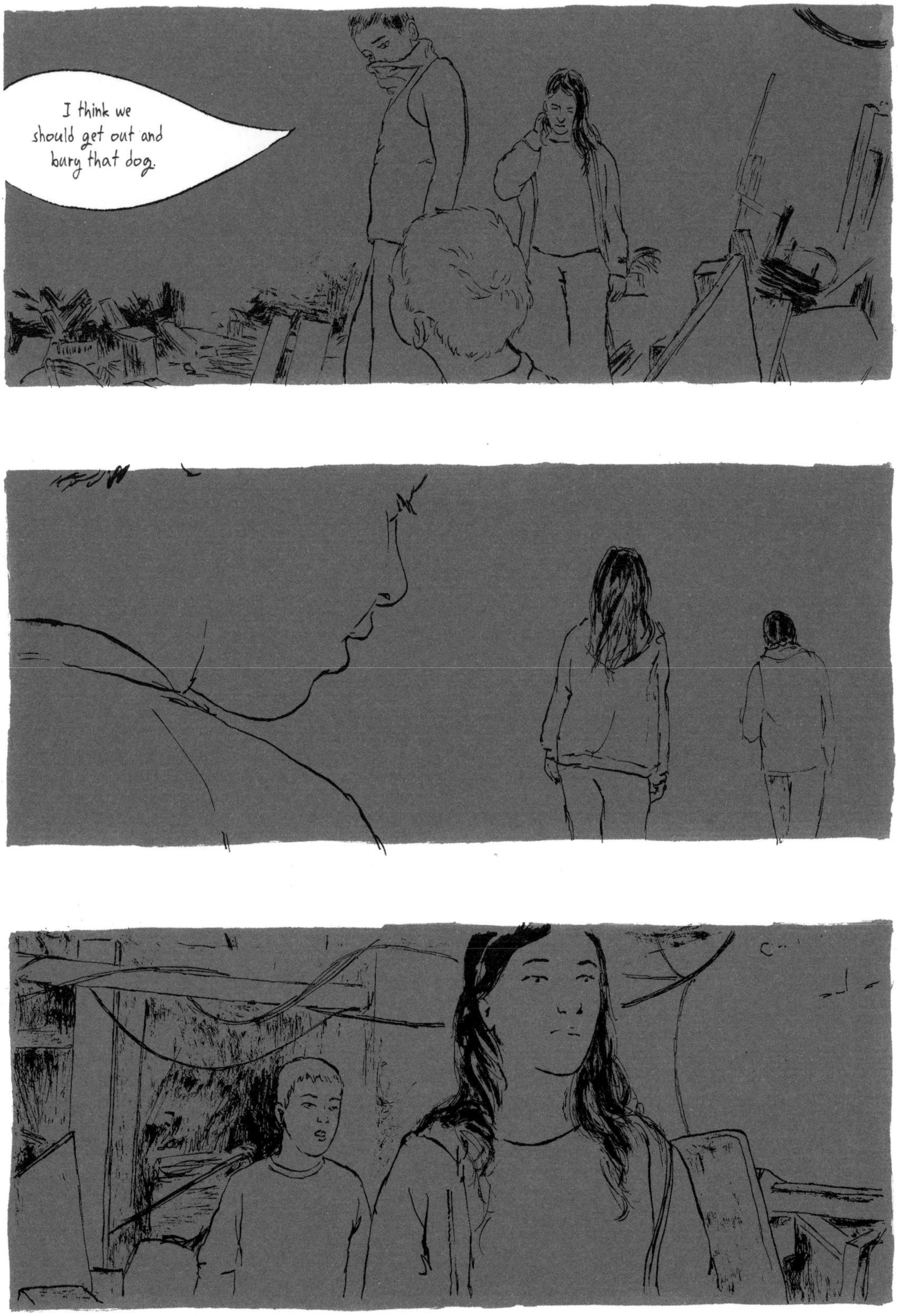
I think we should get out and bury that dog.

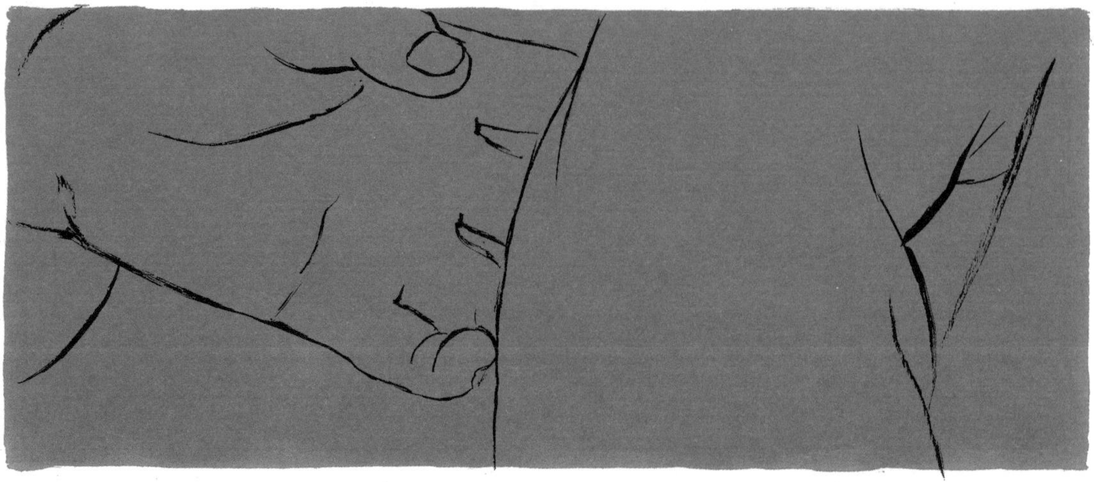

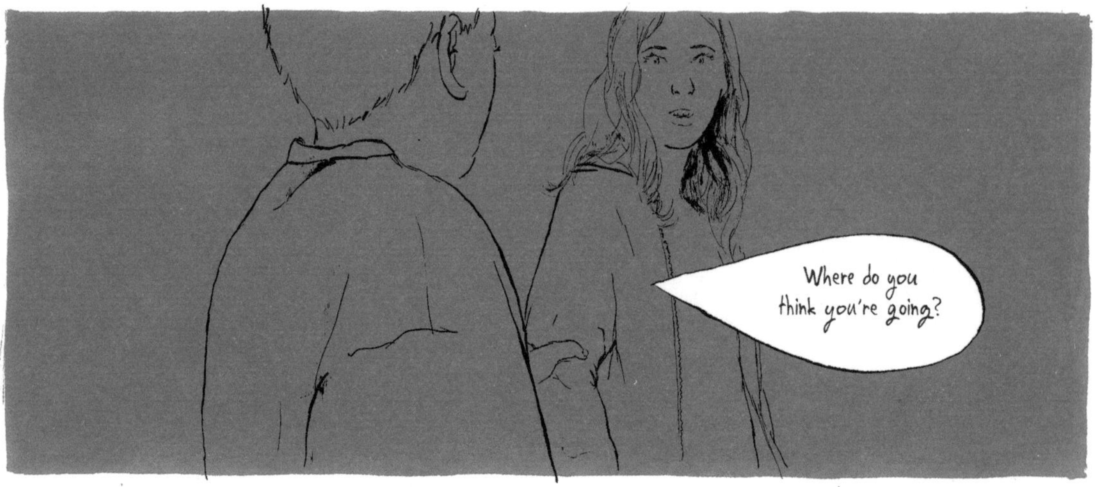
Where do you think you're going?

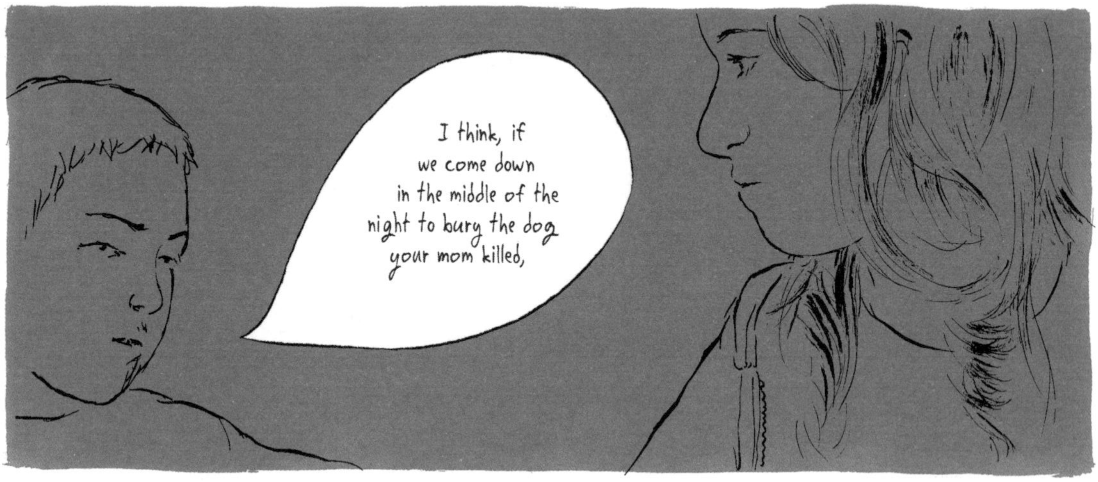
I think, if we come down in the middle of the night to bury the dog your mom killed,

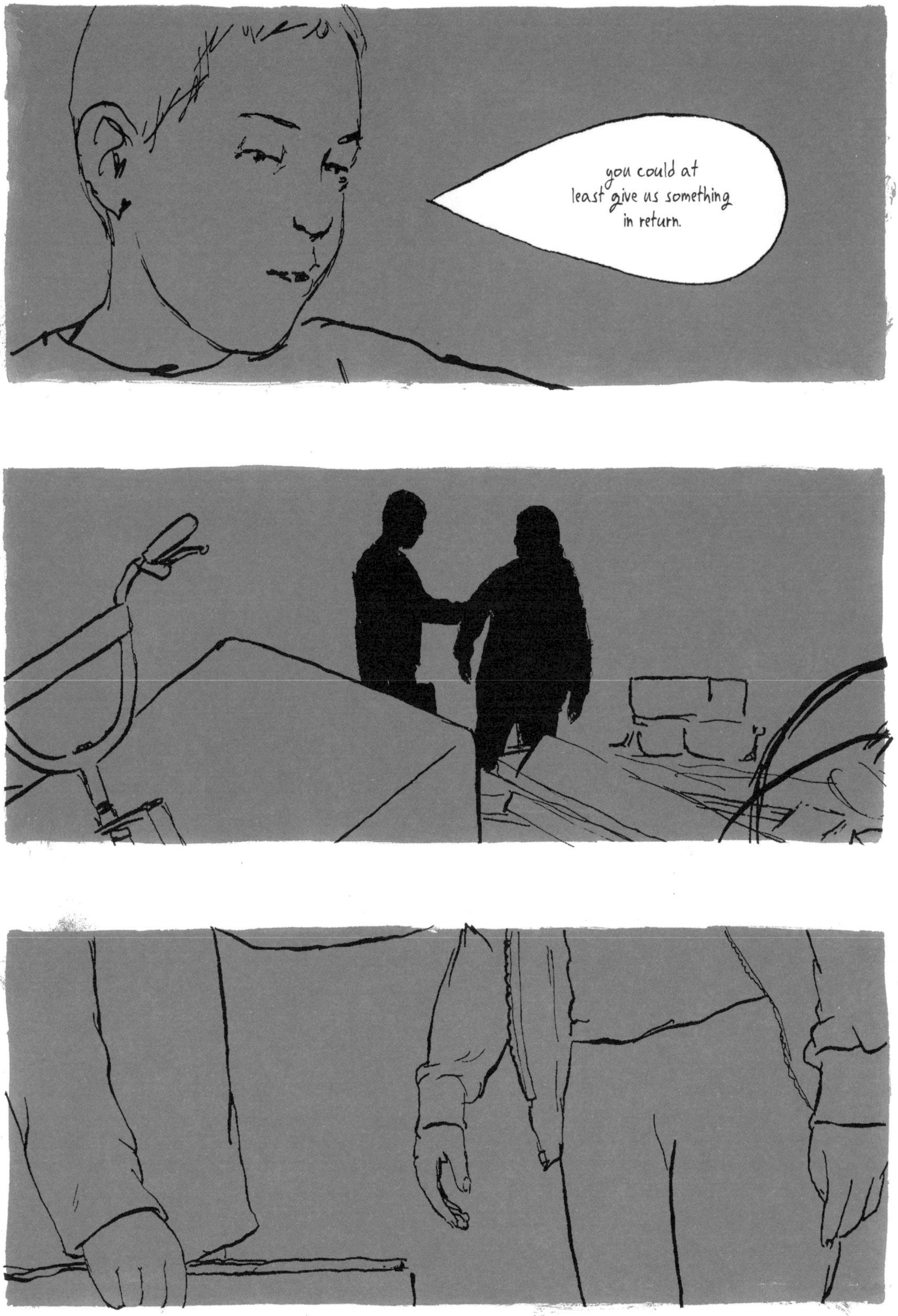
you could at least give us something in return.

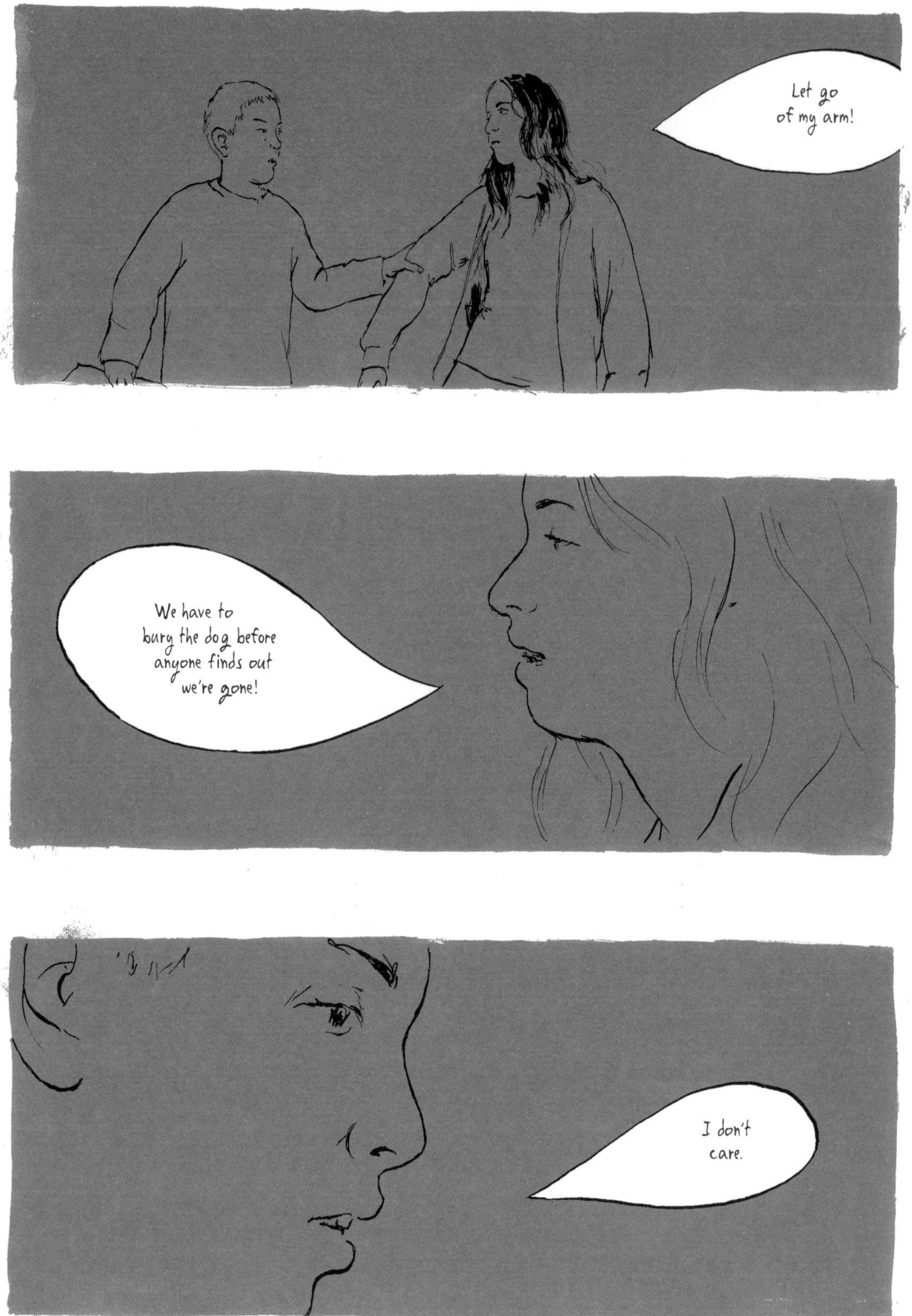
Let go of my arm!
We have to bury the dog before anyone finds out we're gone!
I don't care.

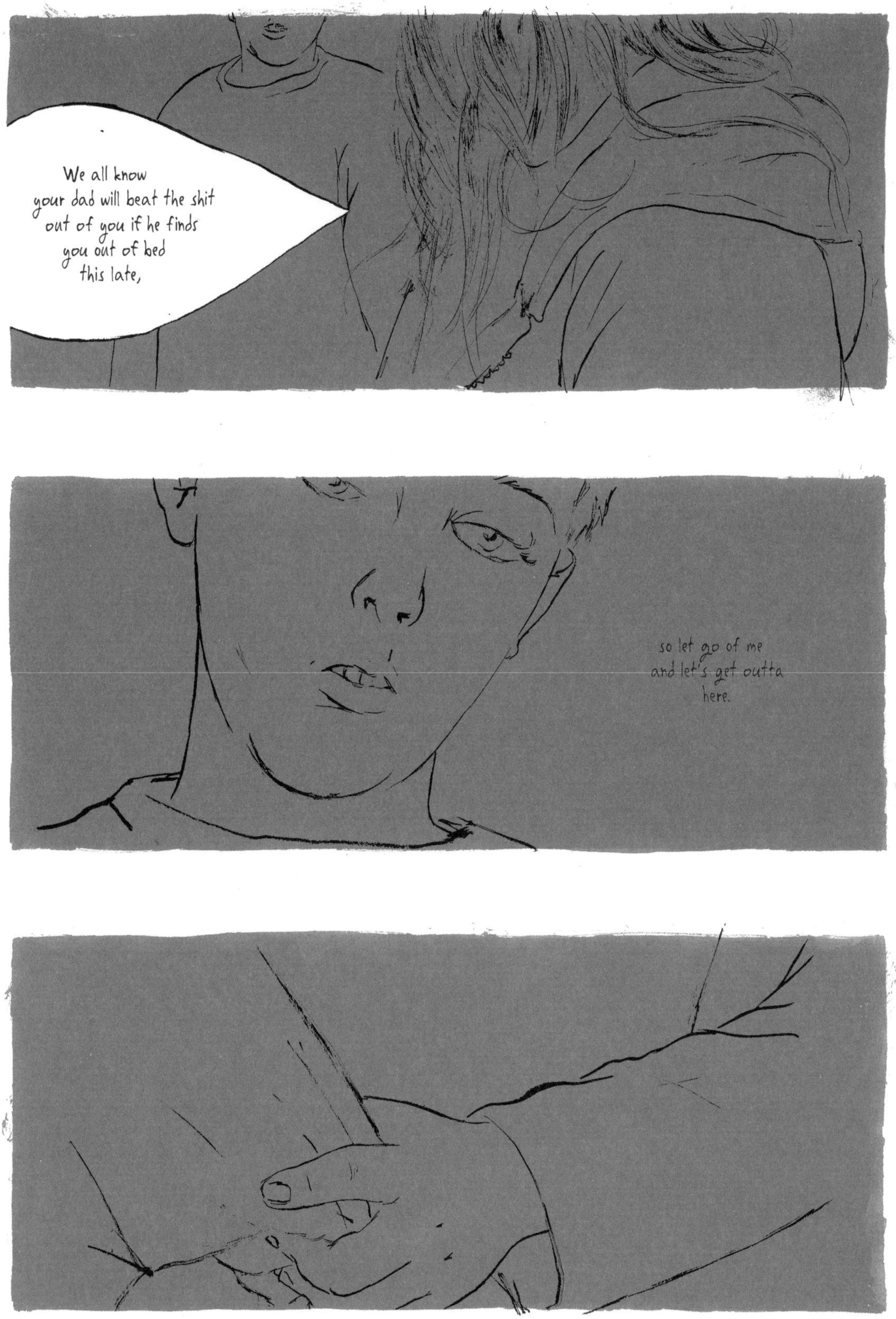
We all know your dad will beat the shit out of you if he finds you out of bed this late,
so let go of me and let's get outta here.

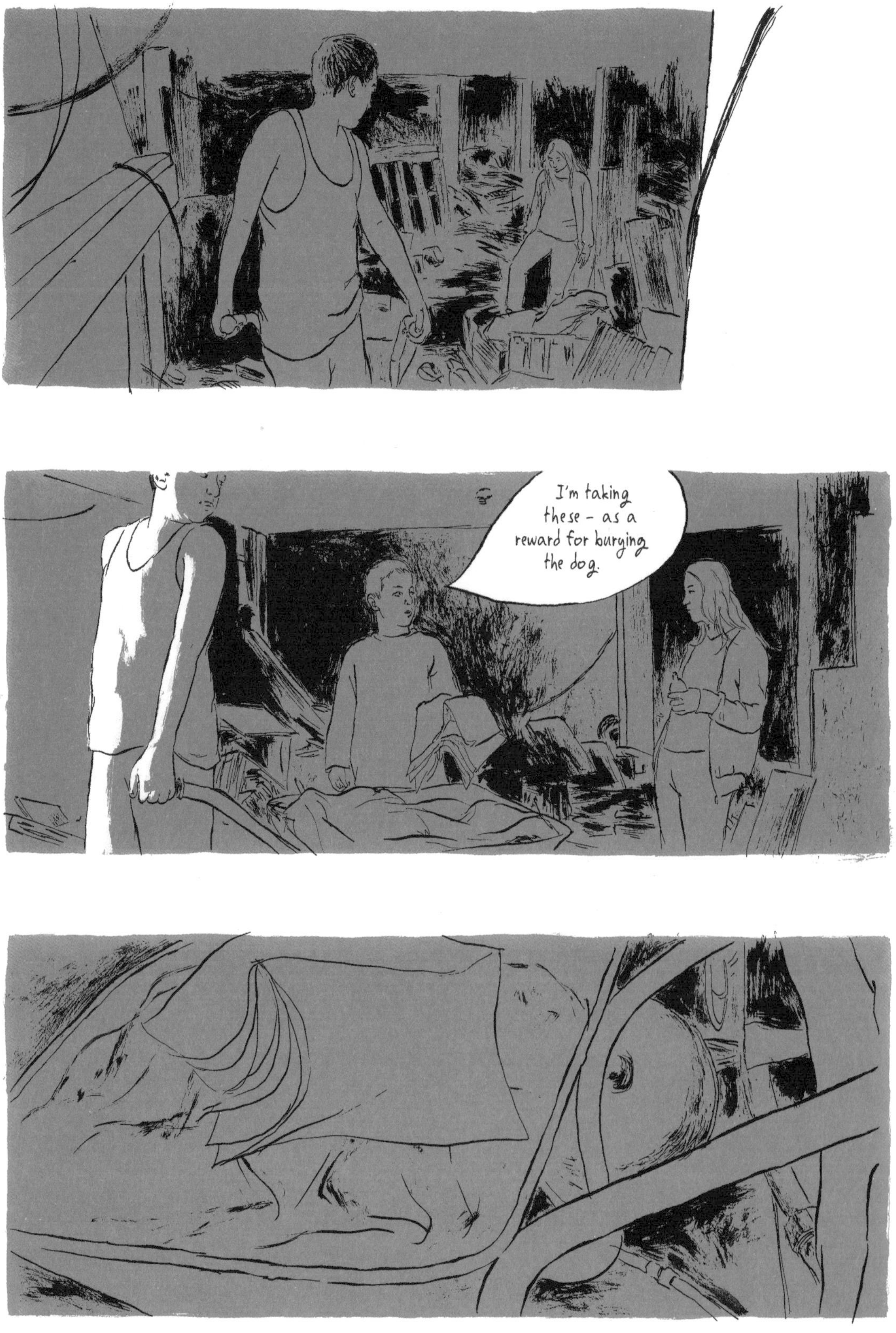
I'm taking these - as a reward for burying the dog.

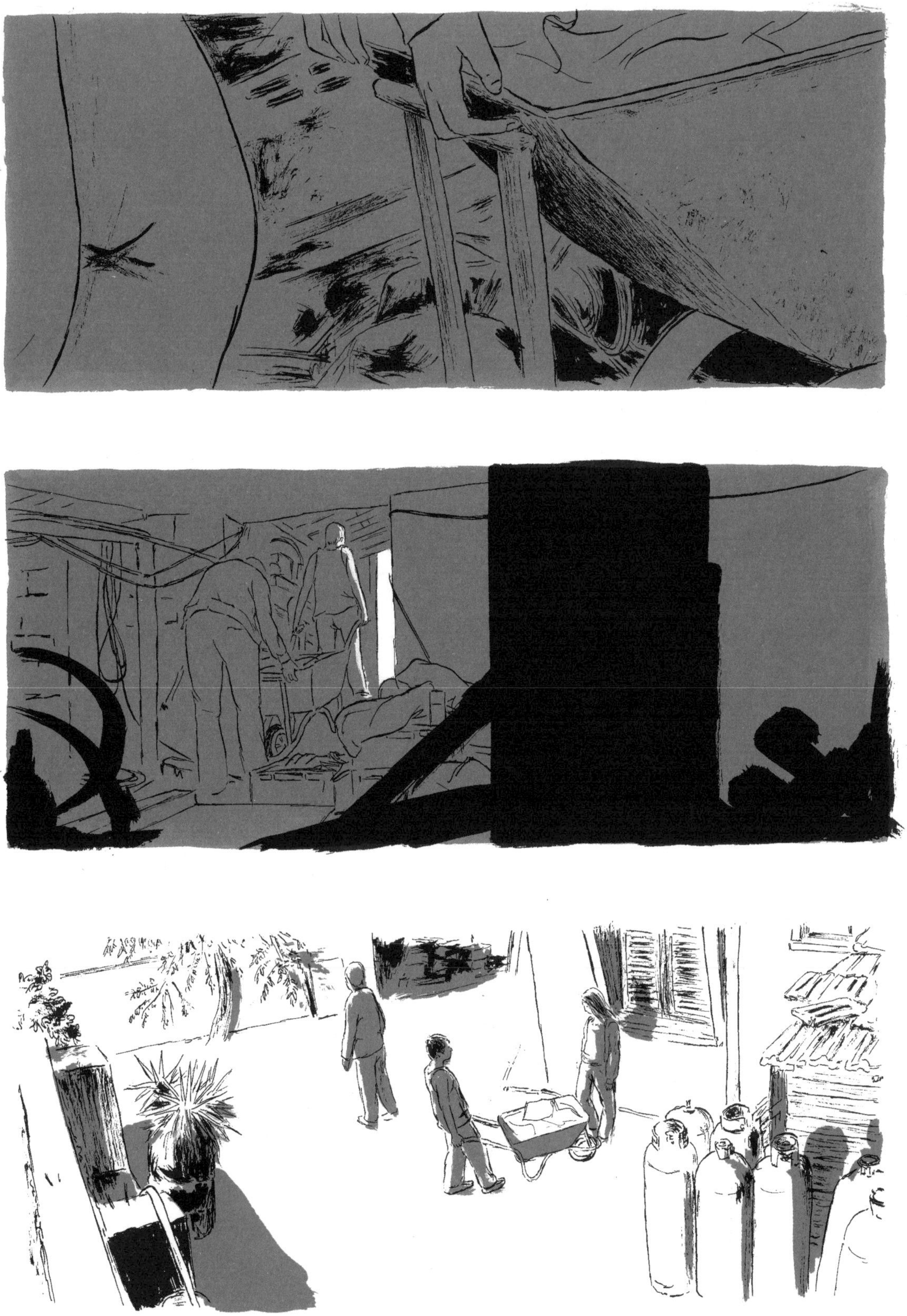

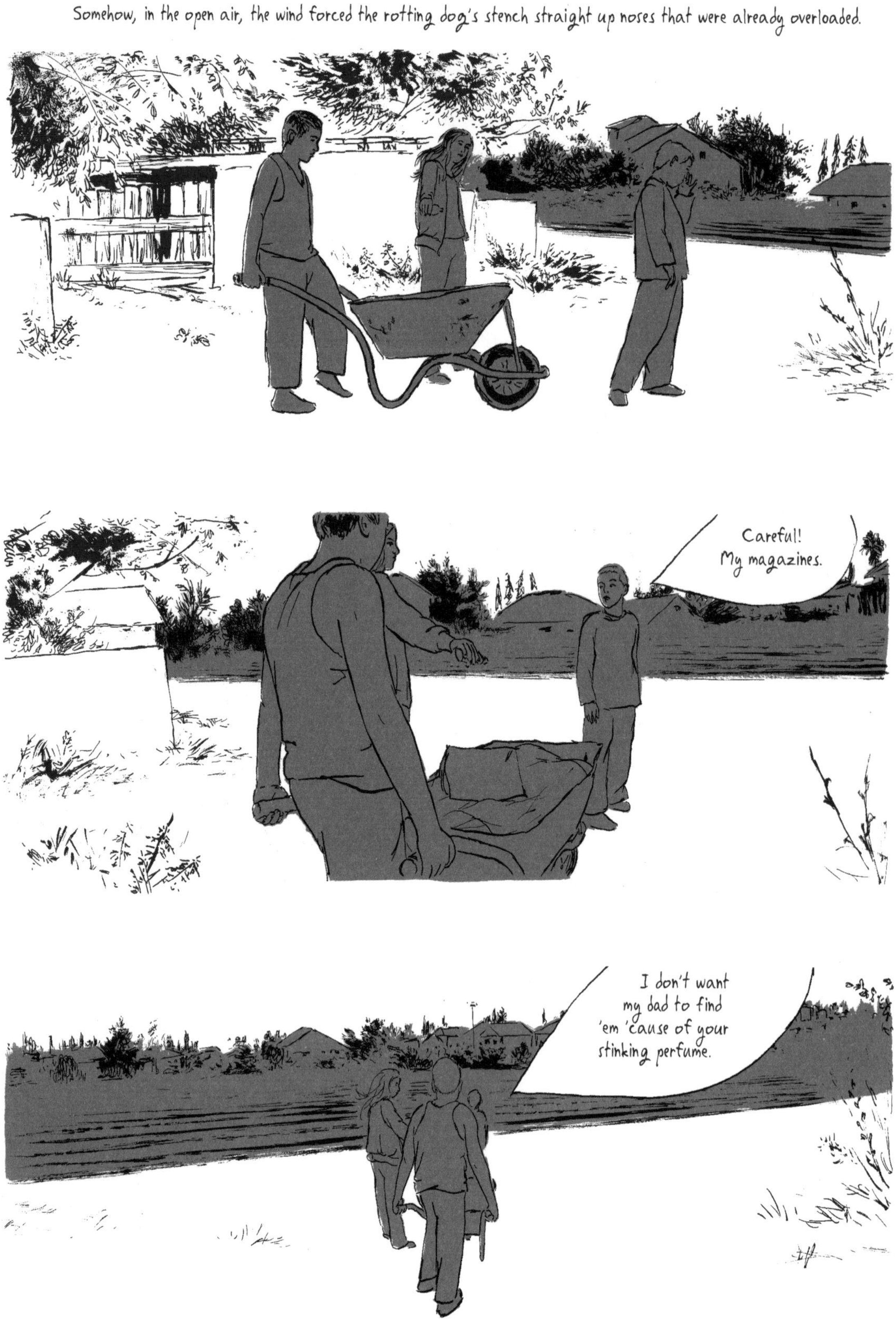
Somehow, in the open air, the wind forced the rotting dog's stench straight up noses that were already overloaded.
Careful! My magazines.
I don't want my dad to find 'em 'cause of your stinking perfume.

HOUSES
1989

After high school and before the army, As'ad and I sort eggs in the Co-op warehouse.

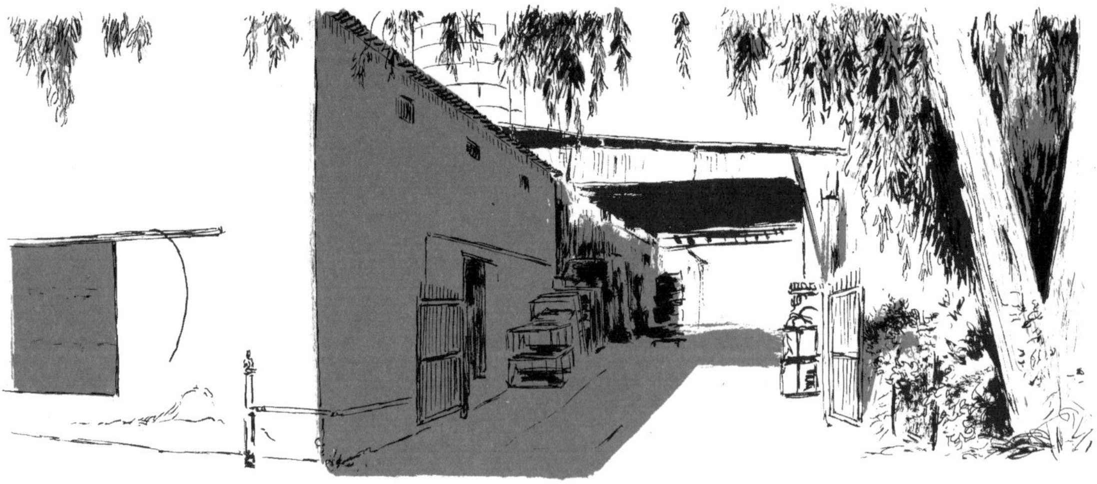

Hunched over the sorting machine, I inspect the eggs rolling by on metal tracks.

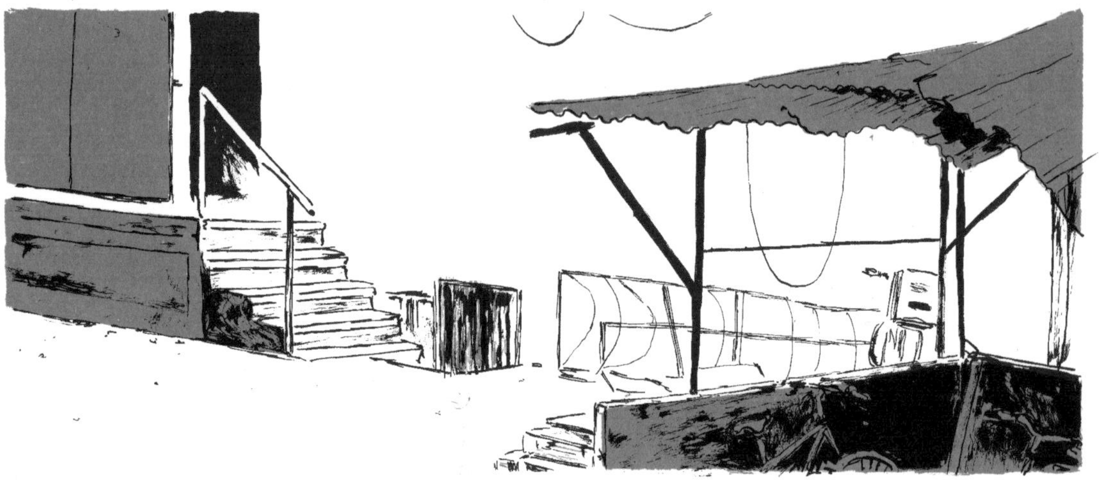

The fluorescent light burns cold under the tracks

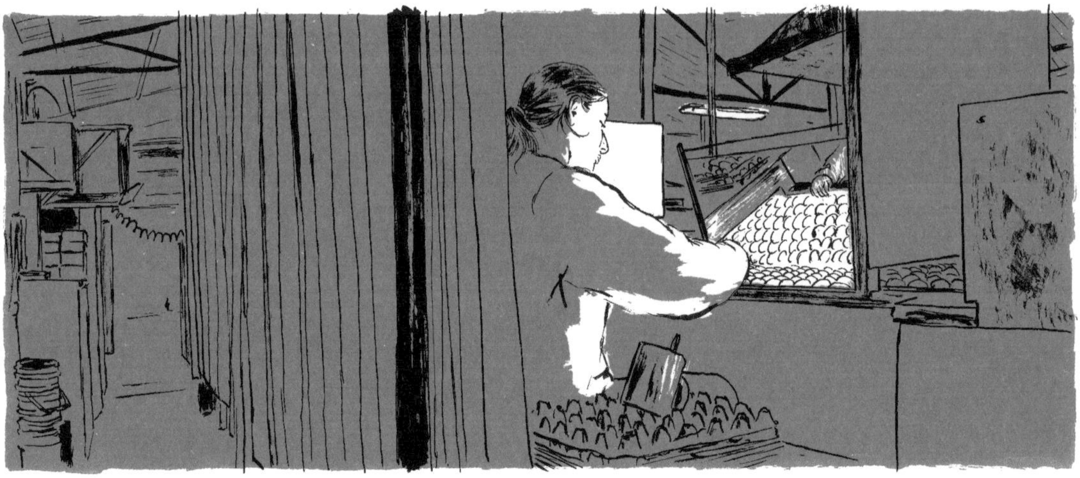

making the eggs transparent.

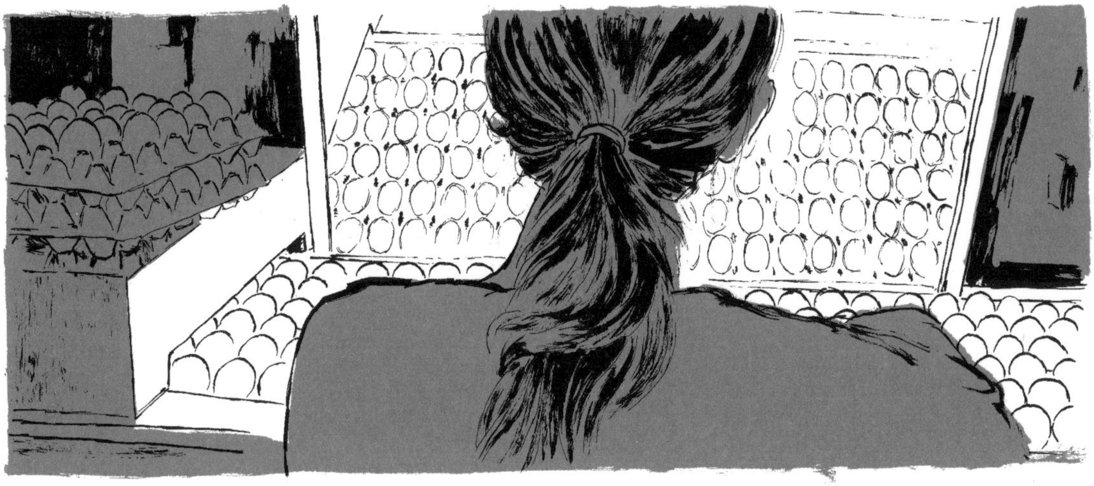

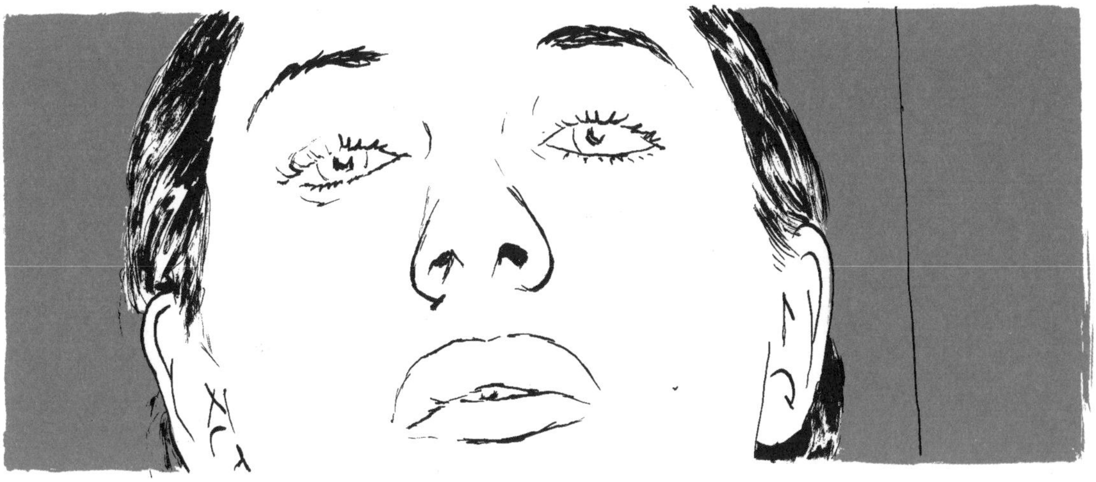

The egg, its insides shining smooth and luminous, rolls on undisturbed, beyond the plastic sheet

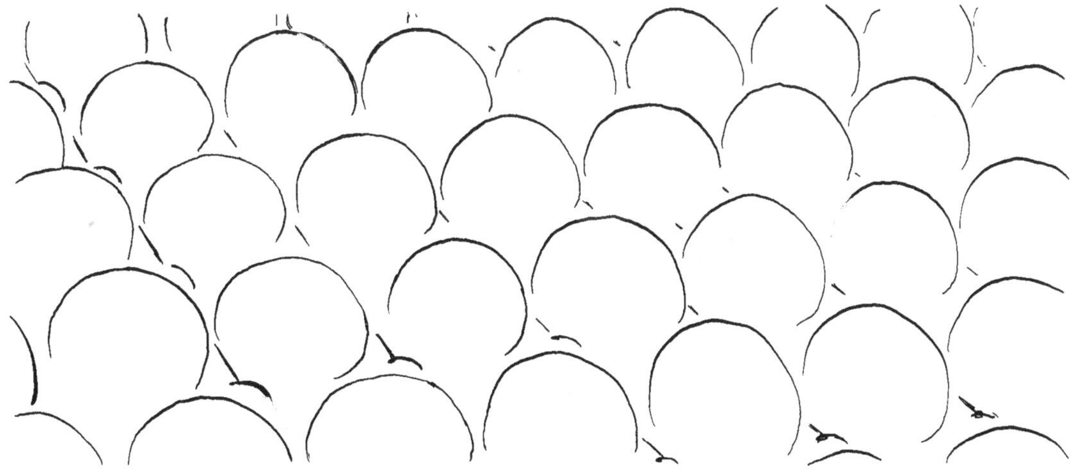

where it is inlaid in a carton mold, a diamond in cold ash.

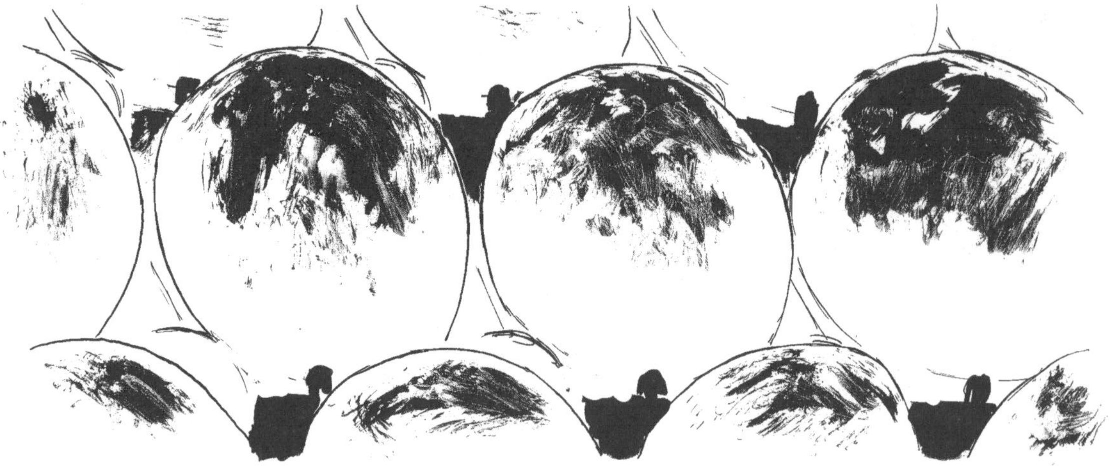

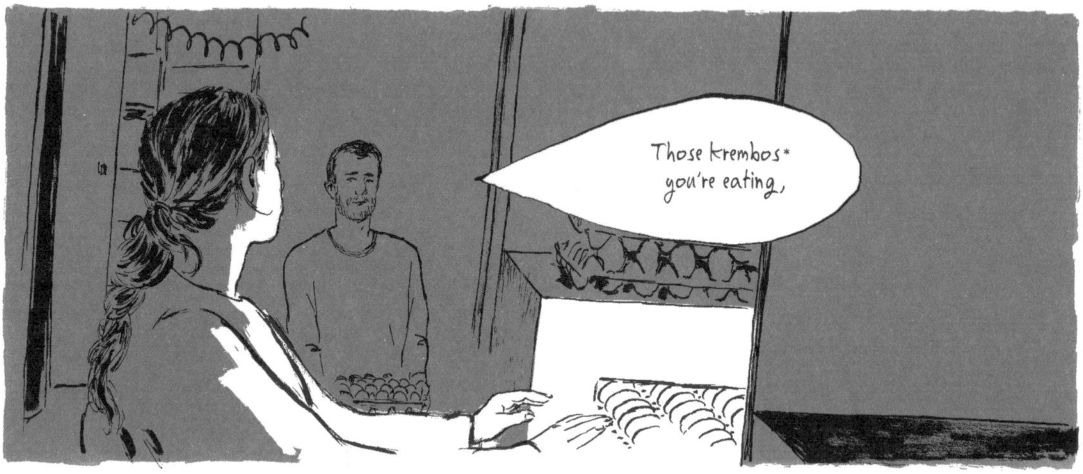
Those krembos* you're eating,

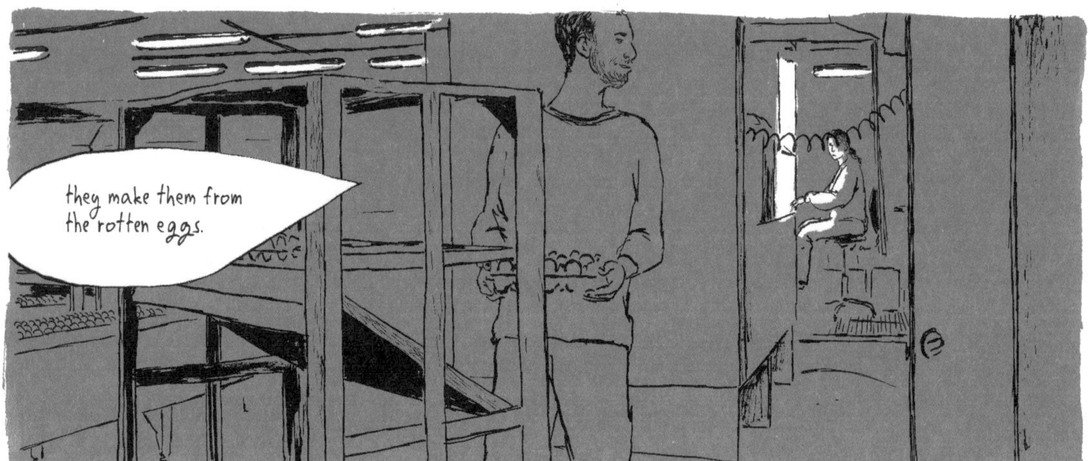
they make them from the rotten eggs.

* Literally "cream inside" it is a chocolate coated marshmallow treat on a round biscuit like US Mallomars.

Tamara the Forewoman sits in her glass cabin, chiding the Gazan workers through the speakers.

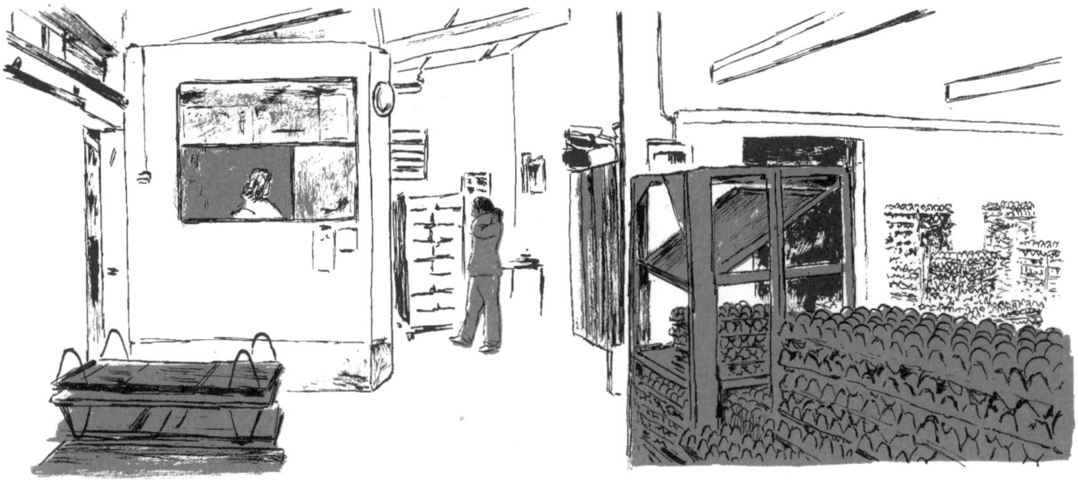

Sometimes she also calls me to join her in the heated cabin.

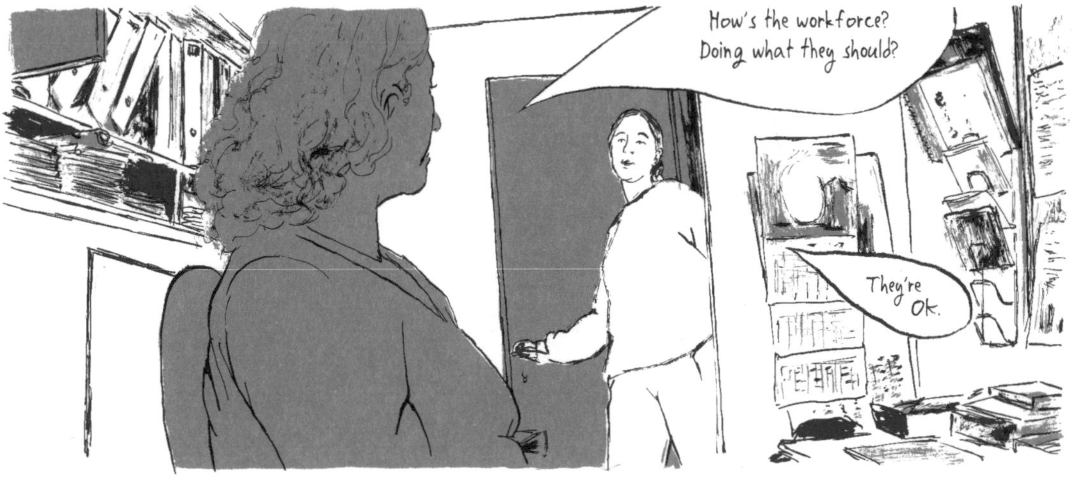
How's the workforce? Doing what they should?
They're OK.

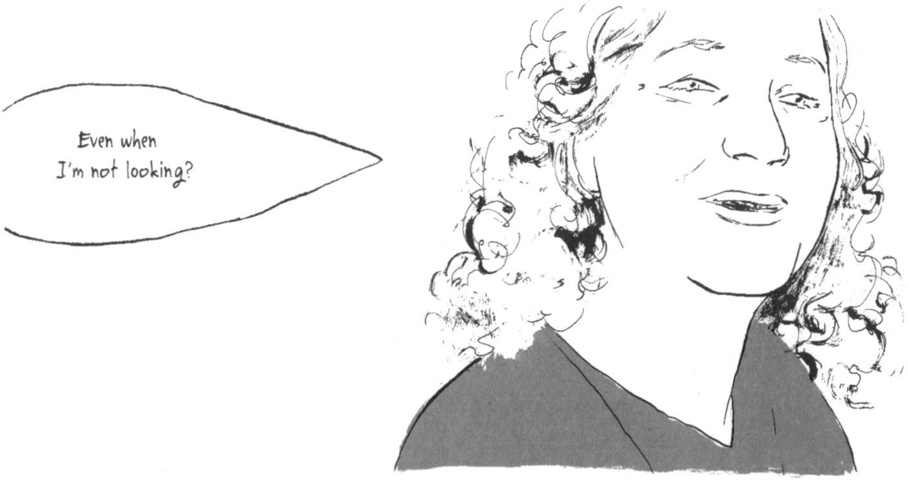
Even when I'm not looking?

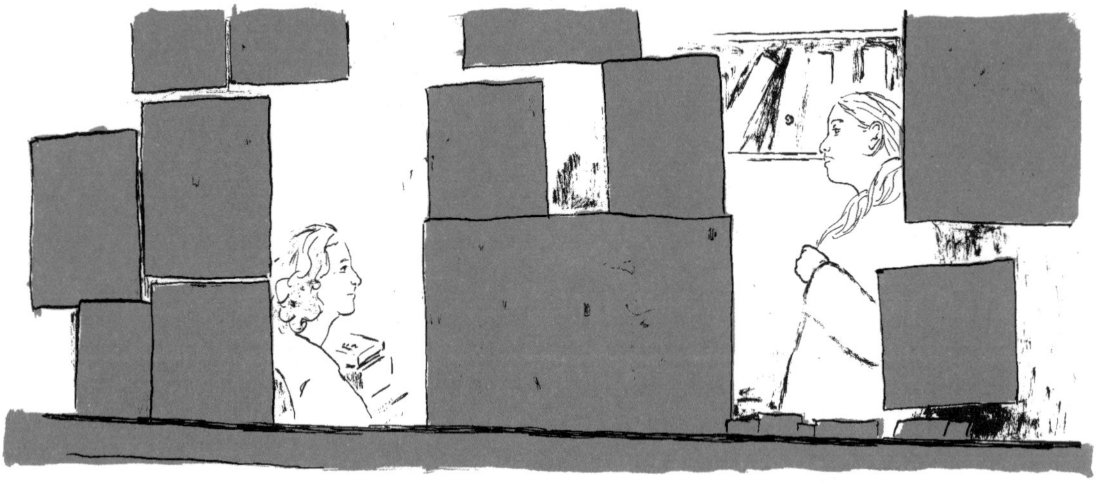

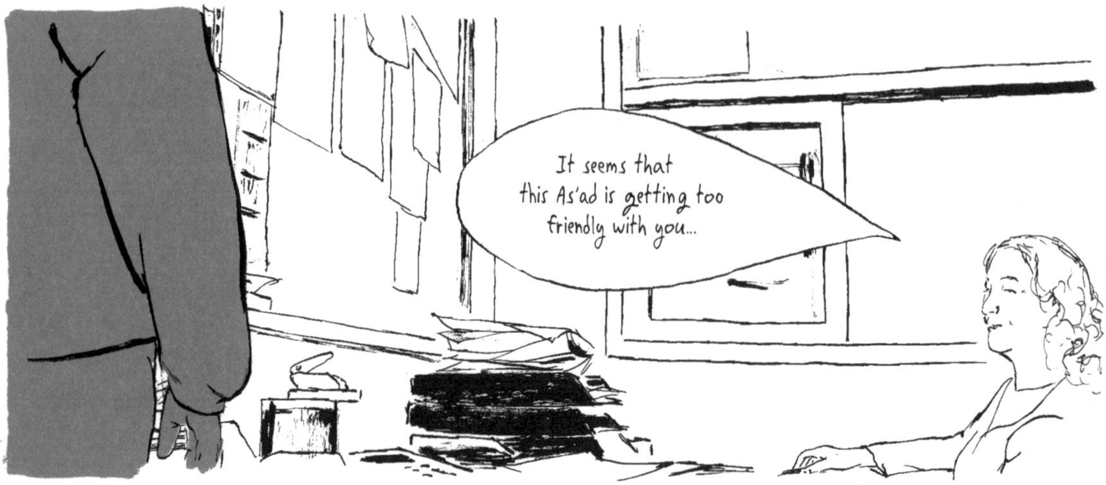
It seems that this As'ad is getting too friendly with you...

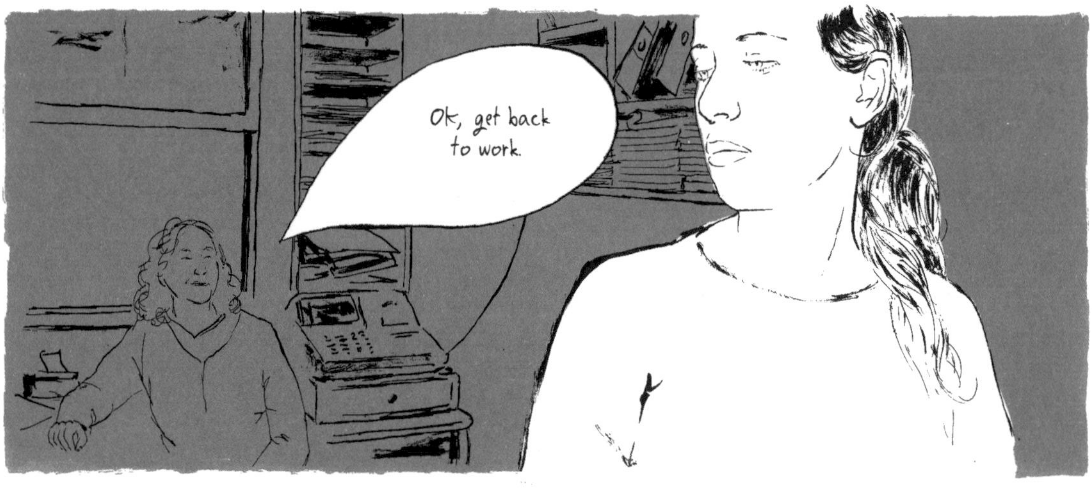
Ok, get back to work.

On the weekend, Omri has a short break from boot camp and comes to me, shrouded in the metallic smell of gun oil.

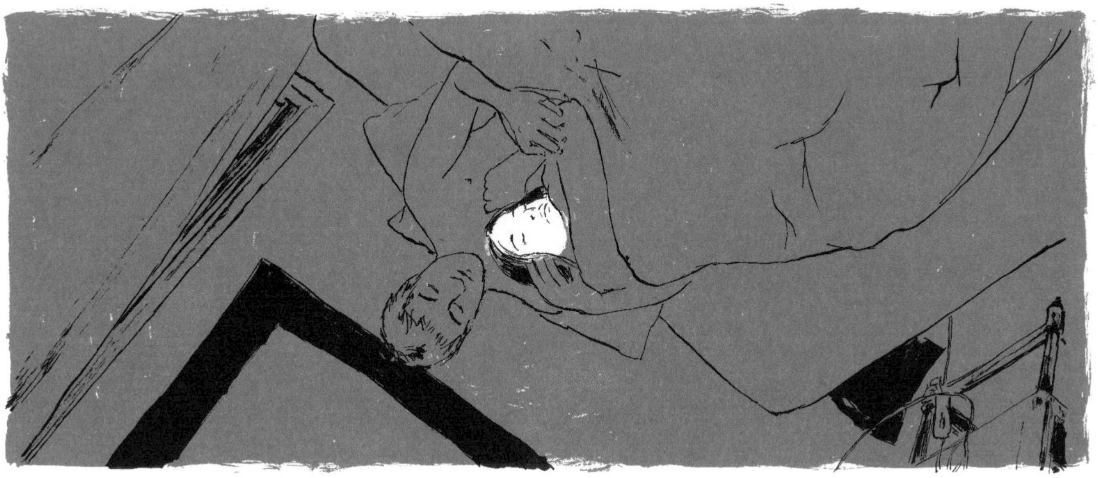

When he fondles me, I close my eyes and, under the lids, I see the eggs

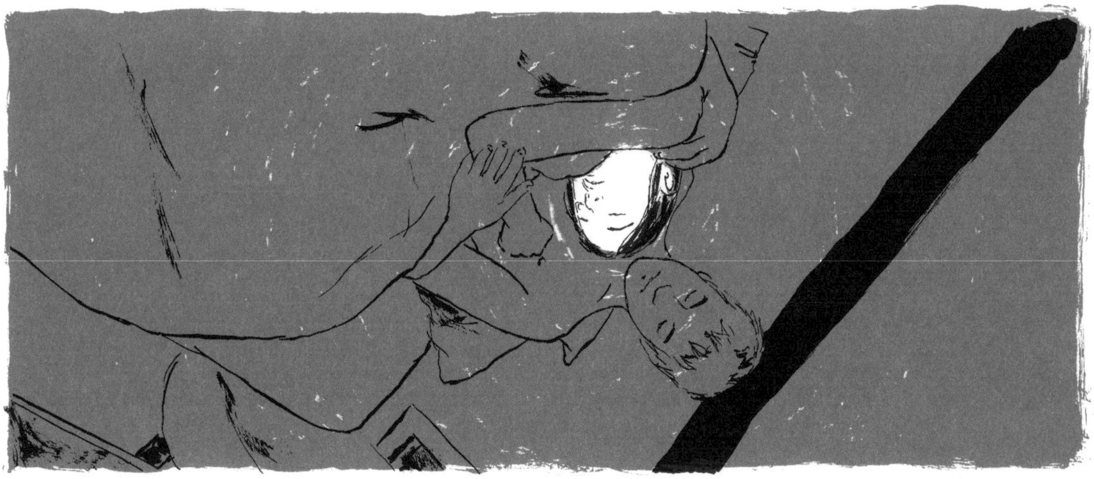

rolling on a soft, luminous bed.

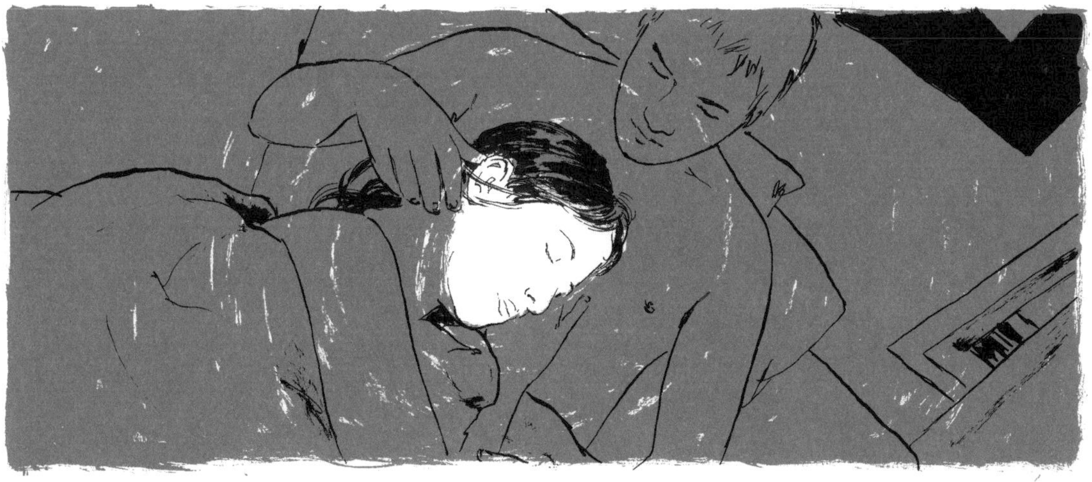

Naked they roll inside my sockets,

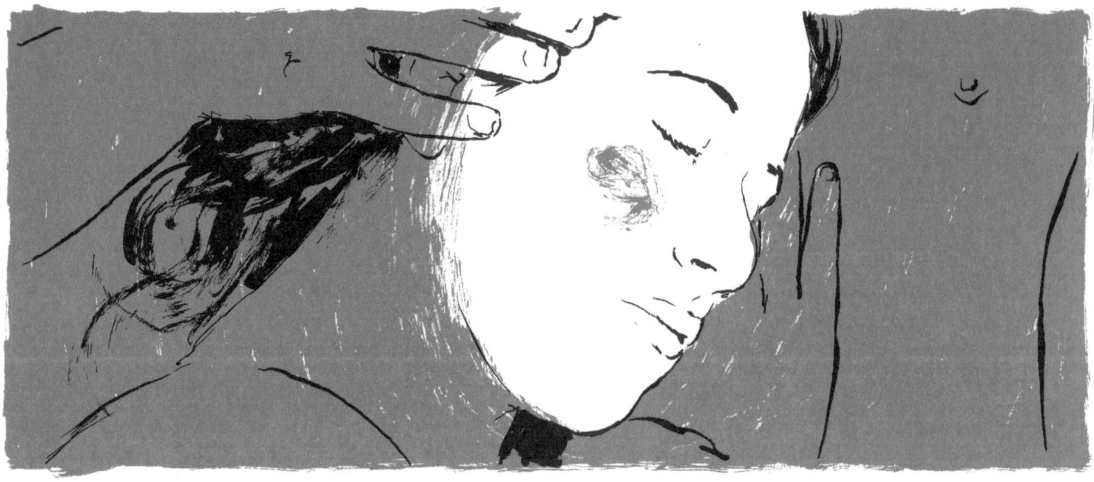

cracks winding through their shells and faint objects looming in their bowels.

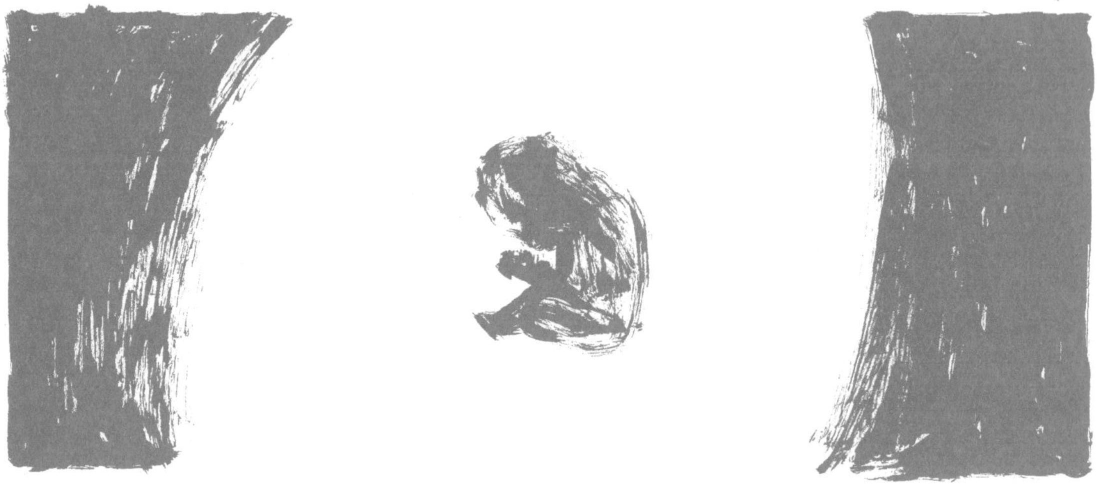

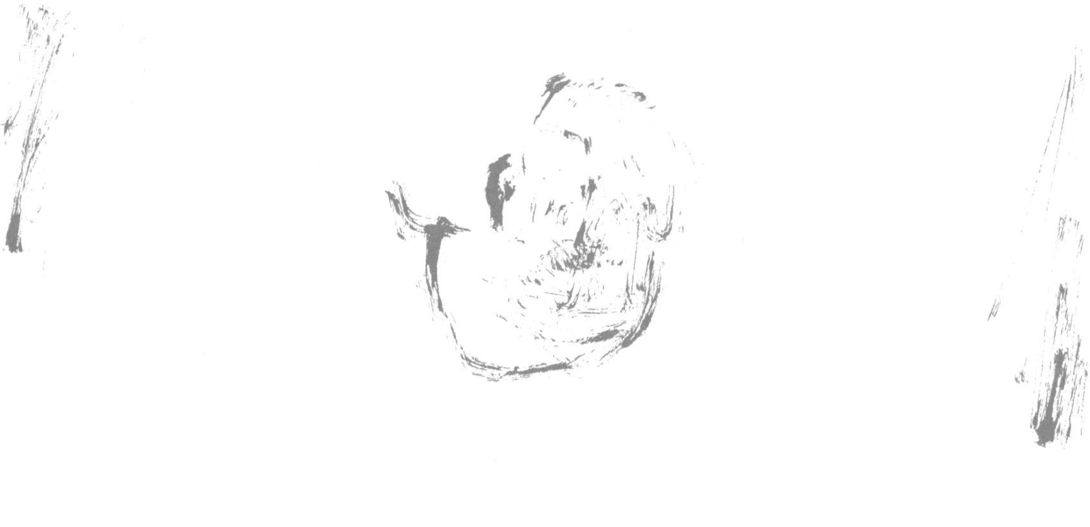

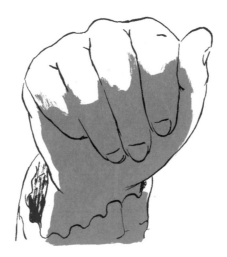

See you later sweetie, live long and prosper!

You'll take good care of As'ad's mates, ah?

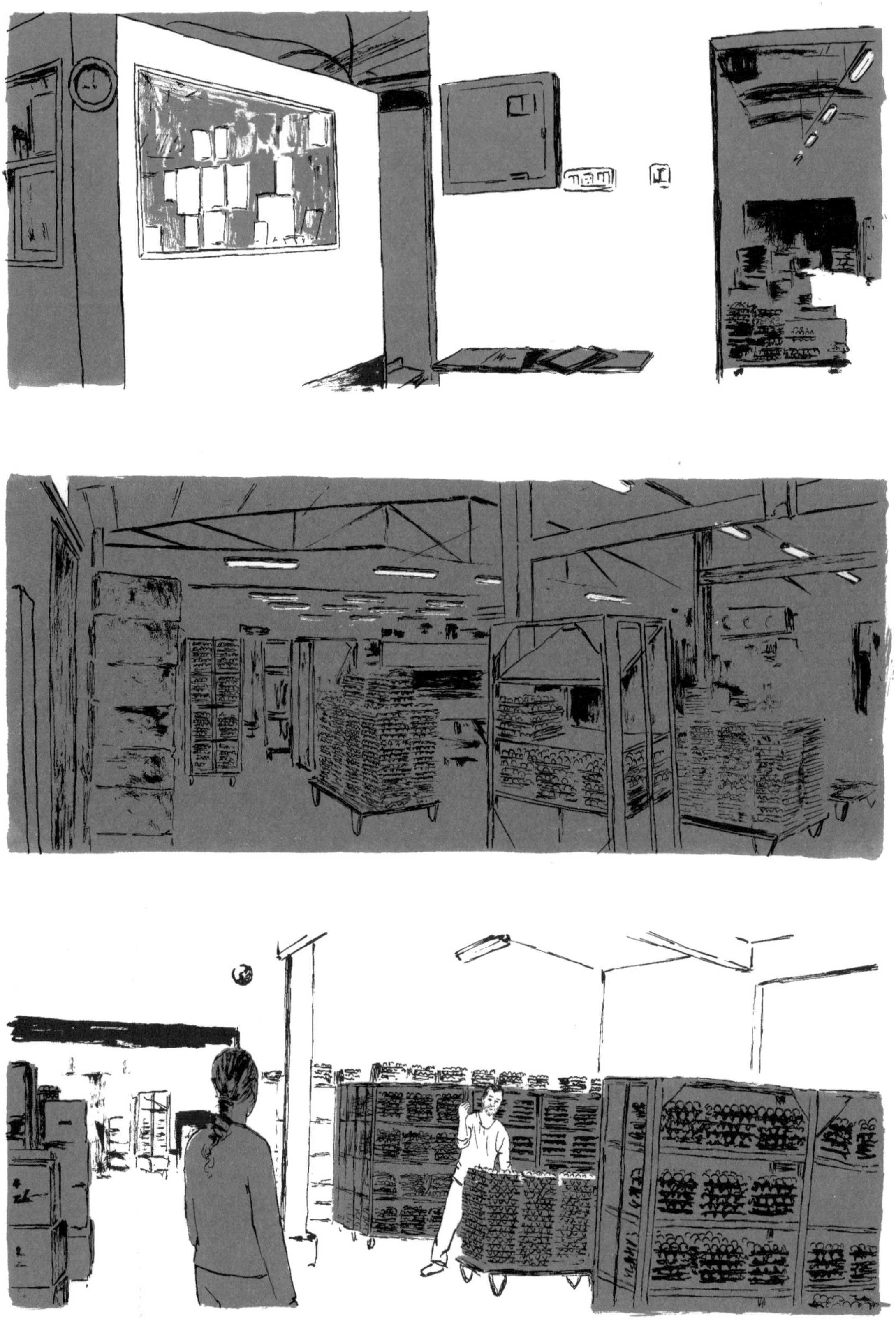

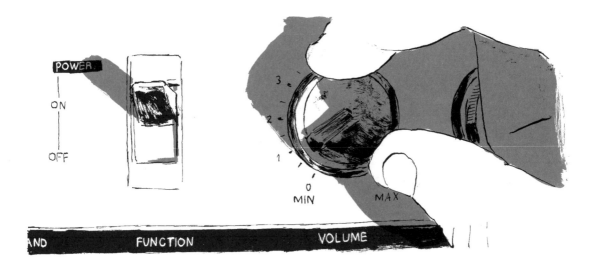

POWER

ON

OFF

3

2

1

0

MIN

MAX

AND   FUNCTION   VOLUME

I'm enlisting
next week.

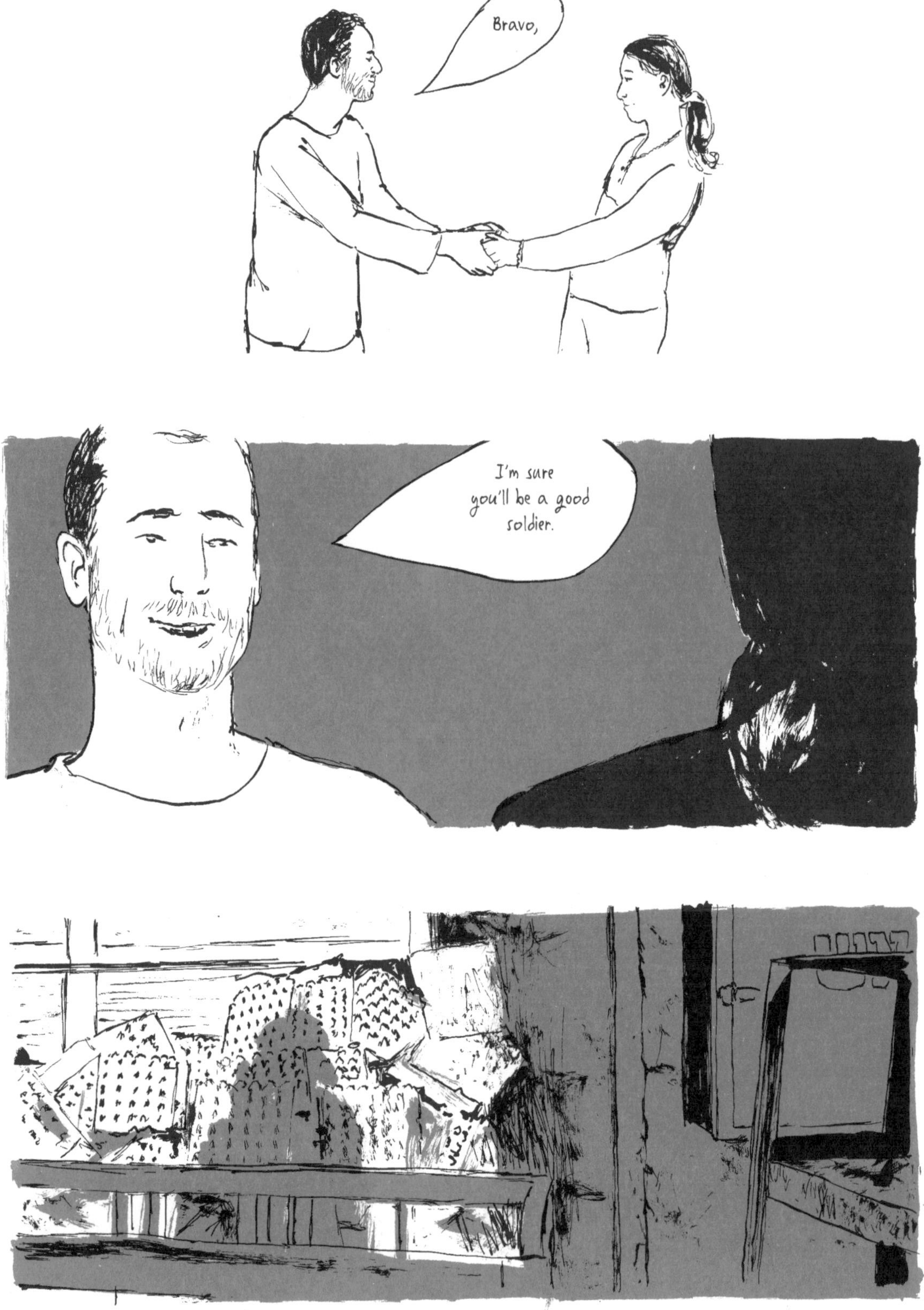
Bravo,
I'm sure you'll be a good soldier.

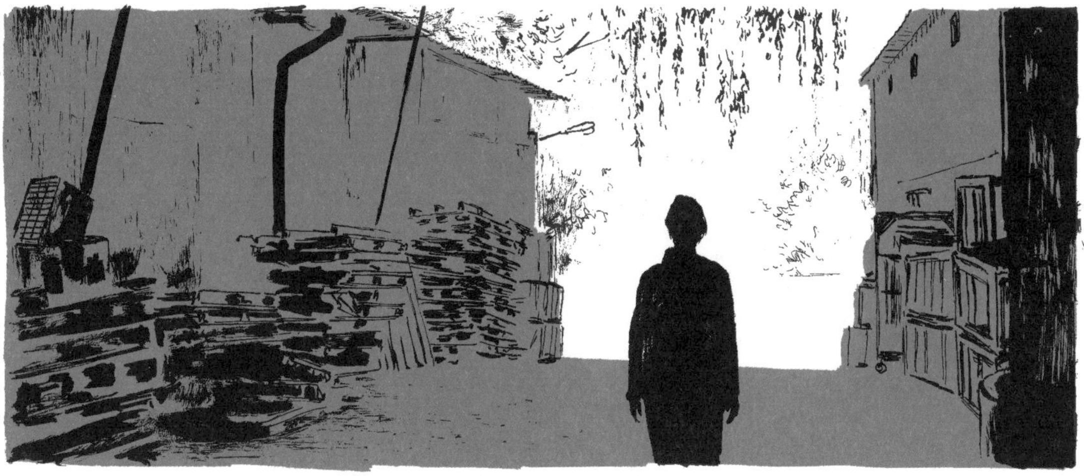

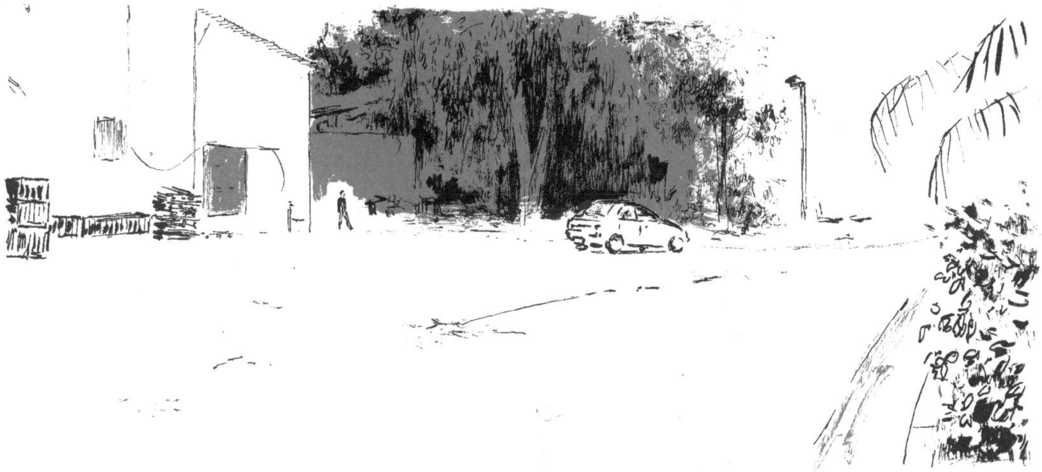

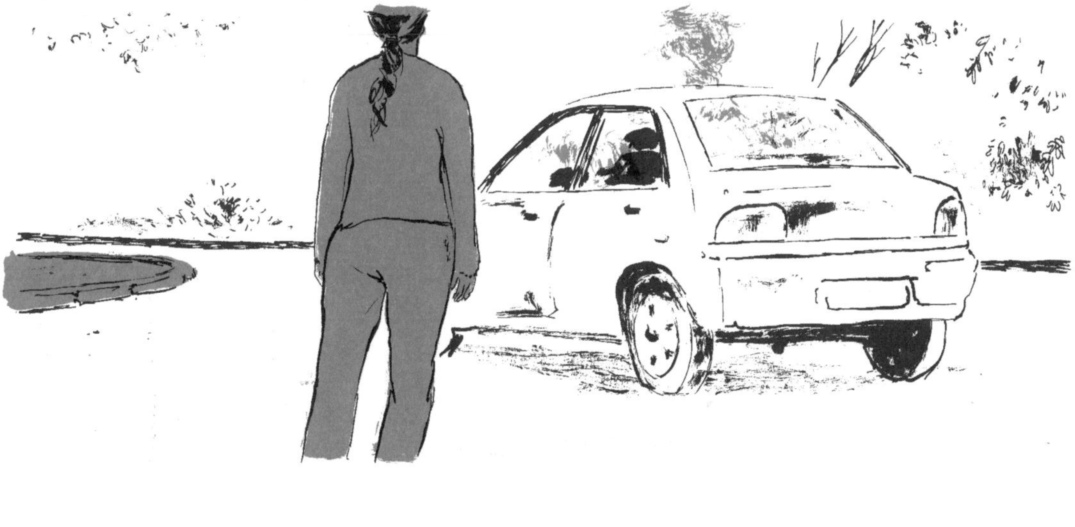

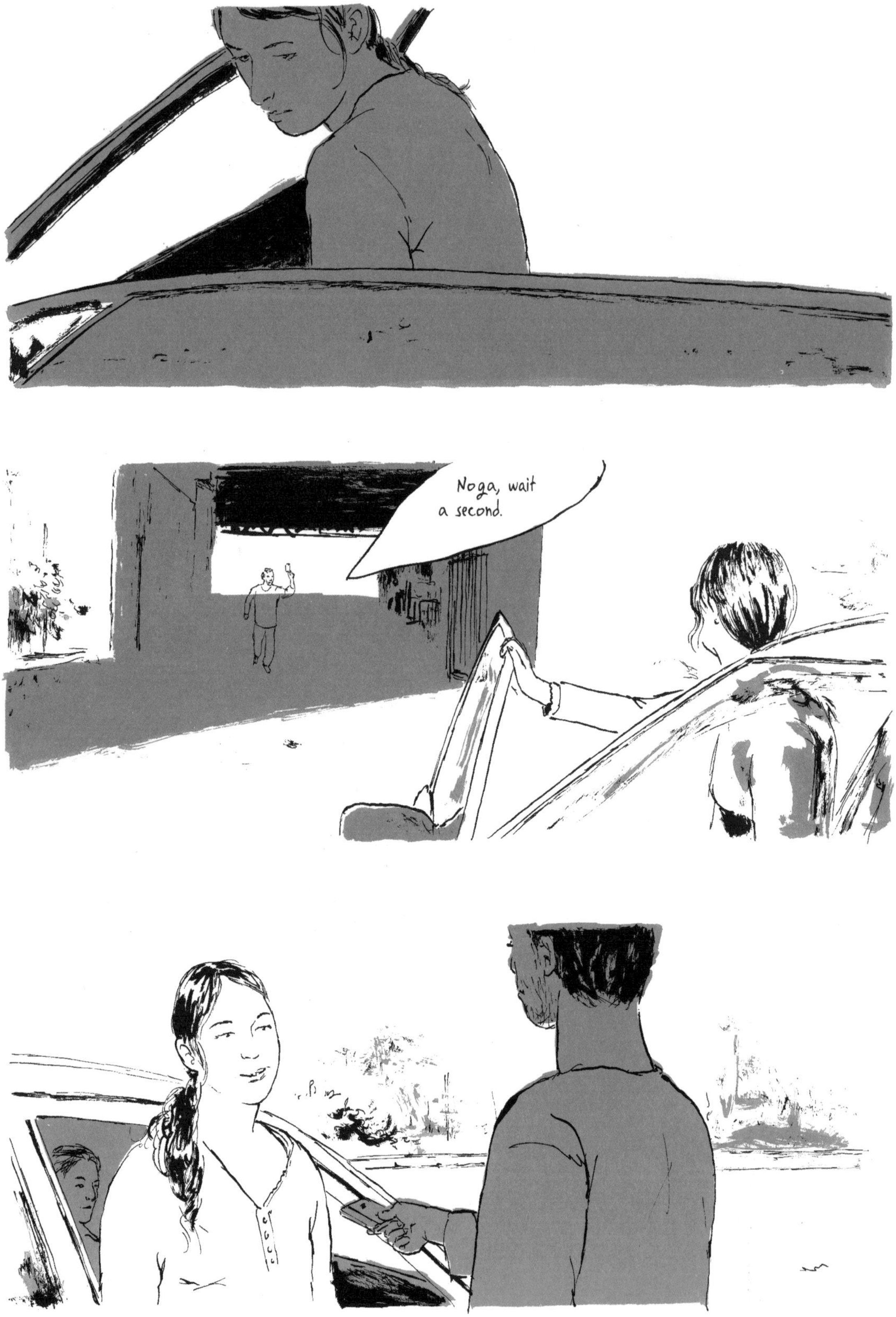
Noga, wait a second.

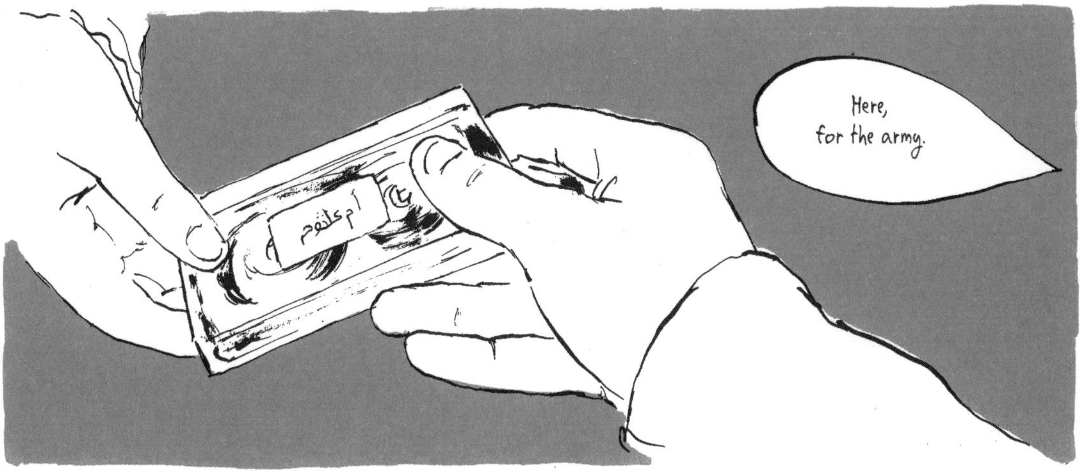
أم كلثوم
Here,
for the army.

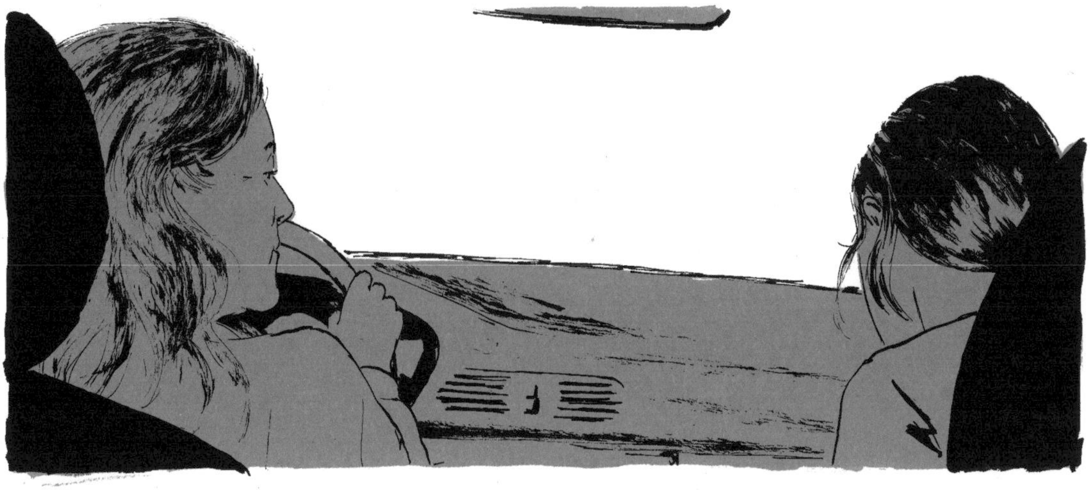

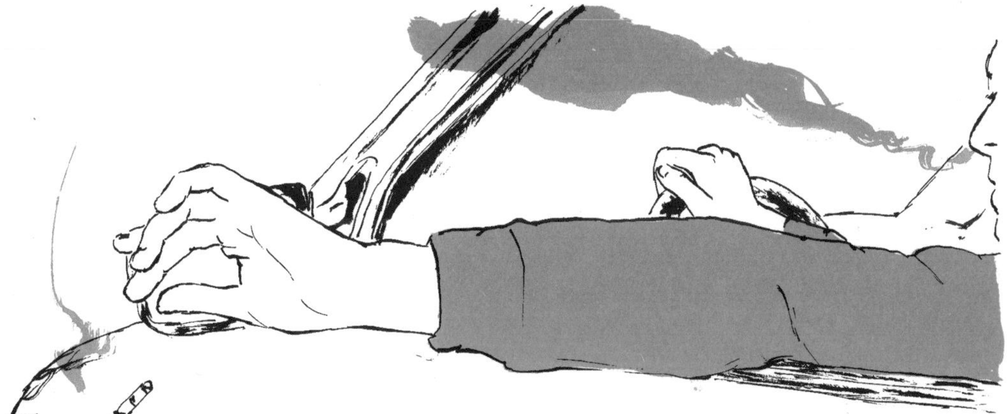

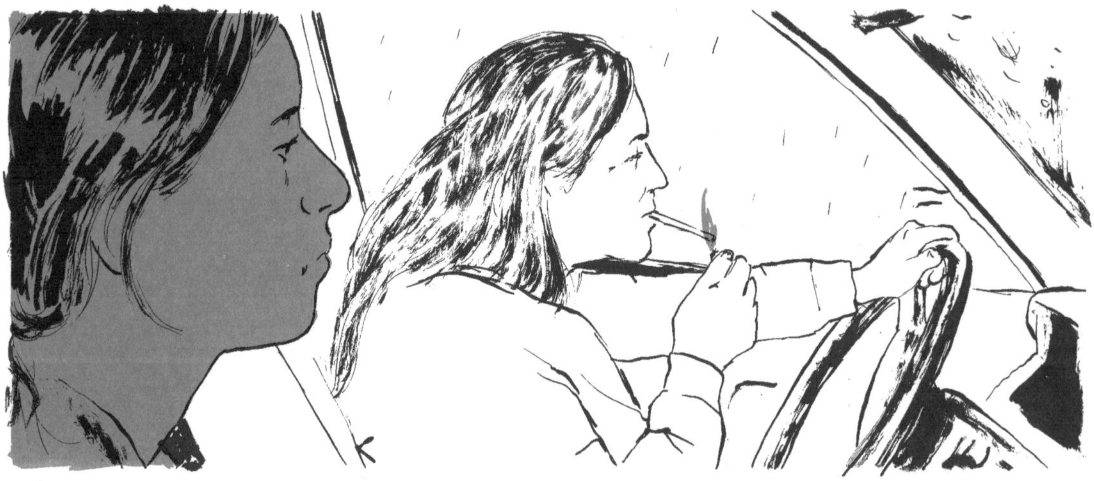
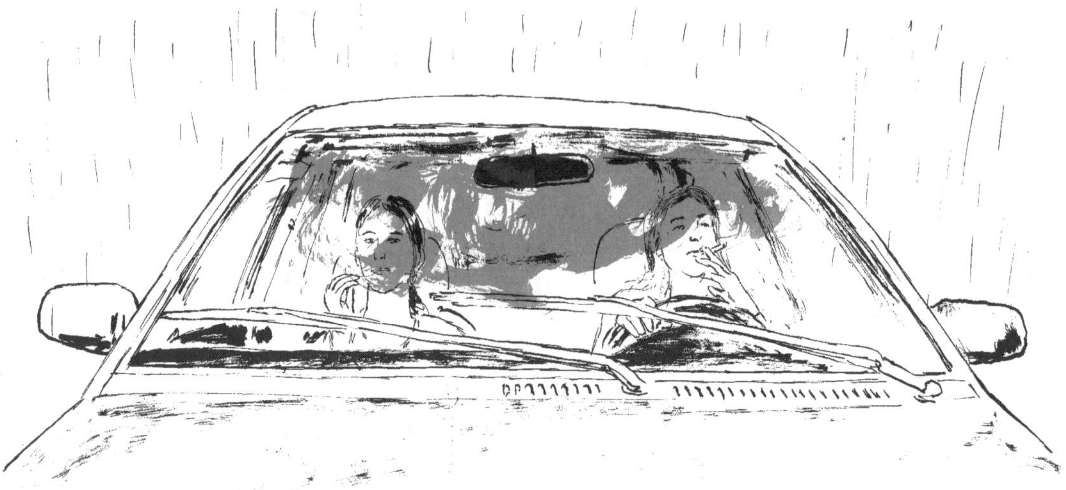
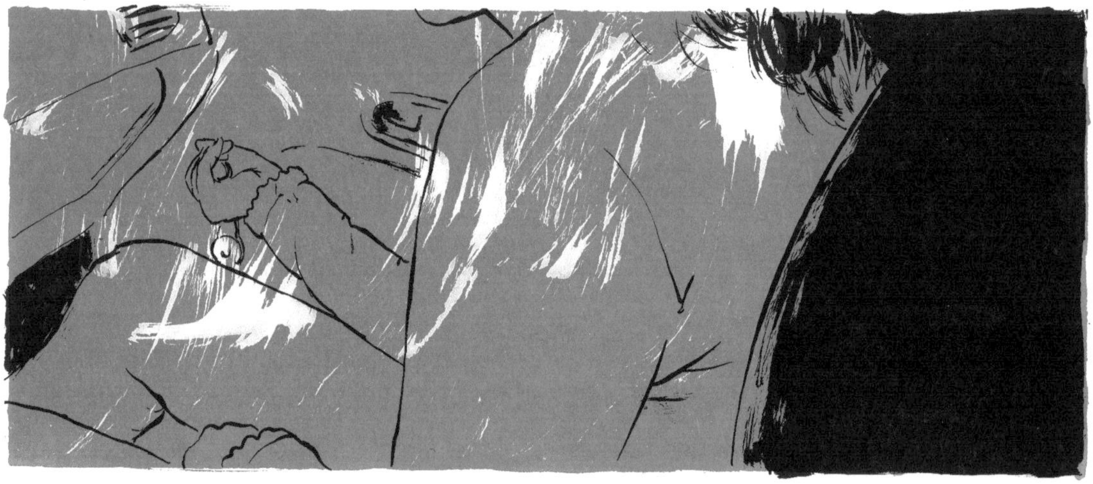

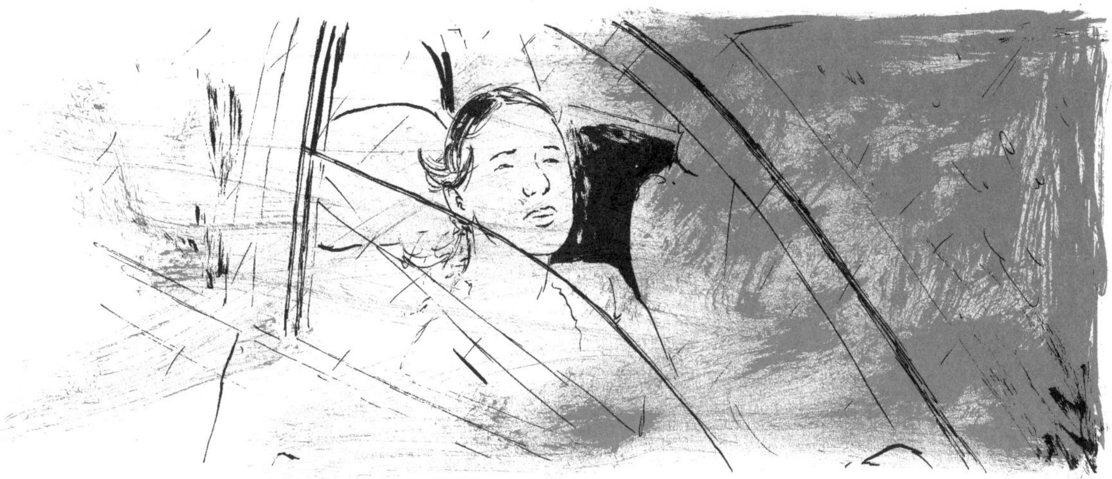

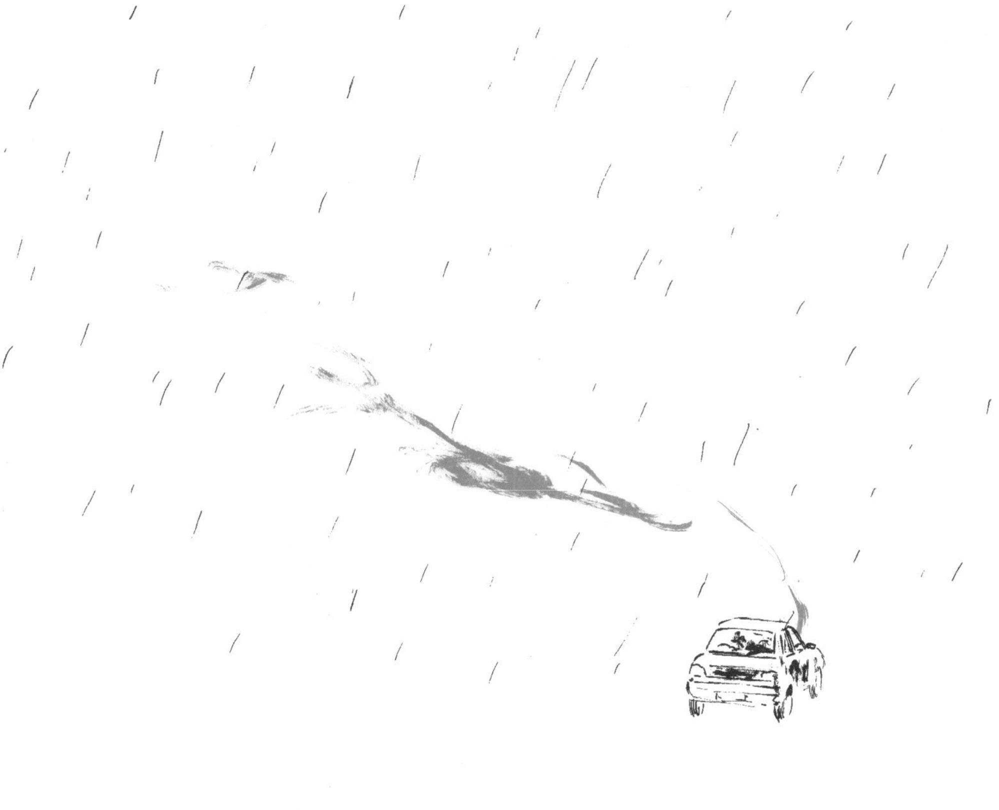

After training as an Educational NCO, I was stationed in a Military Government camp.

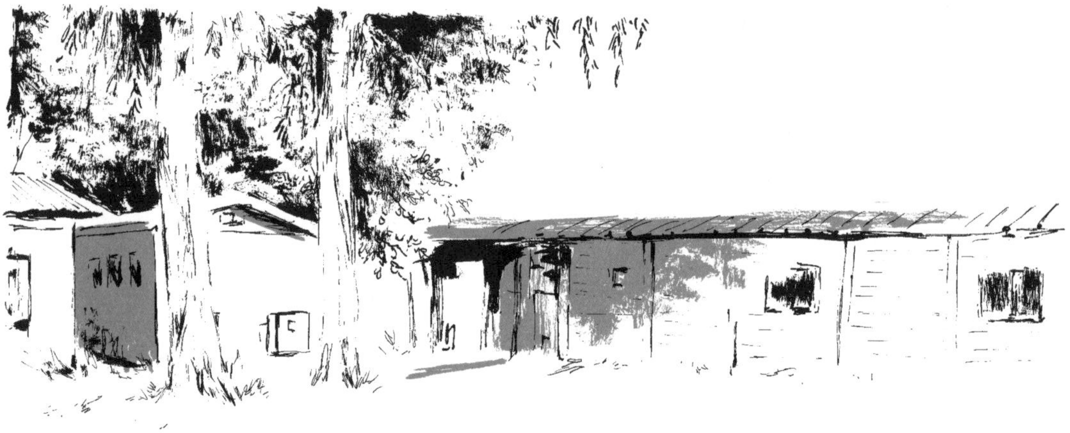

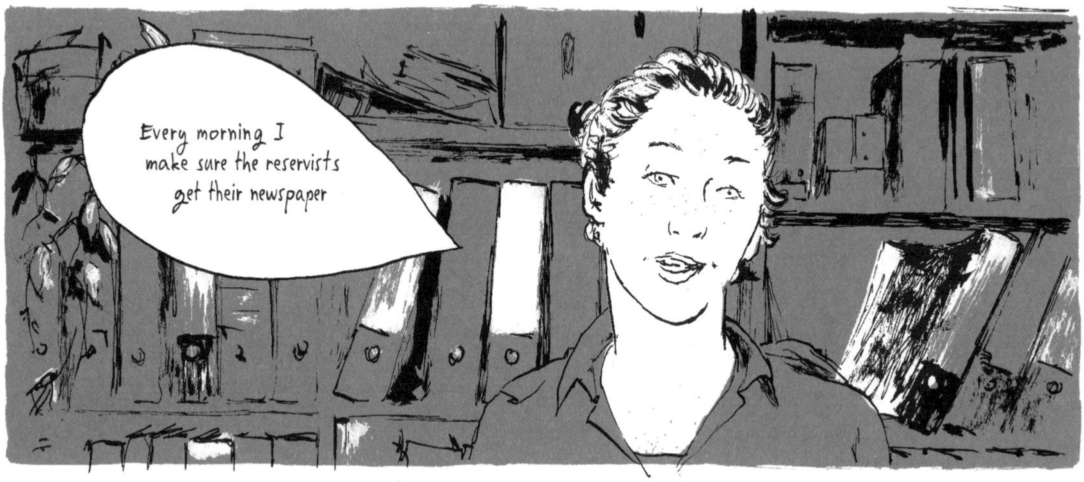
Every morning I make sure the reservists get their newspaper

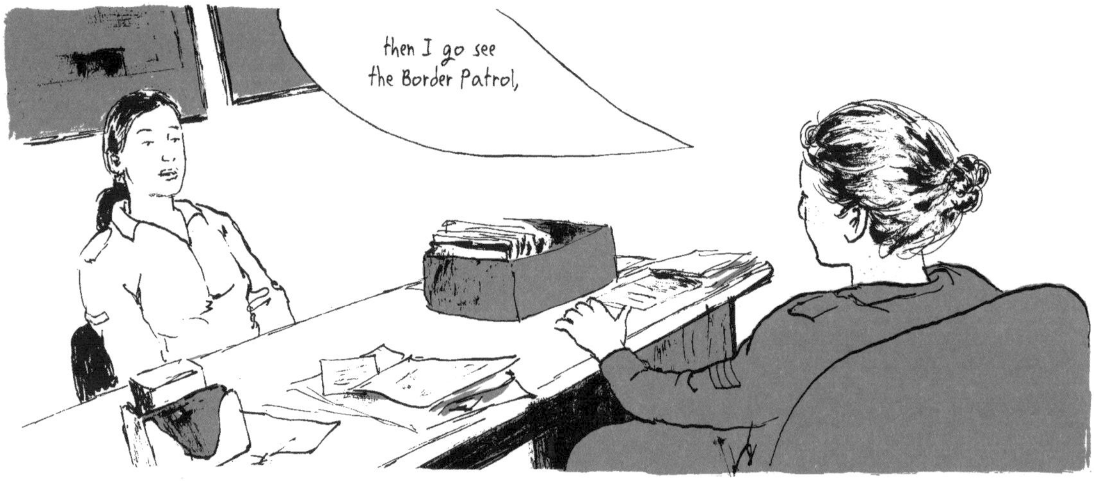
then I go see the Border Patrol,

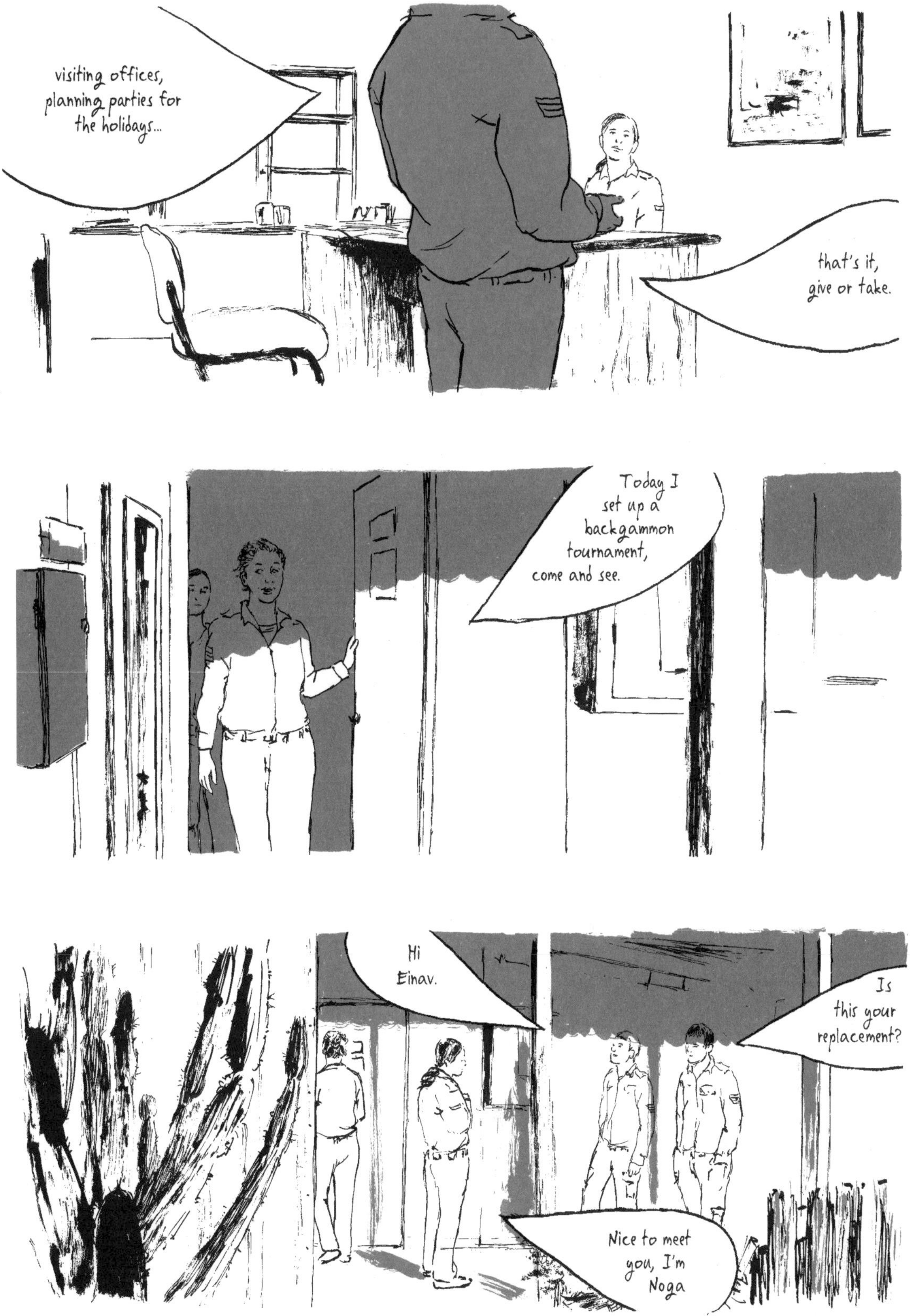
visiting offices, planning parties for the holidays...
that's it, give or take.
Today I set up a backgammon tournament, come and see.
Hi Einav.
Is this your replacement?
Nice to meet you, I'm Noga

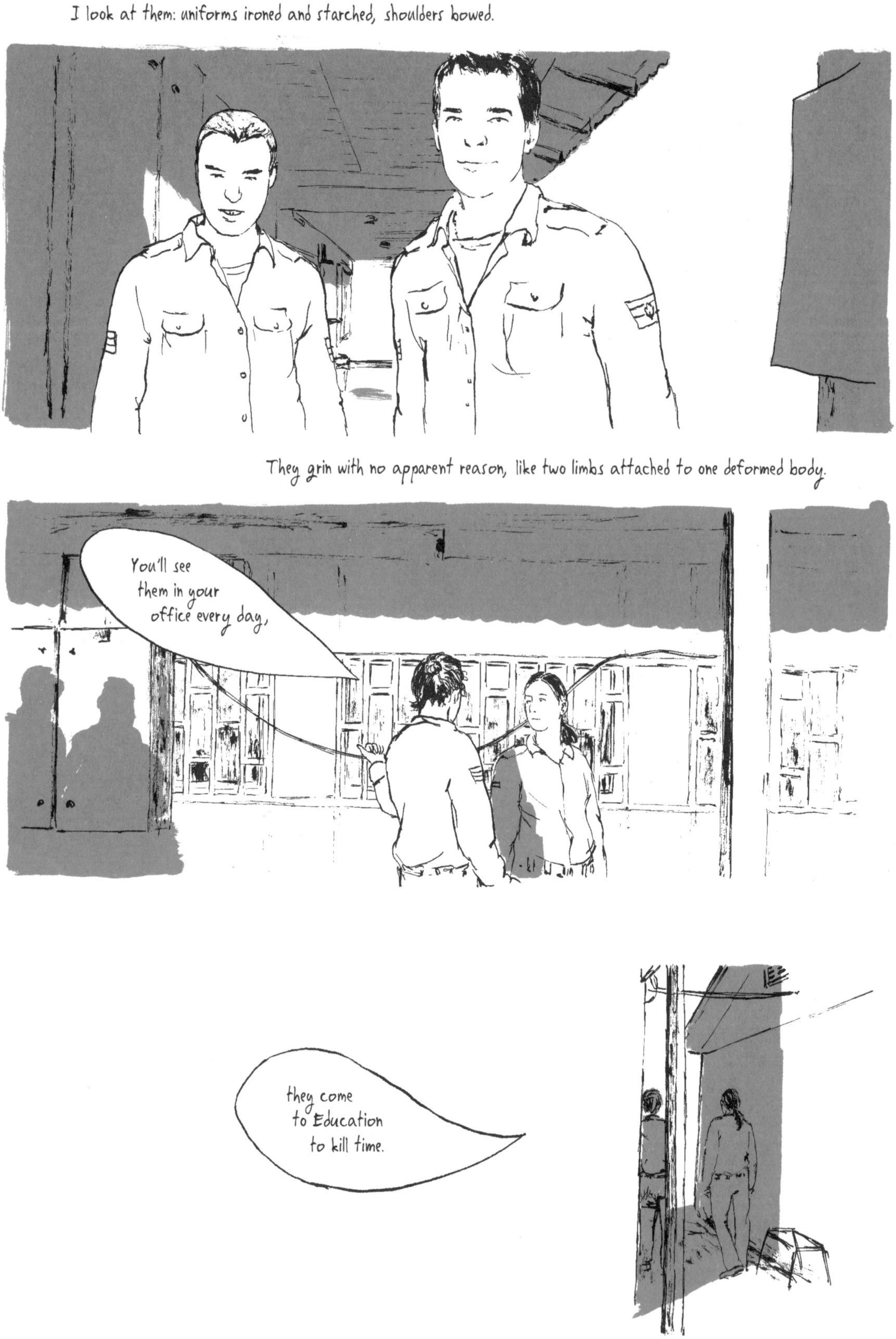
I look at them: uniforms ironed and starched, shoulders bowed.
They grin with no apparent reason, like two limbs attached to one deformed body.
You'll see them in your office every day,
they come to Education to kill time.

After lunch, under a pale early-spring sun, the soldiers gather round the tables in the inner courtyard for the backgammon tournament.

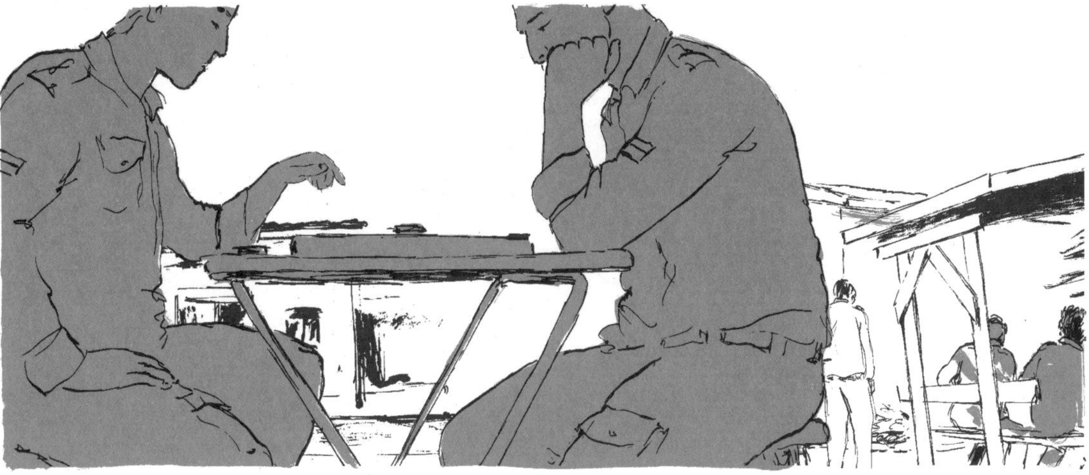

Einav approaches me. With a nod she points out Amir, a Druze soldier with green eyes and amber skin.

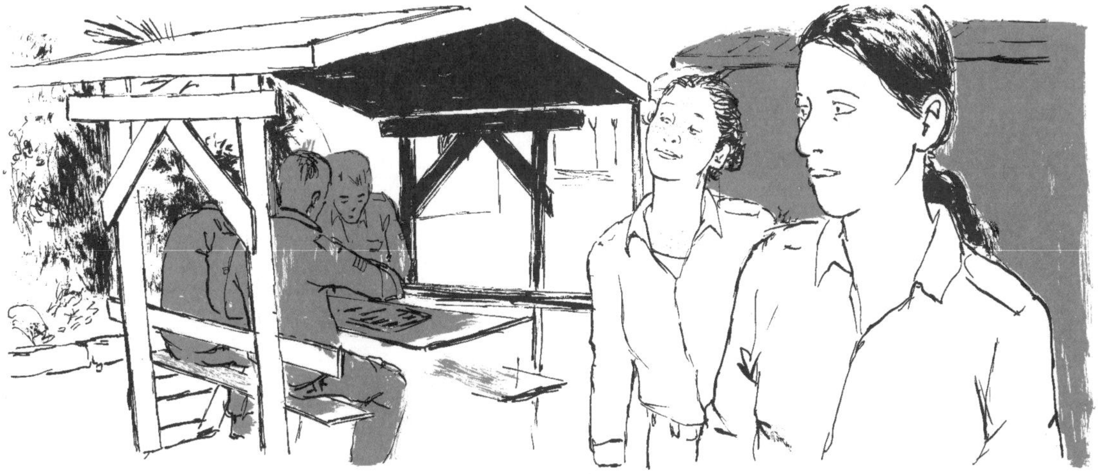

When she bends to pick up a die that a player from the next table dropped, I notice a faded love bite on the back of her neck, covered with a thick layer of make-up.

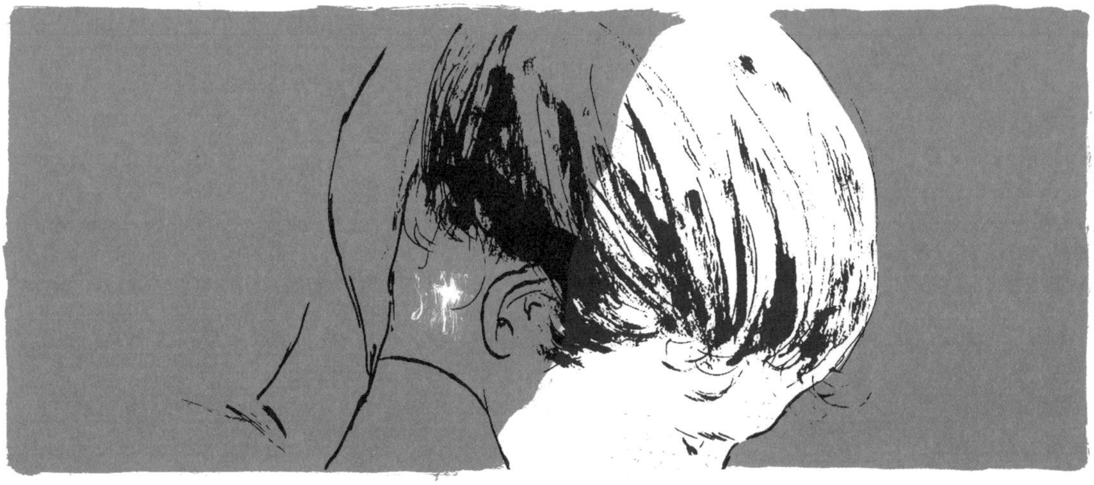

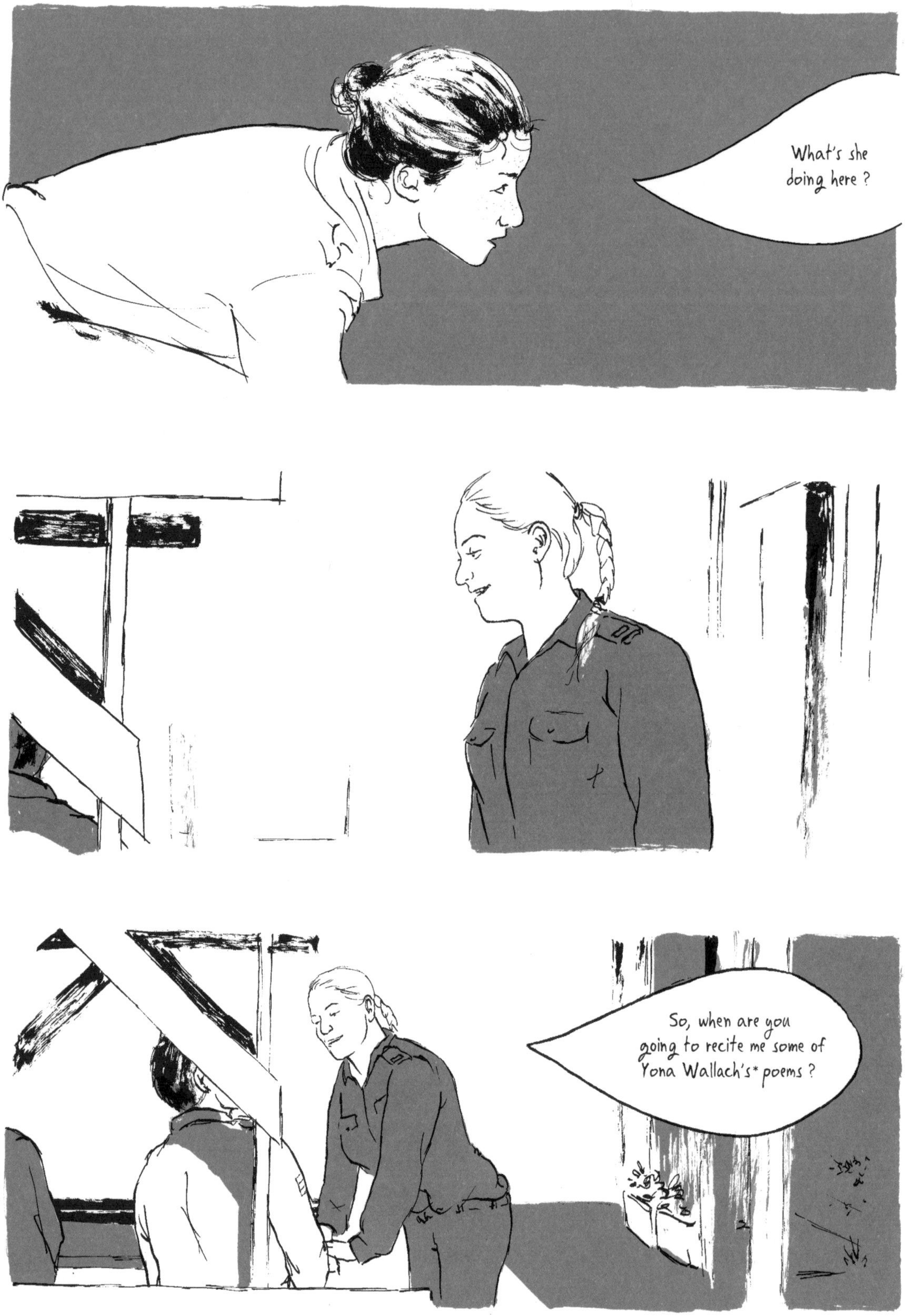
What's she doing here?
So, when are you going to recite me some of Yona Wallach's* poems?

* Israeli poet (1941–1985) whose work is known for its breakneck pace and insistent sexuality.

Einav keeps whispering nervously, I can hardly hear her.

The dice bang against cheap wooden boards, their impact overwhelming the NCO's whispers

as she tries in vain to articulate her arduous passion.

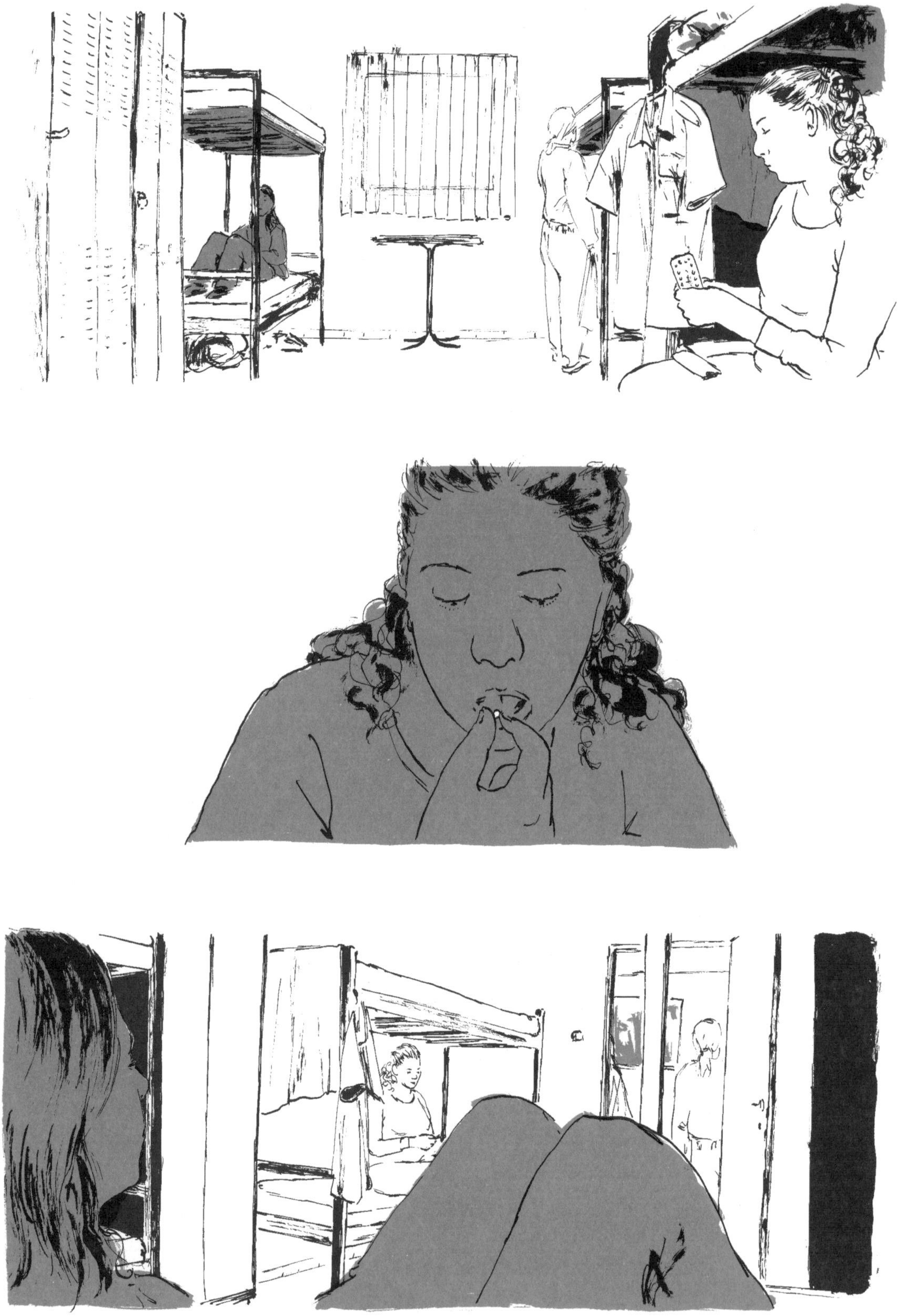

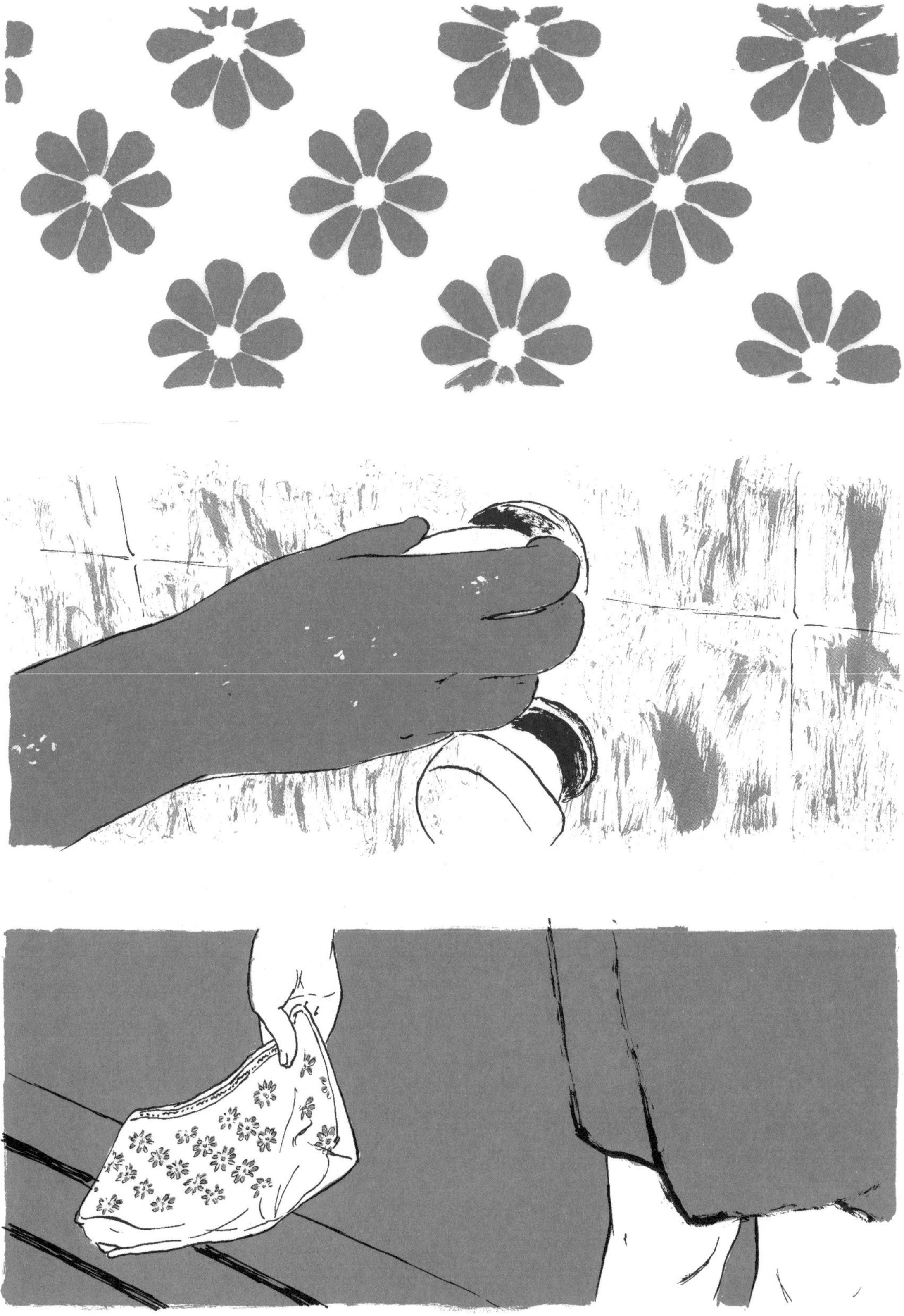

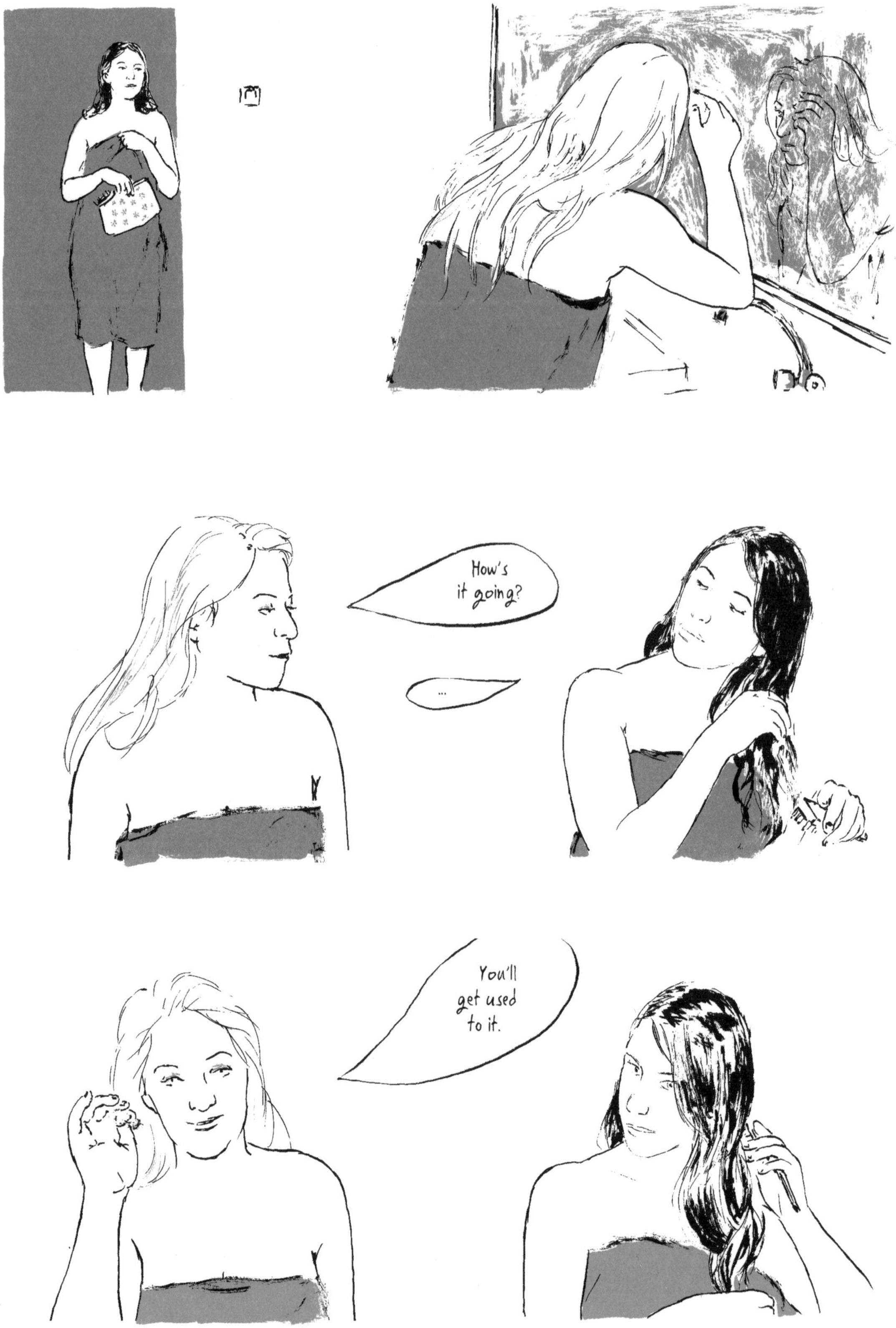
How's it going?
...
You'll get used to it.

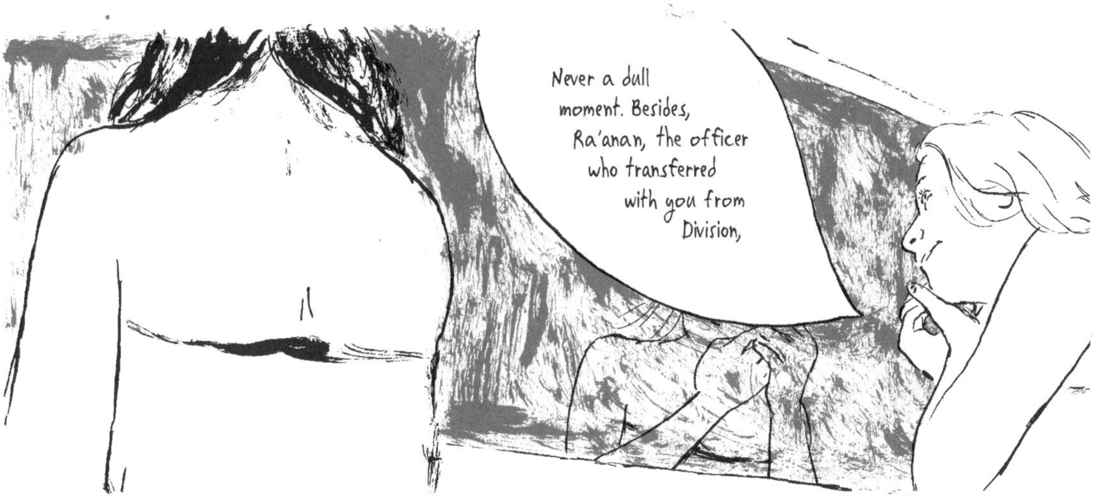
Never a dull moment. Besides, Ra'anan, the officer who transferred with you from Division,

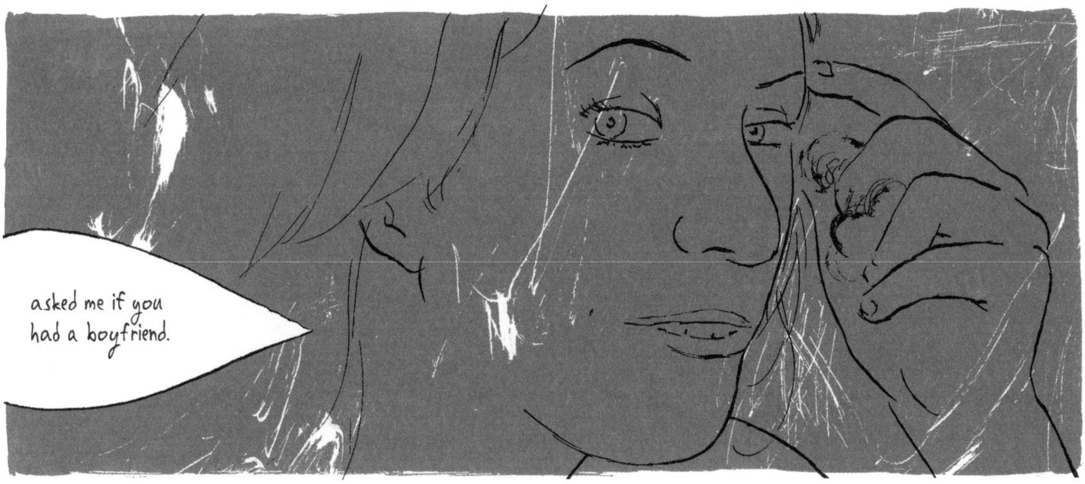
asked me if you had a boyfriend.

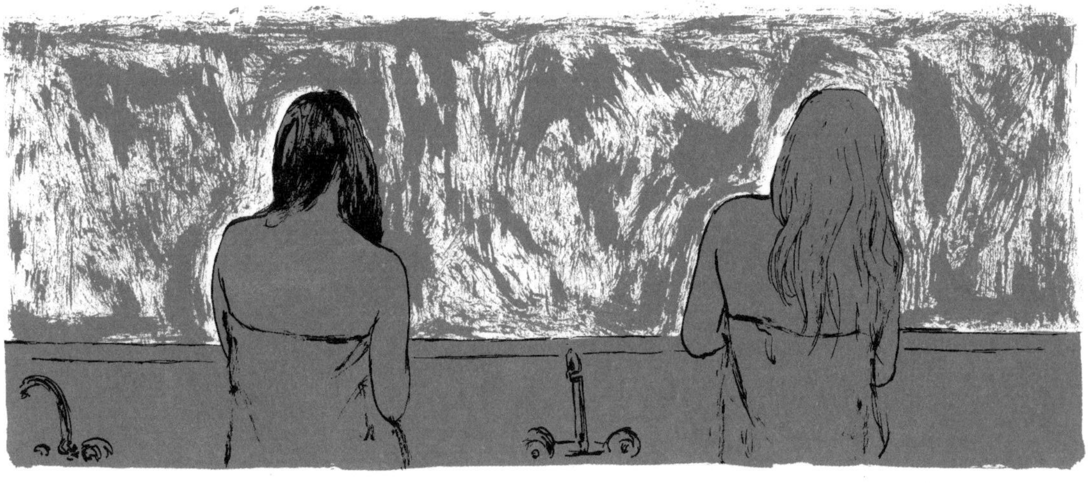

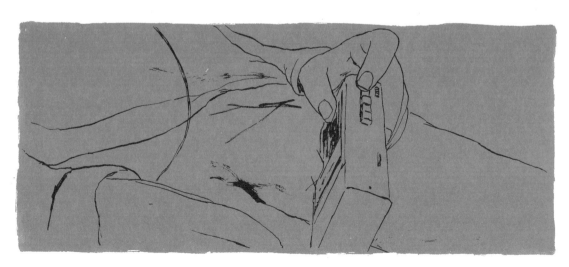

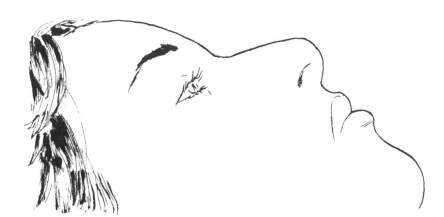

Wake up!

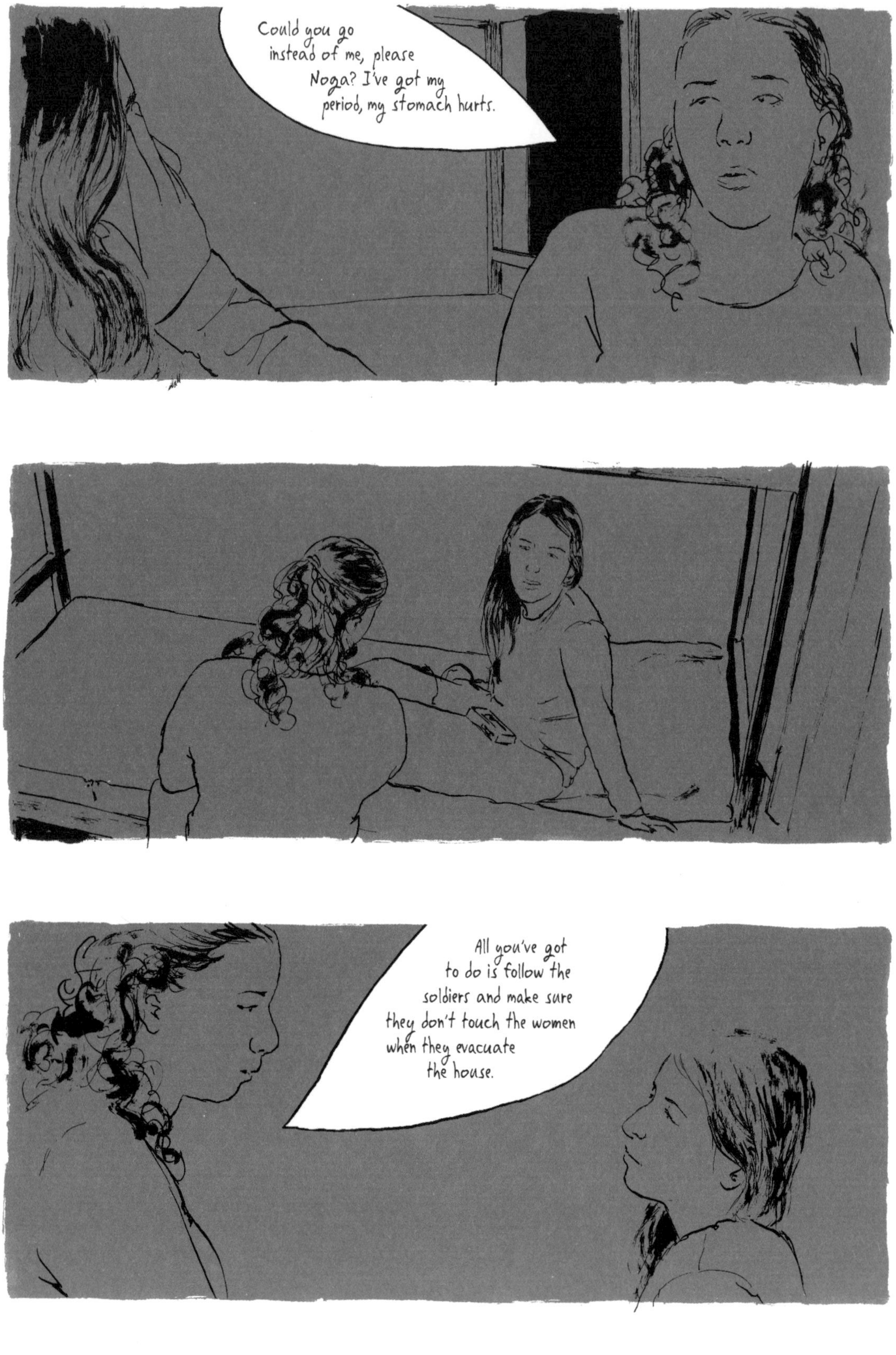
Could you go instead of me, please Noga? I've got my period, my stomach hurts.
All you've got to do is follow the soldiers and make sure they don't touch the women when they evacuate the house.

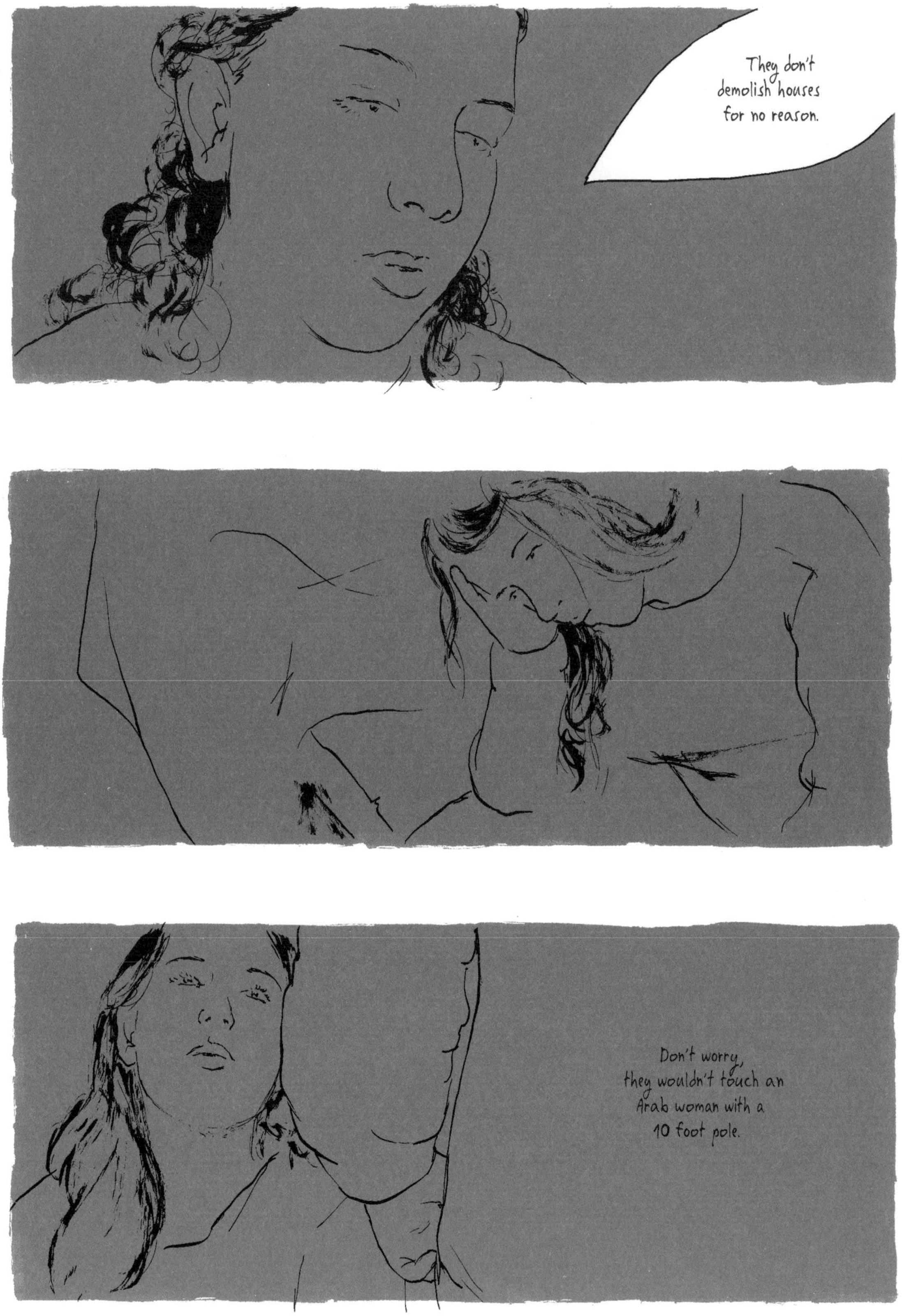
They don't demolish houses for no reason.
Don't worry, they wouldn't touch an Arab woman with a 10 foot pole.

Sorry, I don't have a helmet for you.

In the next jeep sits Efrat, looking even more refreshed than she was in the shower, hair combed, an army coat wrapped tightly around her.

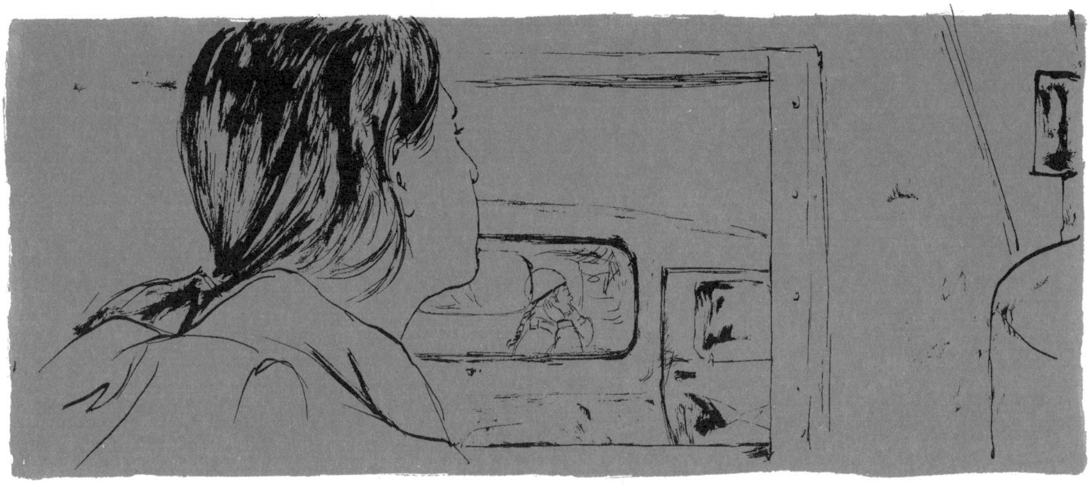

She fixes her hair under her helmet and tightens the main strap under her chin.

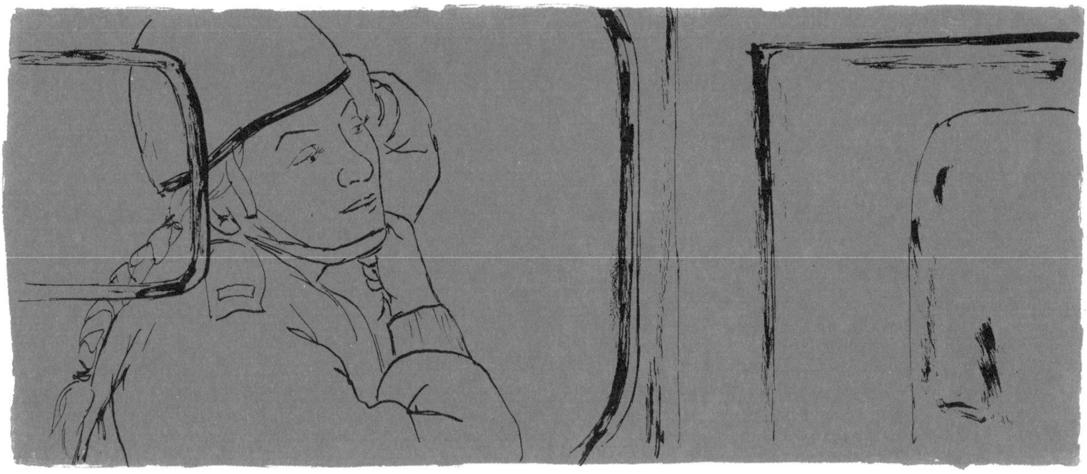

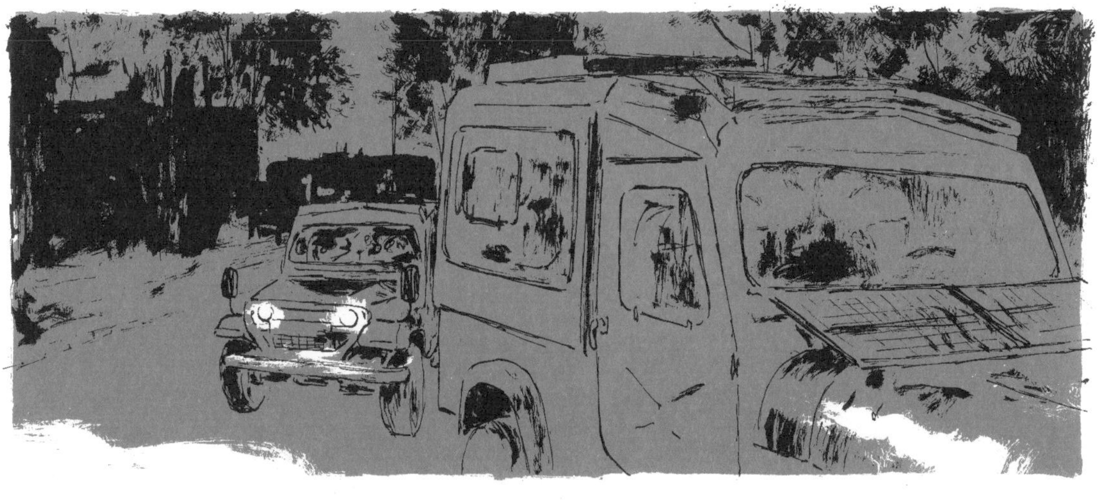

Ten minutes later we stop by the roadside and play with the night vision device, the "bunny rabbit",

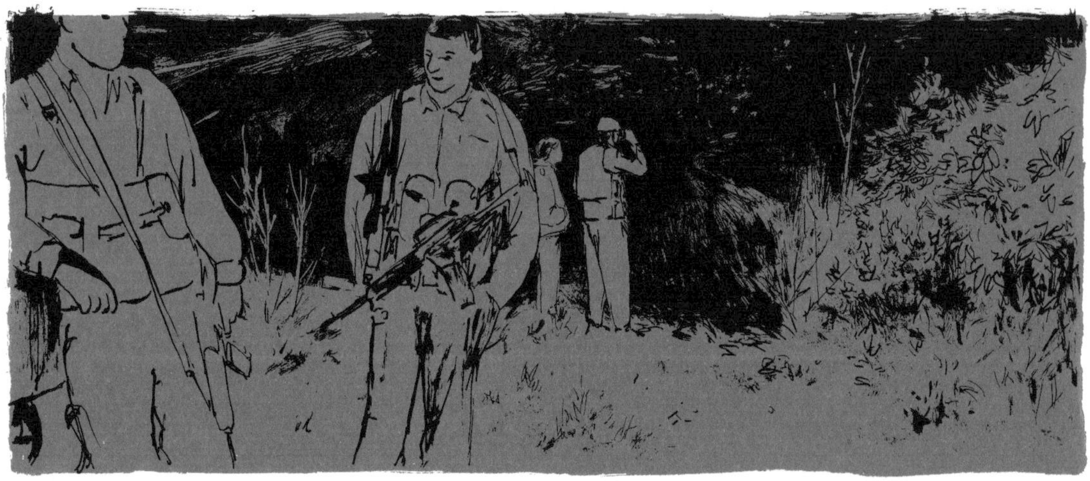

until it's time to storm the village.

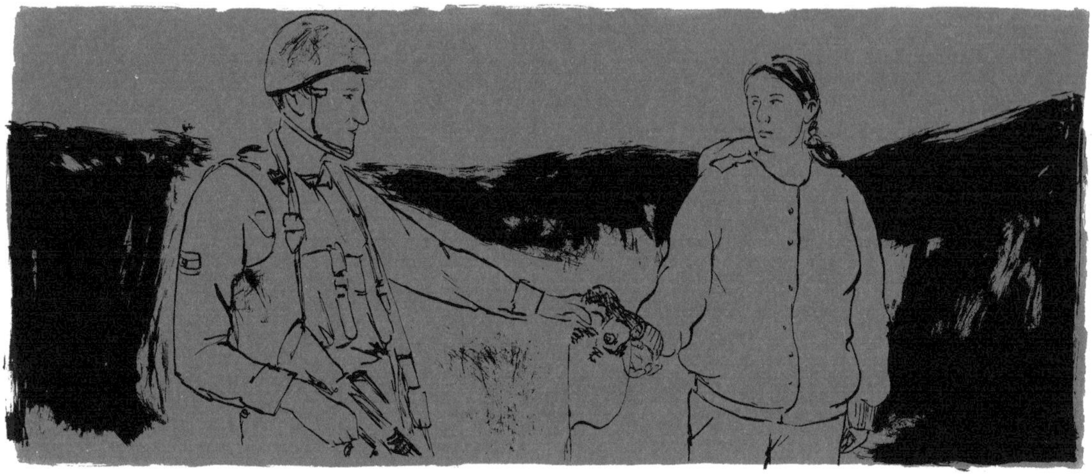

Through the lens I discover the naked night.

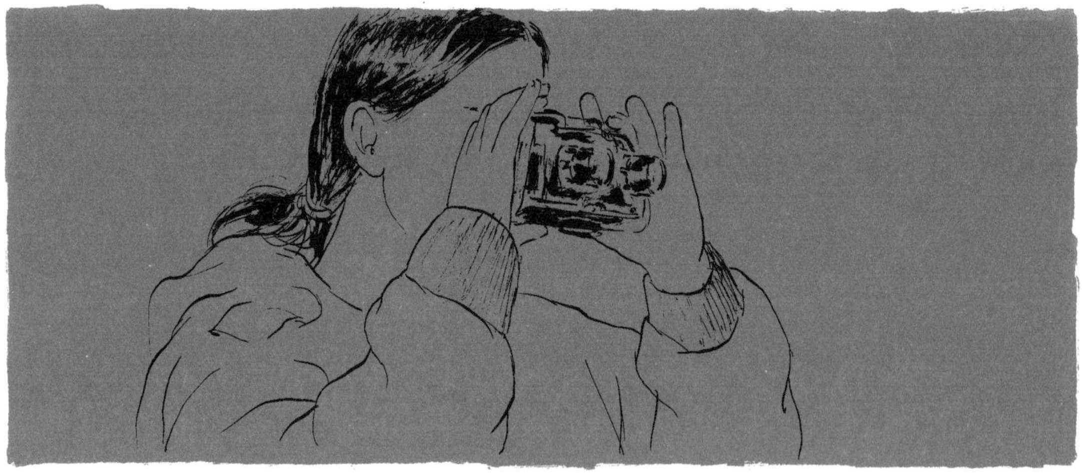

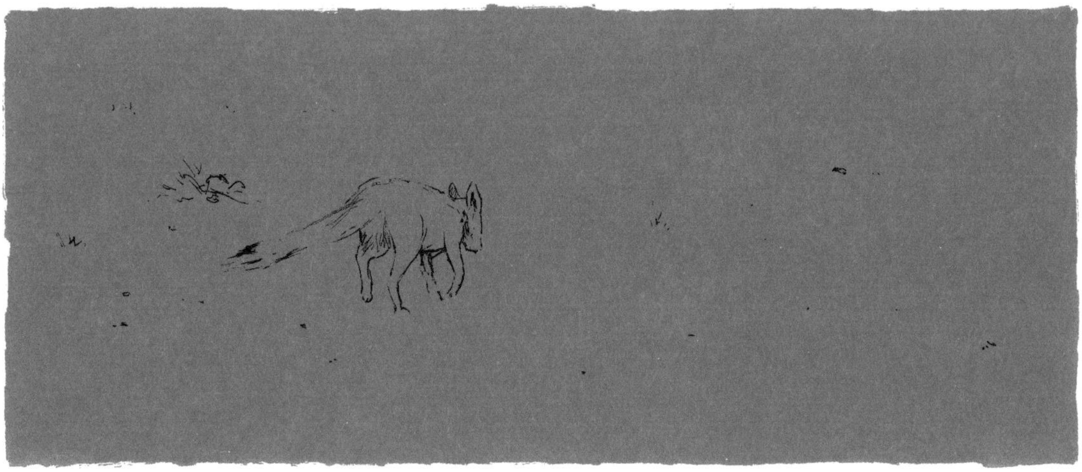

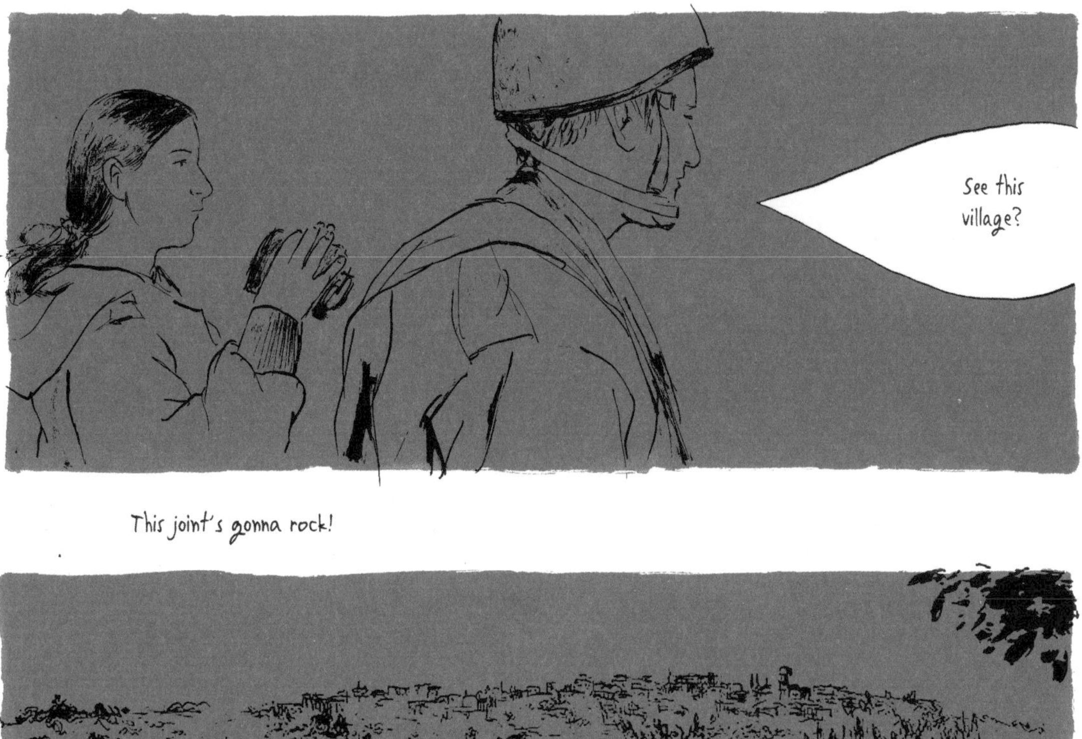
See this village?

This joint's gonna rock!

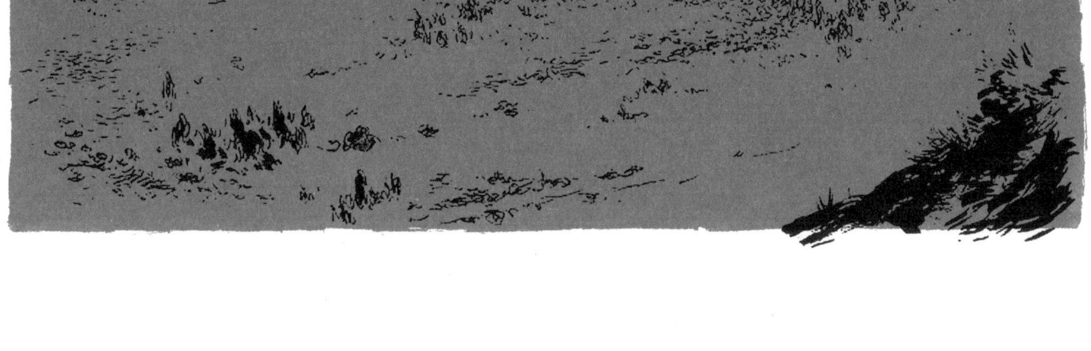

"Good morning ya jama'a[1], the yahud[2] have come to your village!"

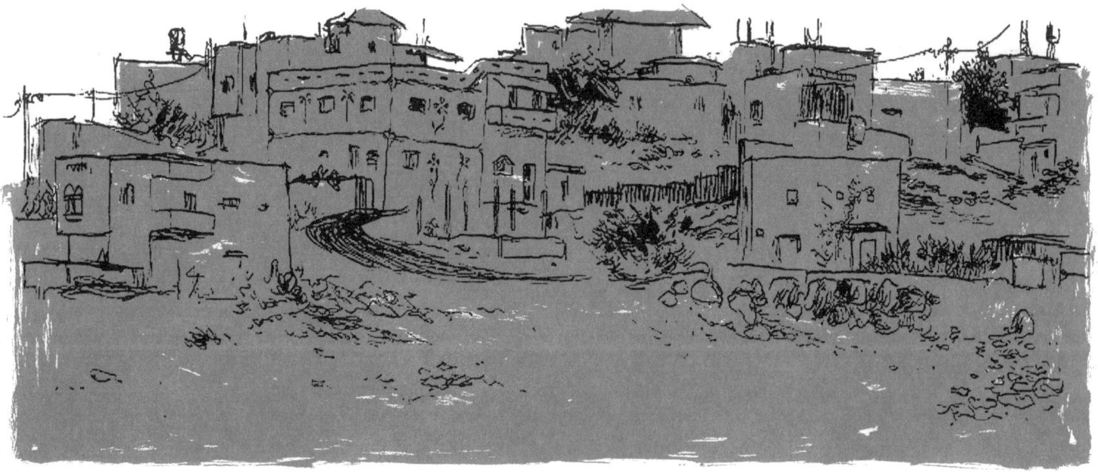

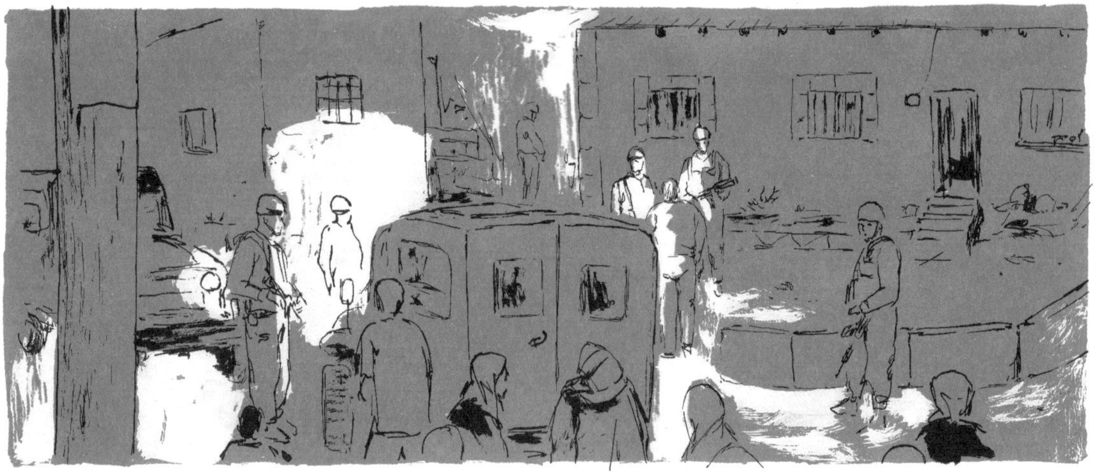

The house is large with many rooms. The men, already awake, are ordered to evacuate.

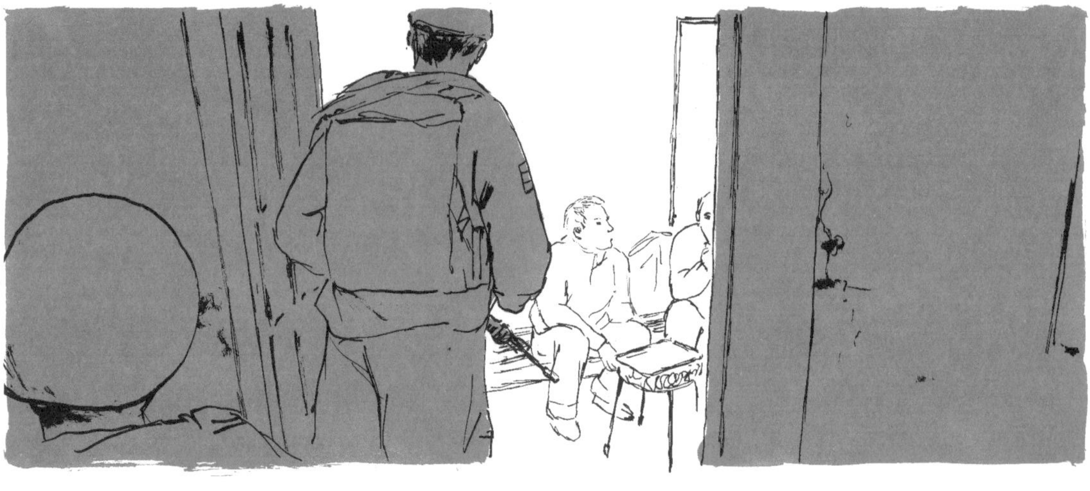

1. Arabic: "you guys" / 2. Arabic: Jews

They start emptying the house: mattresses, pots, chairs,

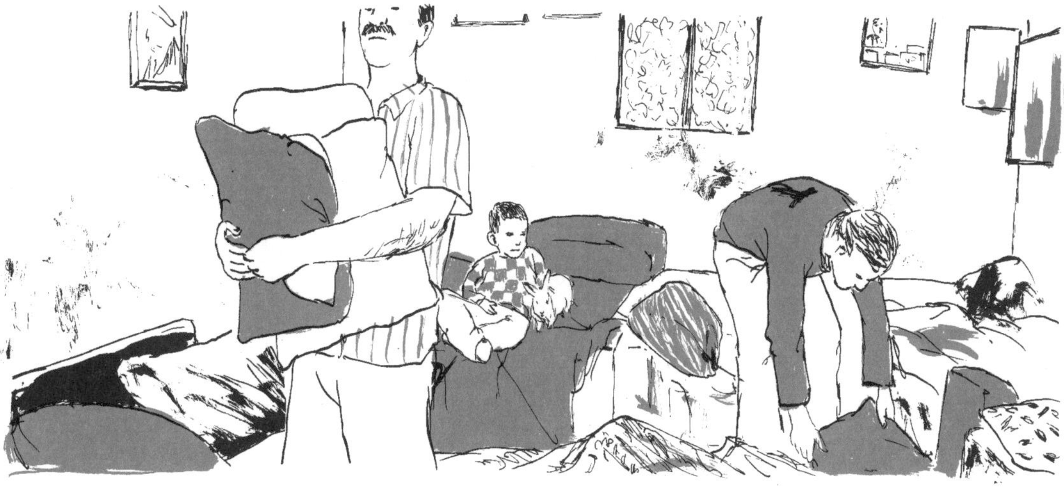

nothing stays. The men work efficiently, passing along furniture and personal effects,

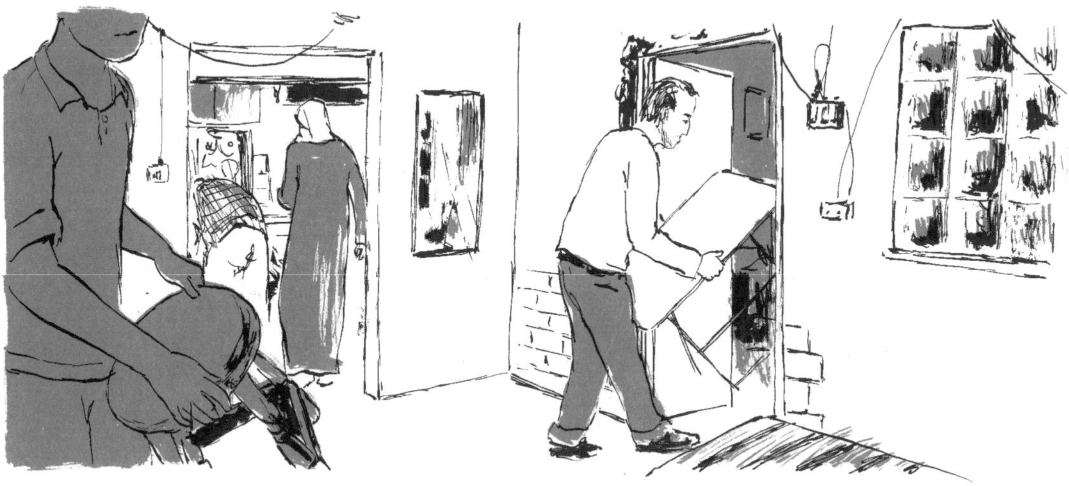

stage hands to their own disaster.

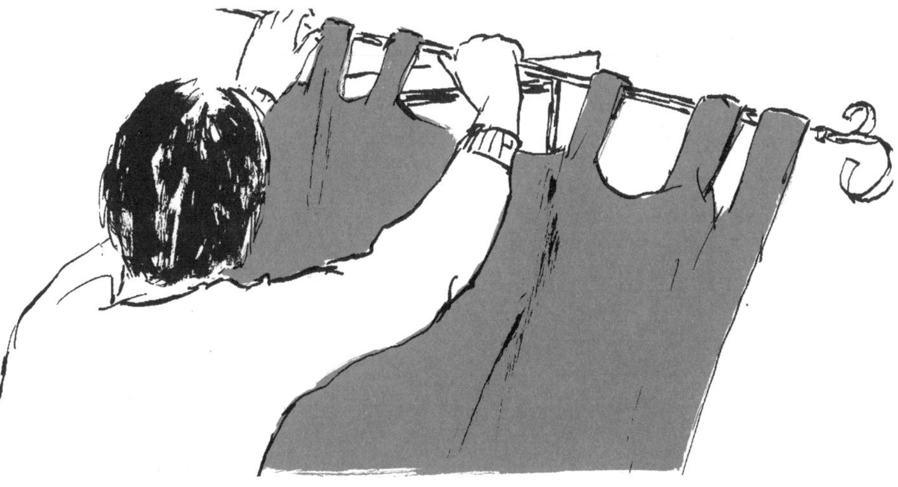

A heavy-set man carrying a giant wardrobe orders his wife, who yells and curses at the soldiers, to keep still.

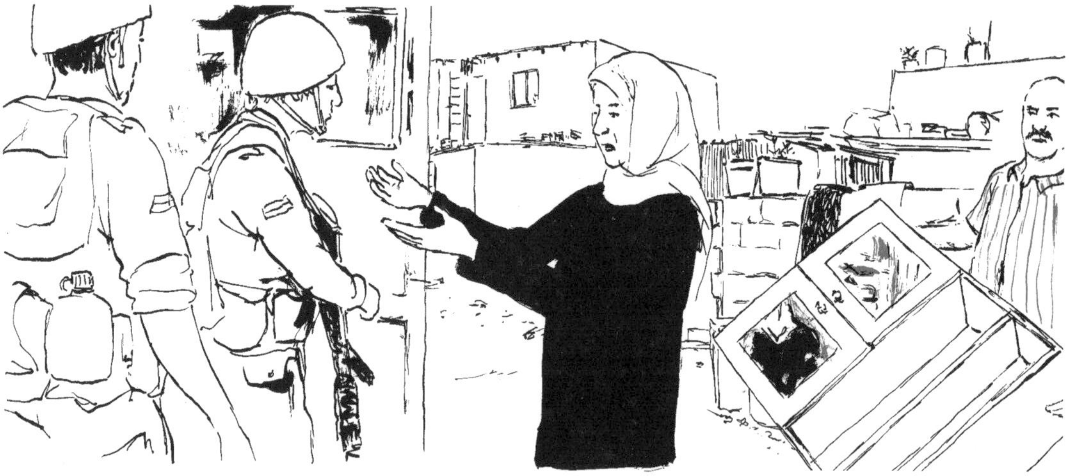

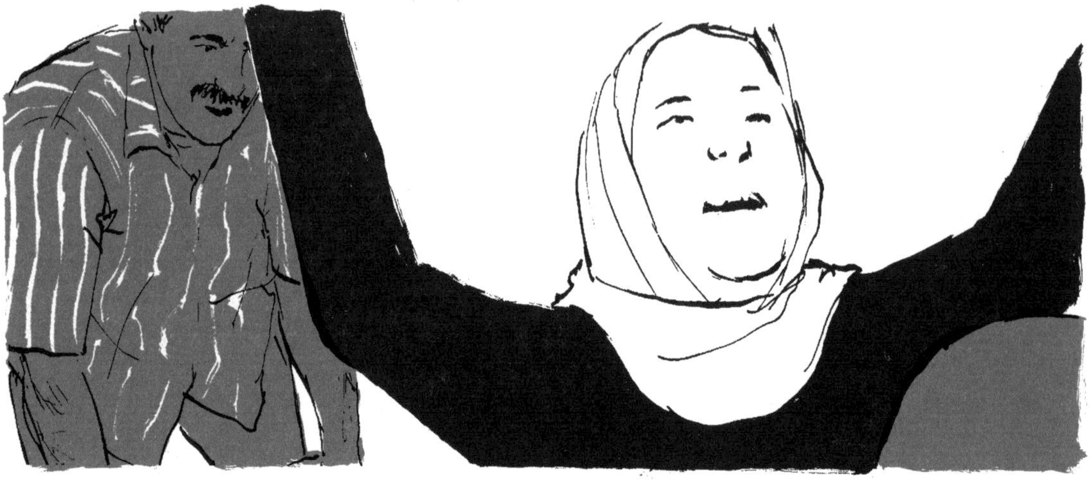

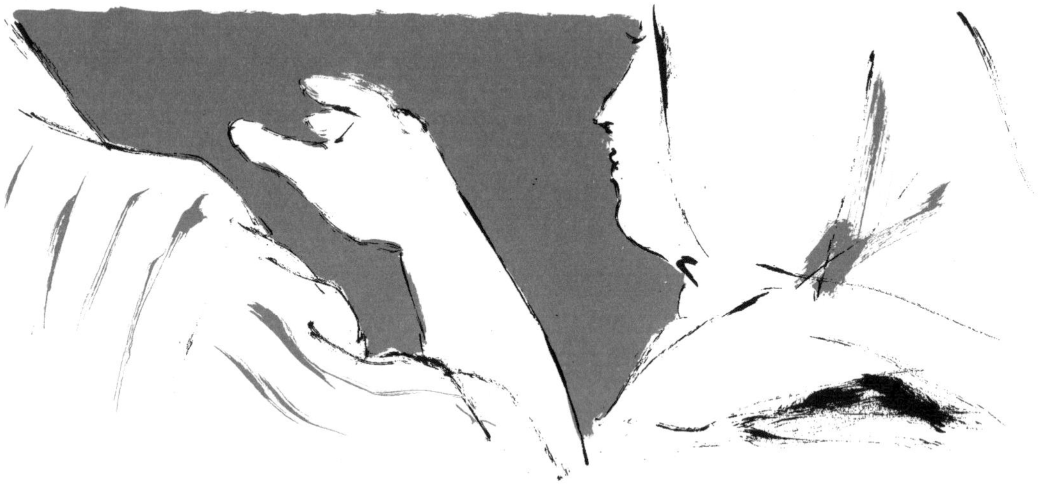

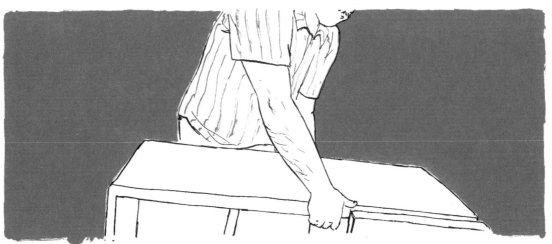

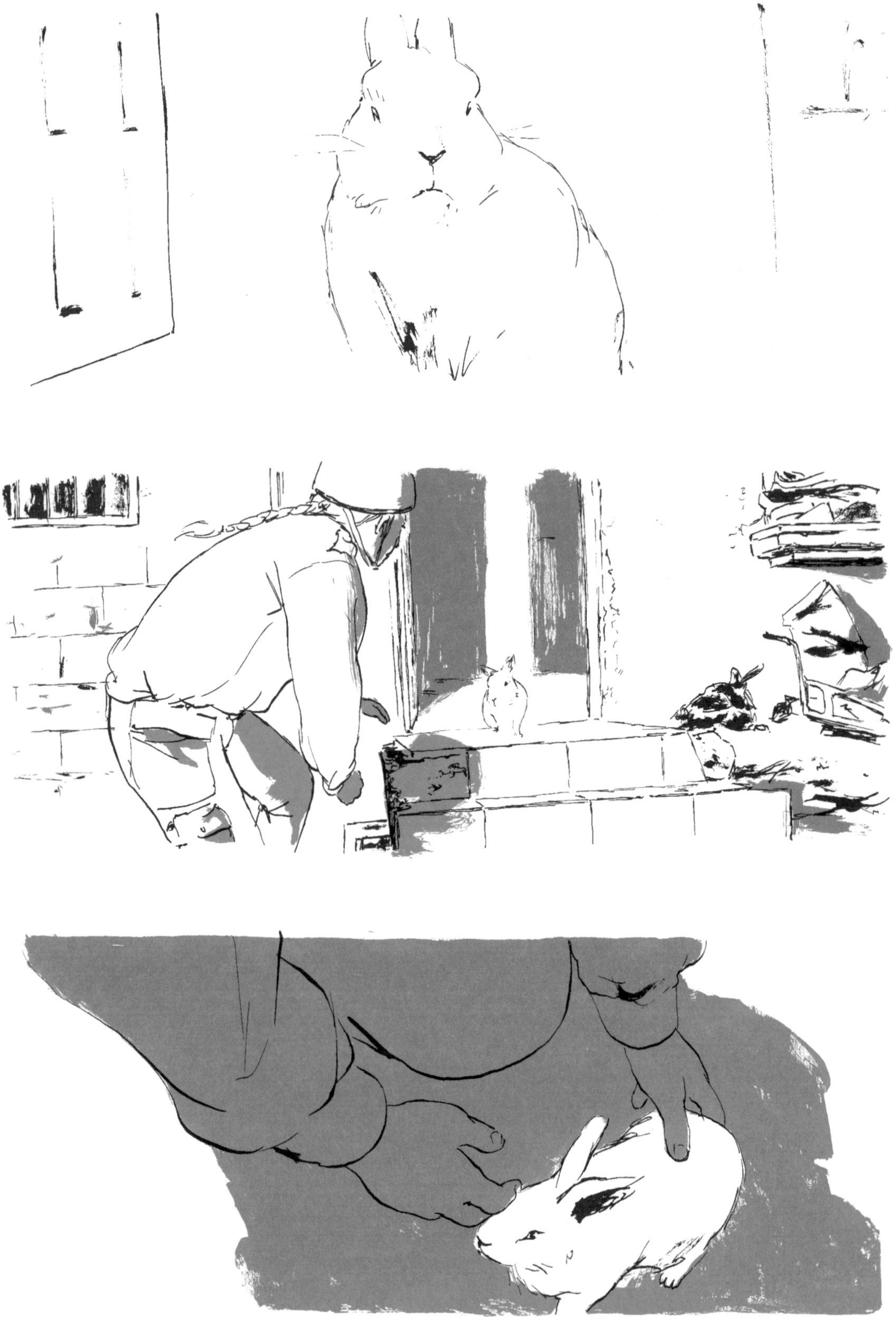

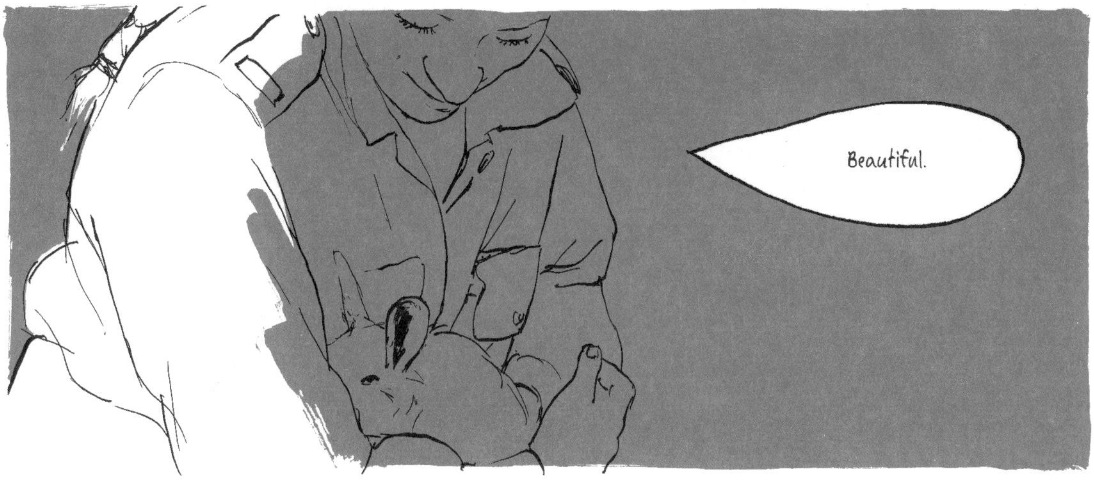
Beautiful.

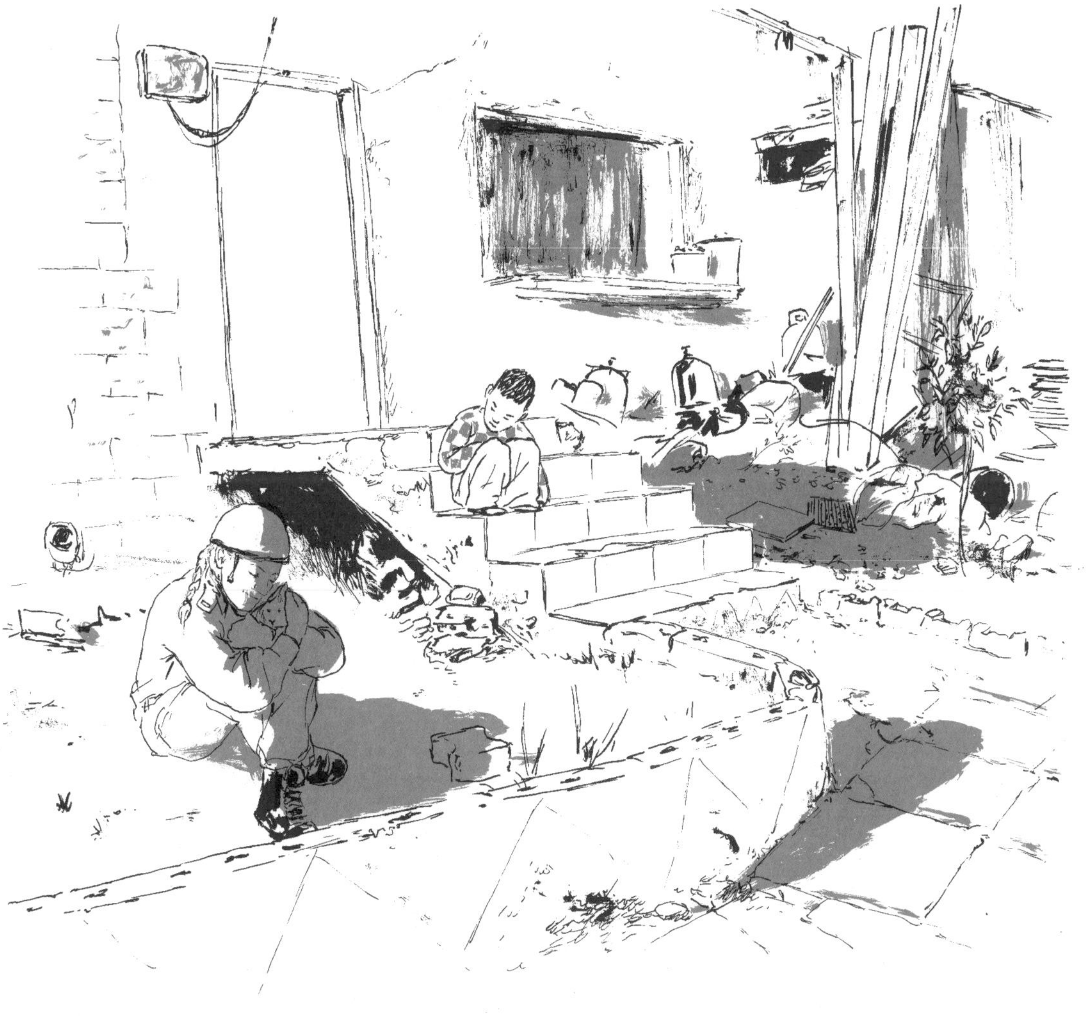

The pale morning shines over the houses, revealing the slopes that close in on the village.

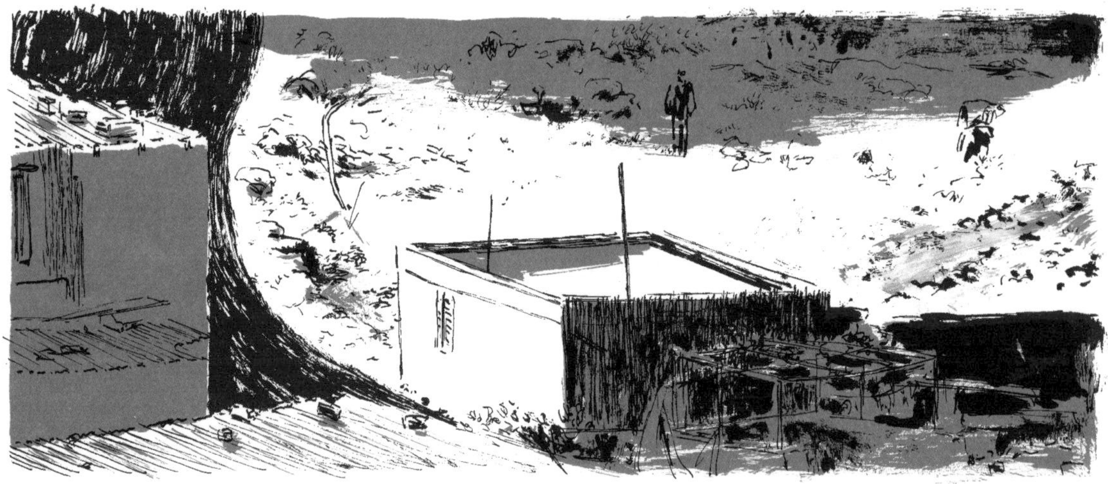

The evacuation is complete.

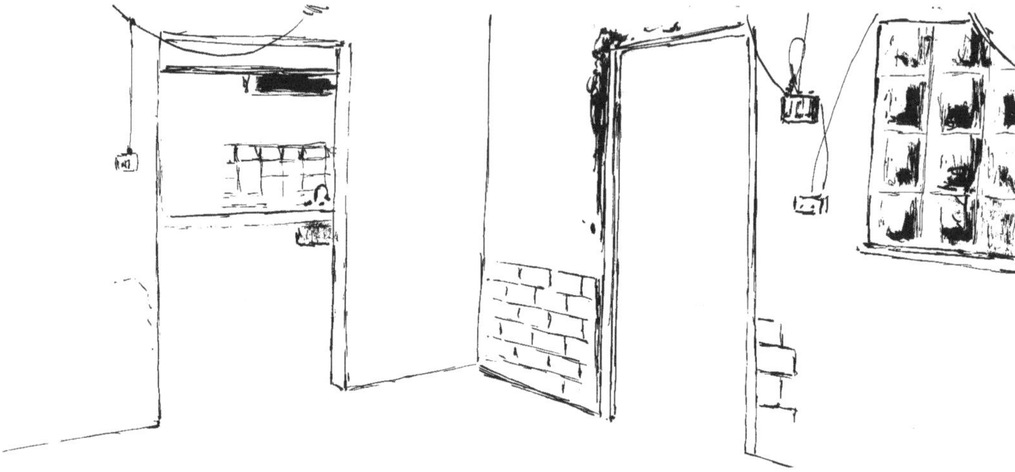

My tired image is reflected back to me from the mirror in the giant wardrobe.

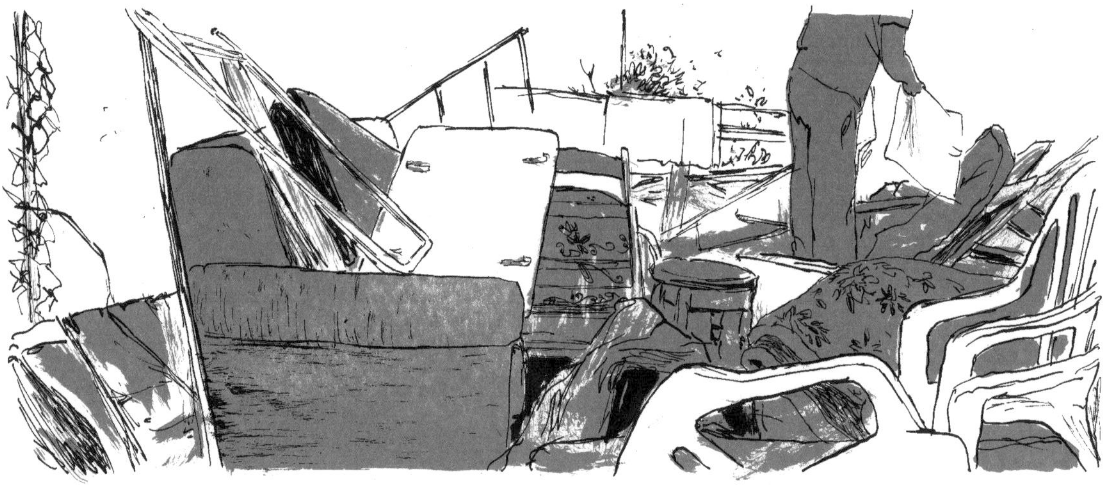

My eyes burn with weariness, thin capillaries wriggling like red earthworms in their white membranes.

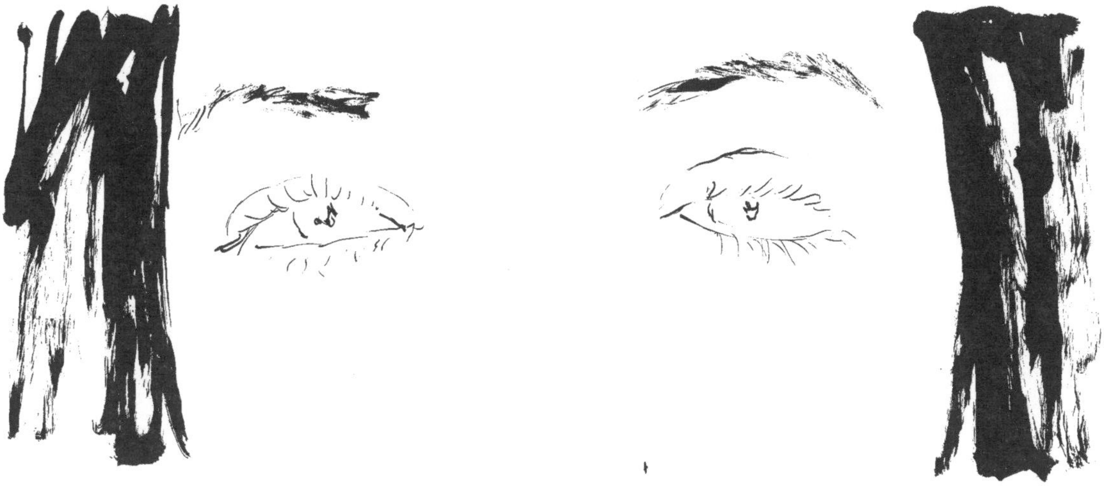

When the Combat Engineering Corps start setting up the explosives, a plump pigeon advances to the roof's edge

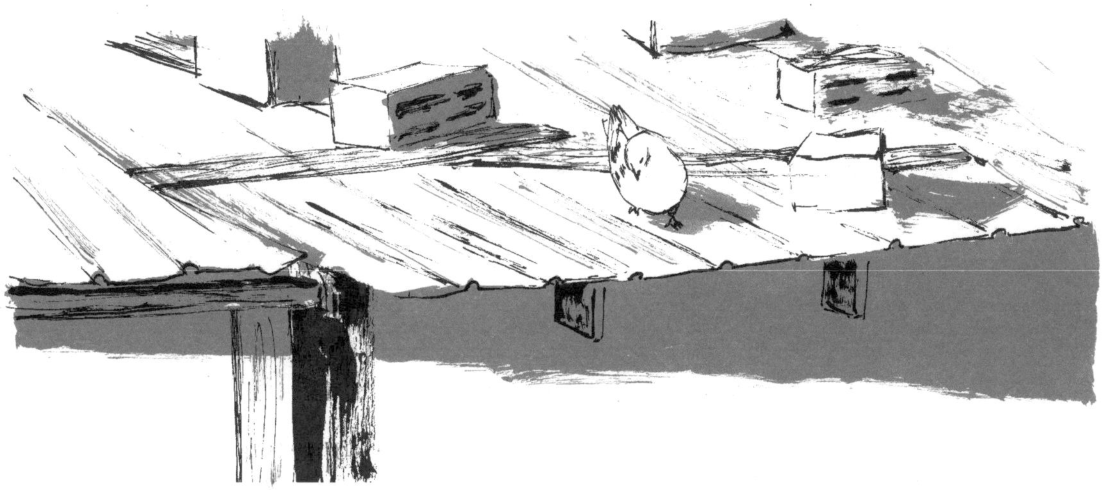

looking down on the proceedings.

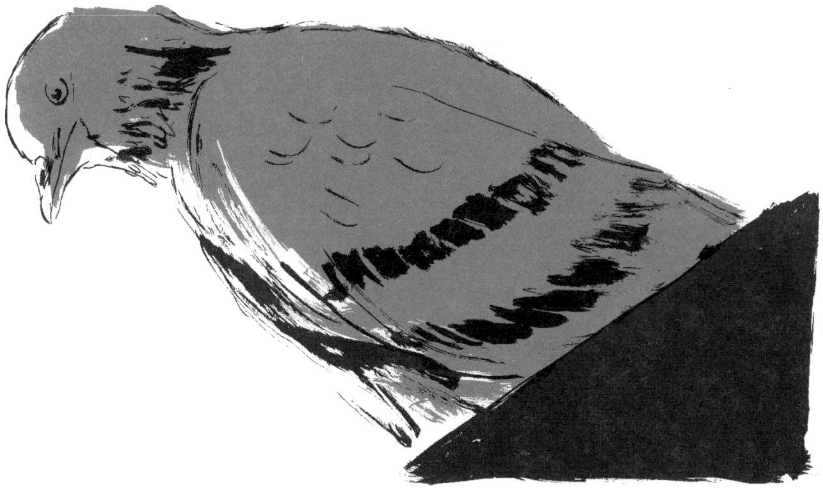

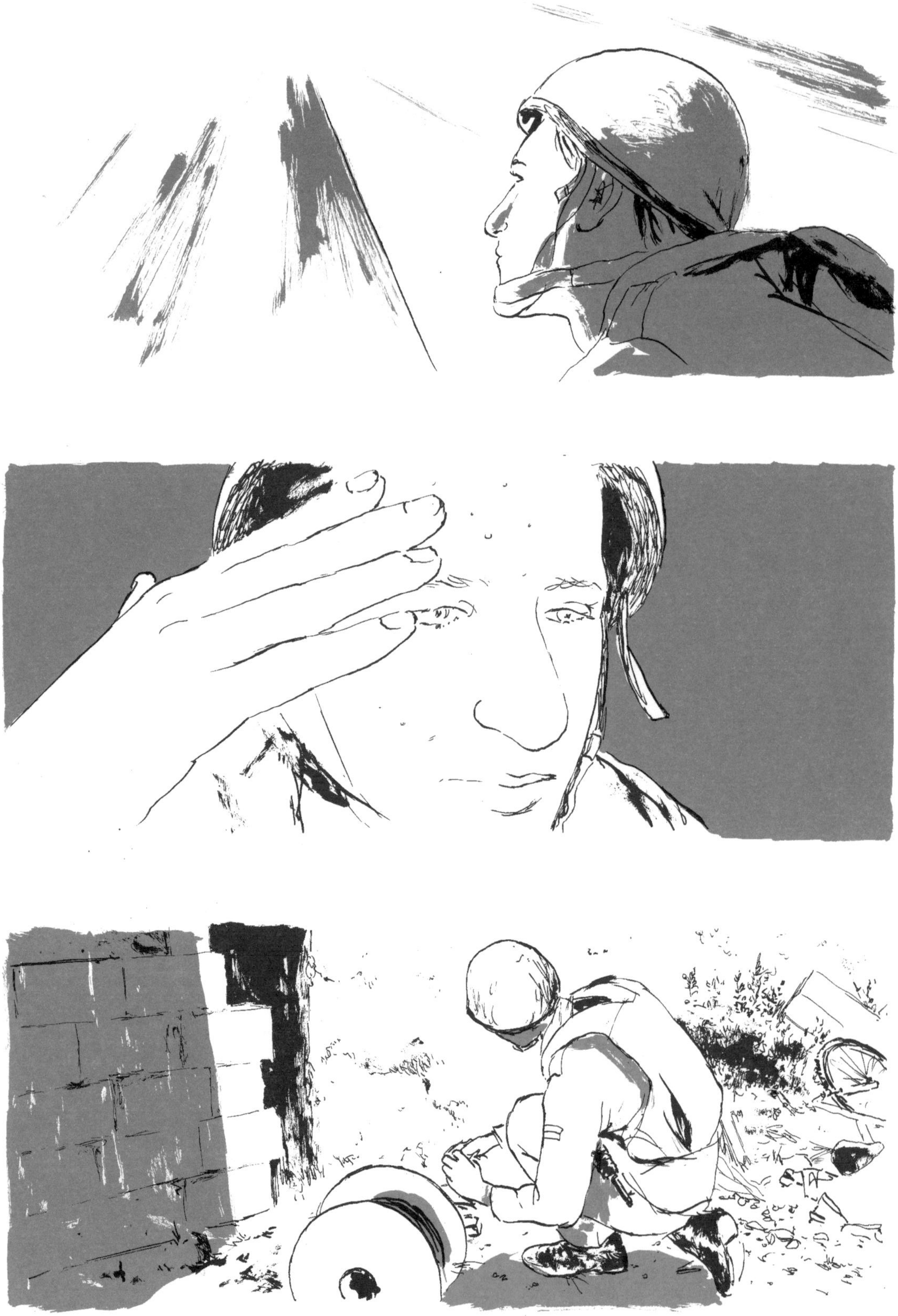

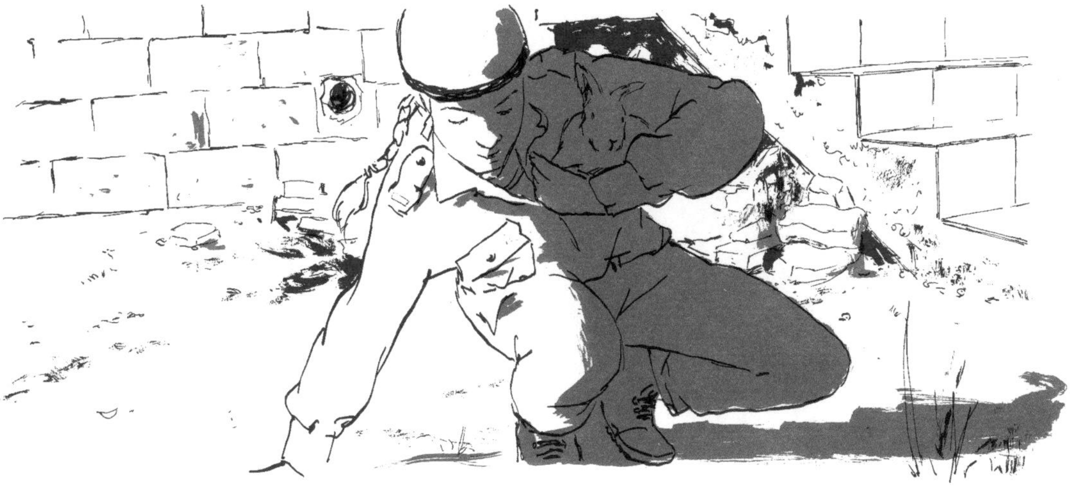

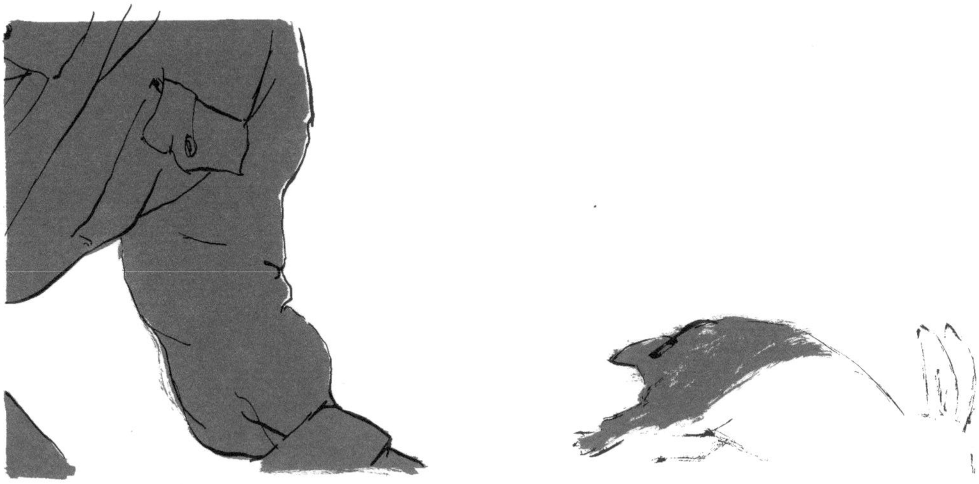

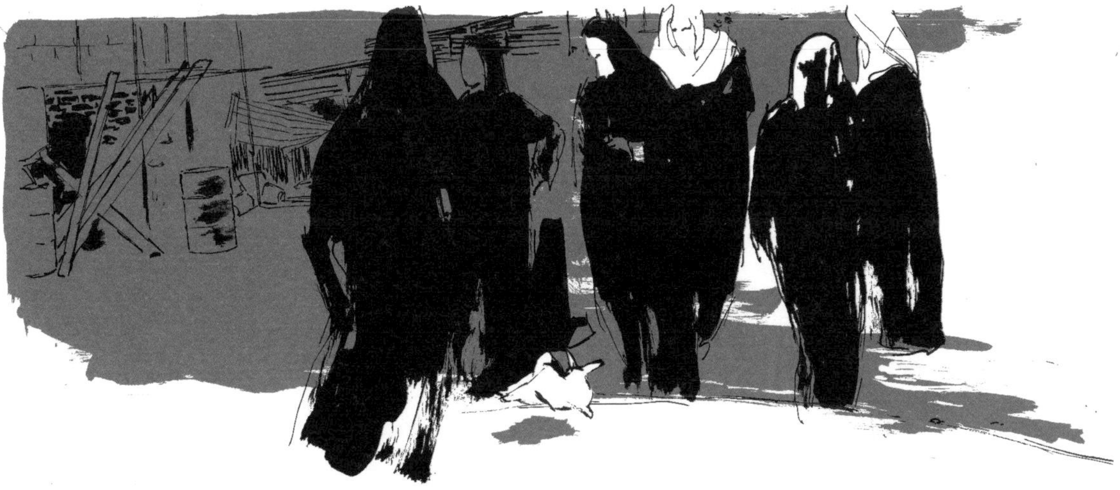

The pigeons depart to other roofs.

Soon, the houses too will fly up into the sky.

BEHIND FARM 54

The graphic novel *Farm 54* is based on three stories written by Galit Seliktar. The stories were first published in Israeli literary magazines and then adapted into a graphic novel by Galit's brother, illustrator Gilad Seliktar. Farm 54 is a real place where both siblings were raised, an actual farm in Ganei-Yohanan – a small village located in Israel's agricultural periphery, which was founded by Jewish immigrants from Russia, Yemen and Libya in the early 1950s. All the stories in *Farm 54* are based on true events which took place between the mid-1970s and late 1980s.

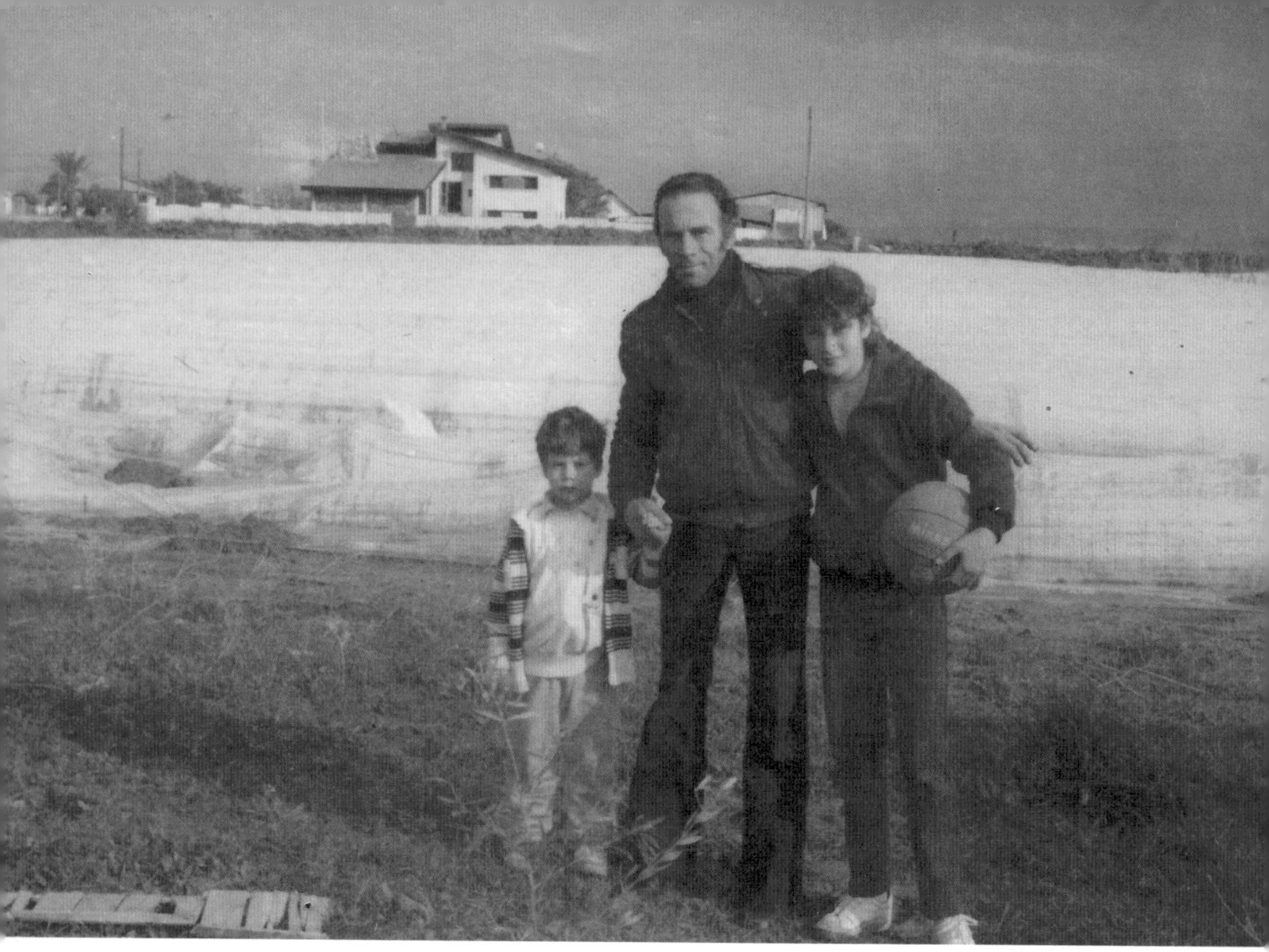

THE SUBSTITUTE LIFEGUARD

Galit & Gilad: This story was the first collaboration between us and the cornerstone of *Farm 54*. It was first published in 2007 as a short graphic story in an Israeli literary magazine, *Masmerim*, and included a framed narrative which is omitted in the book. In that earlier version the story starts with the heroine visiting her brother's grave where she relives his drowning in her mind.

Galit: One afternoon, when Gilad was about two years old, our family was barbequing in the backyard. It was a hot day and my father went to look for one of our dogs he had seen disappear at the far end of the yard, a part covered with high grass and infested with snakes. On his way he passed by our blue fiberglass wading pool and heard heavy spattering. He thought he had found the dog, but it was Gilad, fighting for his life in the half-meter-high chlorinated water. I saw him in my father's arms, fully dressed in his toddler clothes and wet to the bone. Both of them were quiet. The silence broke when my mother started screaming. Only then did we stop eating.

Above: In the background: Farm 54, Winter 1982 [left to right: Gilad Seliktar, Moni Seliktar, Galit Seliktar]
Right: The manure pit and the old cowshed.

Gilad: "The Substitute Lifeguard" was the first time I had ever read any of Galit's stories. I have only a vague recollection of the event itself, but her visual writing style took me back to the pool on some deep emotional level. I was aware of my sister's many years of engagement with visual media such as photography and video, but only when reading about myself in that pool did I realize that her writing was also extremely visual and that the cinematic quality of her texts, along with the themes and settings that were also my own, could form the basis of a powerful collaboration. The first published version of "The Substitute Lifeguard" was very short. The compact format relied on the cemetery frame to create an immediate dramatic impact. In book form, the actual story could gradually unfold without this scaffolding, a device meant to generate sentiments that are yet to be sustained by the plot. As I was adapting and then re-adapting the text into graphic form, I found myself drawn to the cinematic format of a three-panel page that now shapes the entire book, perhaps owing to the way the prose was laid out on paper.

Galit: Of course I had to kill Gilad when I wrote this story. I also chose to transfer the drama from the actual wading pool to a manure pit that my father transformed into a swimming pool. It was part of a cowshed that my parents inherited from the former owner of the farm, together with a young calf. My father immigrated to Israel with his parents from Sofia, Bulgaria, in 1949, and grew up in Jaffa, where he met my mother. This urban boy knew nothing about farming and neither did she. In their first year as farmers my father had a severe allergic reaction to eggplant blossom which terminated his agricultural dreams. The calf froze to death in 1973; the same year my father was enlisted to take part in the war that broke out on Israel's southern border. All the chicks that I used to play with (I was almost three years old at the time) perished from thirst after my mother had left the farm during the war to stay with her parents back in the city. Long after we stopped

using the manure pit as a pool, our dogs used to sneak in through the ruined fence that surrounded it and, every so often, one of them would be found drowned in the rain water that half-filled the pool.

Gilad: Galit's text of "The Substitute Lifeguard" was extremely poetic and saturated with elaborate descriptions. Finding my own voice in this dense story meant mostly condensing and editing out. While I did not change any of Galit's words that made it into *Farm 54*, I did "translate" almost all of the narrative and descriptions into a graphical language, which obeys very different conventions, through my own visual perspective. Yet all my drawings follow closely the original text in terms of plot, description, atmosphere and dialogue. The fact that Galit is my sister was very artistically liberating as I wasn't afraid to explore avenues that I might have hesitated to approach had I been working with someone whose text I'd have to adapt whilst "walking on eggs".

Below: Images from the first version of "The Substitute Lifeguard" in which Noga visits her brother's grave.

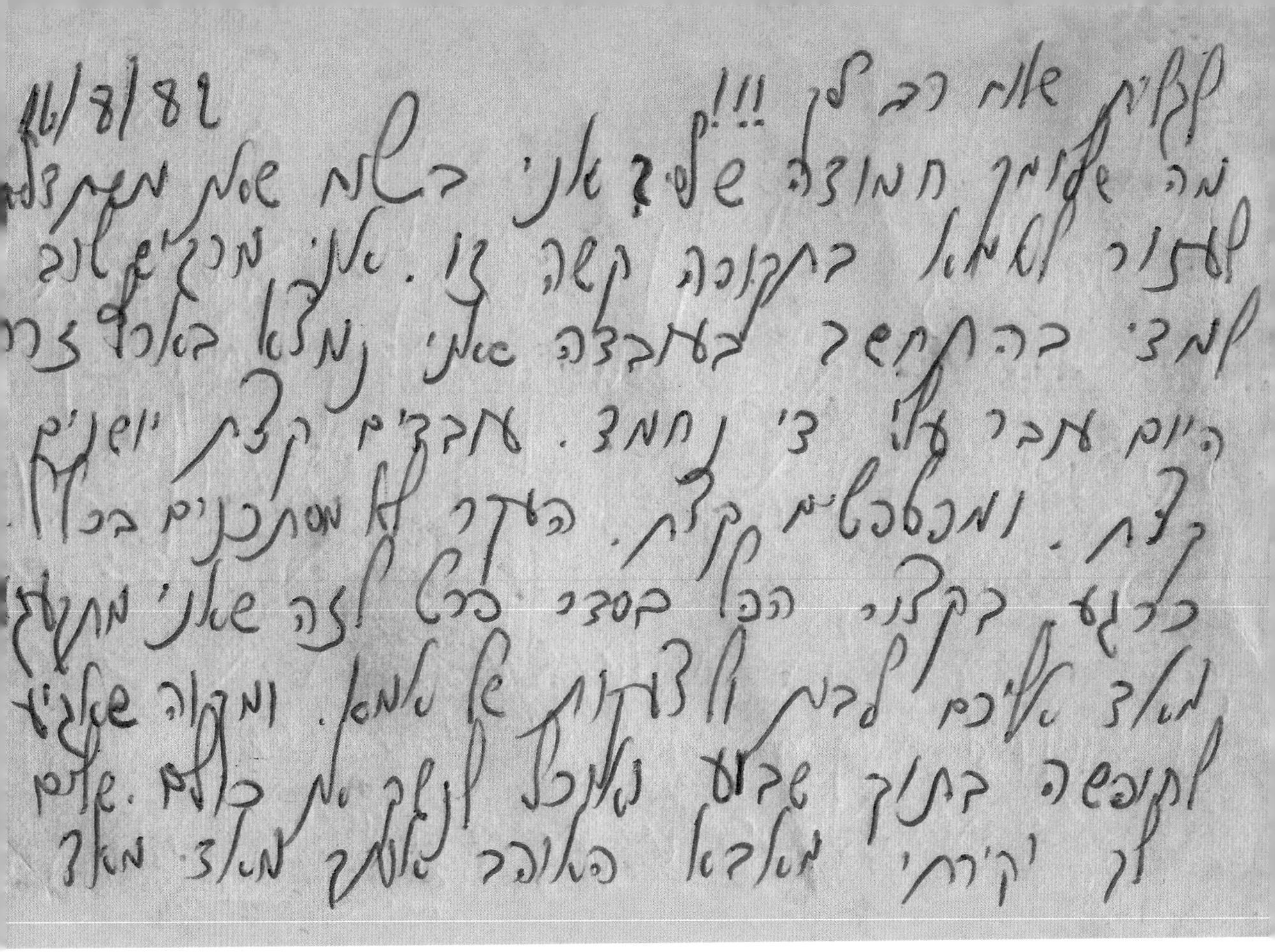

SPANISH PERFUME

Galit: In 1982 my father was enlisted to the First Lebanon War and my mother was left on the farm with four young children. Communication with the northern frontier was carried out through rare phone calls, messages from those who came home to the village for a short vacation and censor-approved green military postcards that my father would send each one of us. When I found some of those postcards several years ago – my mother's, Gilad's and mine – I recalled those chaotic days on the home front and this triggered the writing of "Spanish Perfume". I was reminded that, when my father was away in Lebanon, my mother hit our German Shepherd with the car and then asked me and two of my siblings – Sharon & Oren - to take the dead dog out of the basement and bury it outside. Gilad, the youngest, was forbidden from going down to the basement. I also remember that my mother used to pass the stressful wartime evenings playing cards with "men that nobody wanted at war".

Above: "I am feeling quite well despite the fact that I'm abroad"– A postcard from the First Lebanon War, August 16th 1982.

Gilad: If generally most of my work with Galit's texts involved boiling down, and if the clichés about one image equaling a thousand words have much to sustain them, then there are also many instances where the opposite was the case. Galit's prose version of "Spanish Perfume" began with two brisk lines:

"In the morning Mom ran over our German Shepherd.
In the evening we celebrated my birthday."

This may work powerfully in a short story, but graphically such transitions, between day and night and between different settings, seem artificial. Eventually I devoted five pages to drawing only the first line, replacing the abruptness of the transition in the original with a gradual entry into the graphic narrative. When I first visited the basement for references after years of avoiding it, I was shocked to discover how neglected it was. Filled with piles of rusted tools and other forgotten items, including the wheelbarrow in which the dog was carried for its nocturnal burial. When I was very young my father used the basement as a firing range and I even had the chance to shoot a gun there, a nine millimeter pistol. I remember this basement as being very well organized and dry, as opposed to the neglect and water puddles characterizing it today. I chose to draw the basement as I saw it when working on the book, to capture the atmosphere I recognized in Galit's texts.

Below: "The forbidden basement". On right: the wheelbarrow used for the dog's burial.

HOUSES

Galit: This story is the most autobiographical of all three texts, the most true-to-life. I was drafted to compulsory army service in 1989 during the first Intifadah and, after basic training as an educational non-commissioned officer, I was assigned to a base near Bethlehem. Already on the first night I asked for a transfer away from the occupied territories but, while my request was being processed, I had to remain there for about two weeks. As in the book, on the very first night I went on a nocturnal house demolition mission, replacing another female soldier who did not want to go. The night left its mark on me and for many years I repeatedly retold the events, until I decided to write them as a short story.

With the hindsight of a writer I realized that, beyond the actual events, what was perhaps worse was revealed by the way I described the heroine – as a person completely insulated from the situation and from the suffering of the others. While this dovish character manages to refrain from directly and deliberately harming the Palestinian residents placed under her responsibility, I now think that her (that is, my) decision to obey such orders with little protest is almost as harmful as keen participation.

Gilad: There were parts in this story that I found to be too direct or dramatic, too loud. As I approached it, I decided to lower the volume by giving several scenes an understated

Above: Galit Seliktar during her military service, 1989/1990.

quality, which is more characteristic of my work, as opposed to some of Galit's writing that often tends to be more explicit. One of these scenes was the part where the female officer takes the rabbit from the Palestinian boy. In the original text (and, according to Galit, also in reality during that night in 1989) the boy was crying, asking the officer to give the rabbit back to him. Instead of showing the boy crying I drew him sitting quietly on the stairs, staring at how the officer hugs the animal, holding it close to her chest and cheek. The picture of that lone rabbit took me the greatest number of drafts by far. It was meant to facilitate calming the scene while introducing a charged and frozen silence that captures the moment with all its fear, resentment, and banality.

Right: Photographs from a Palestinian village used as reference for "Houses". Name withheld at residents' request.
Below: An egg-sorting warehouse used as reference for "Houses".

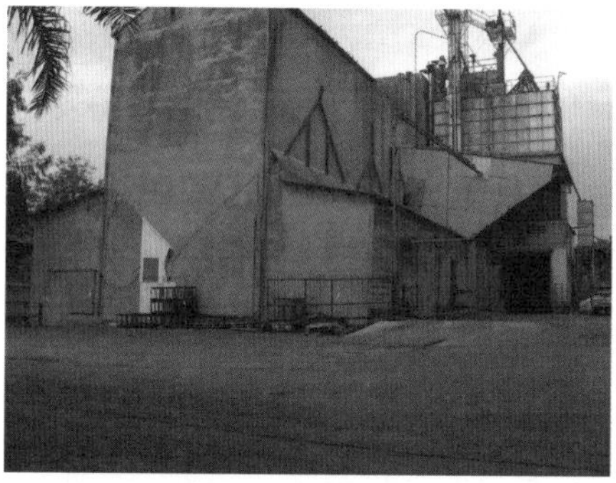

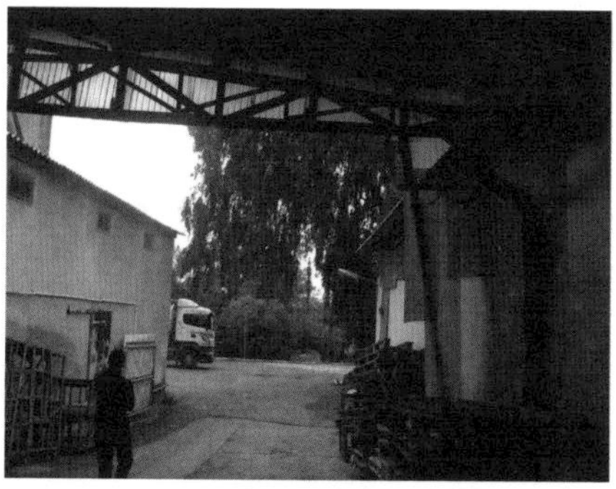

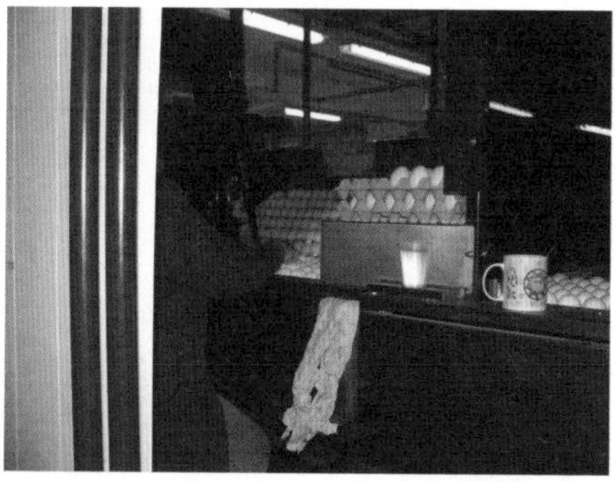

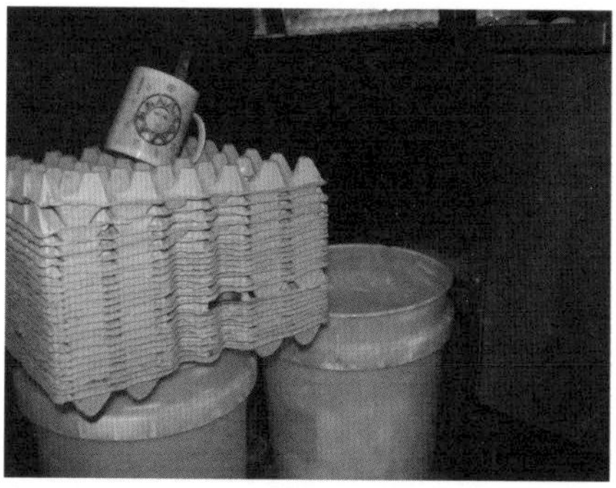

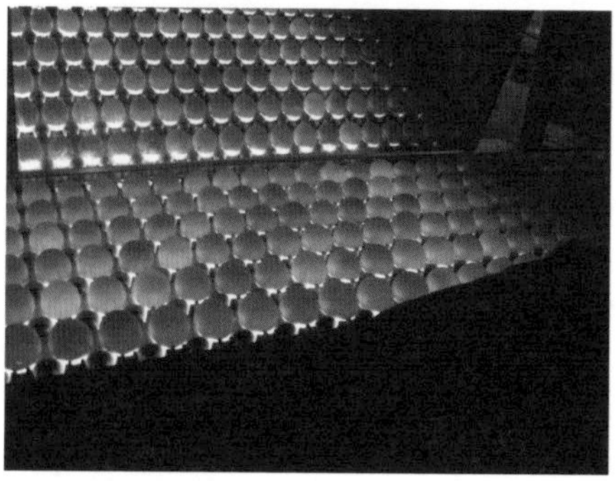

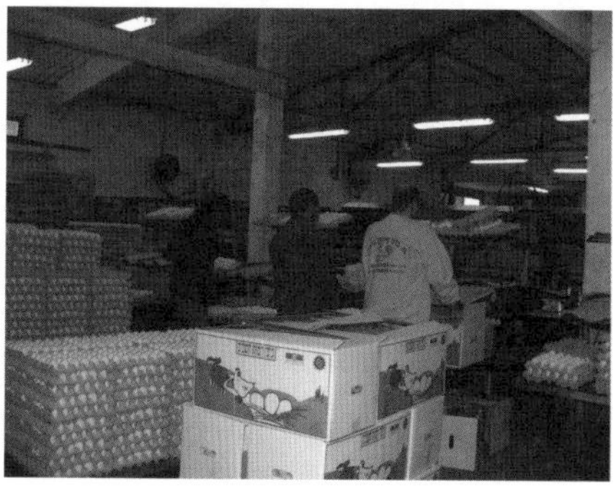

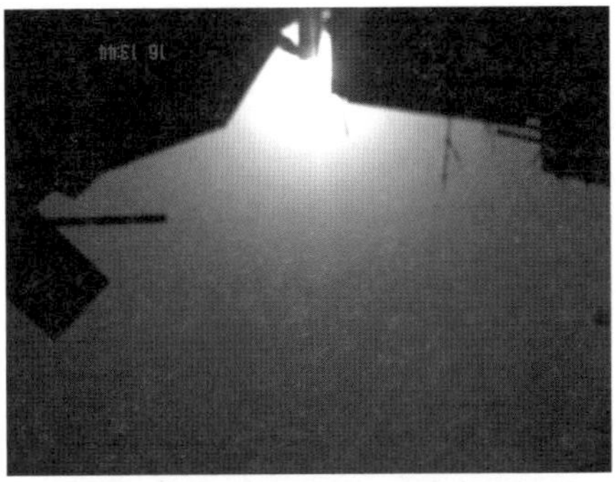
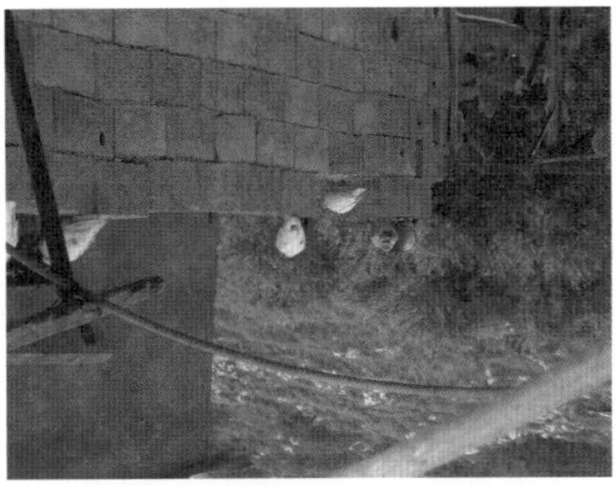
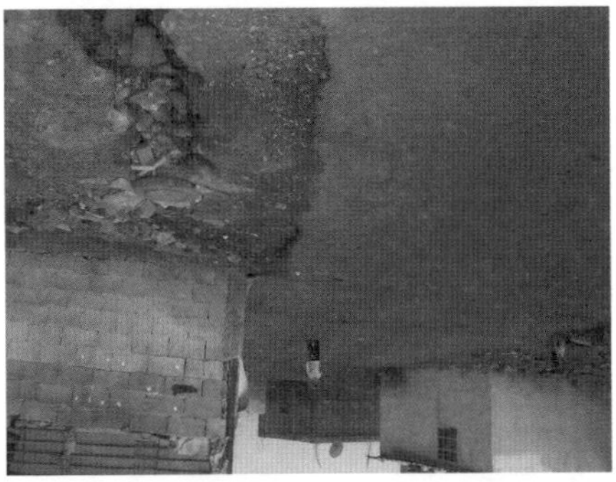
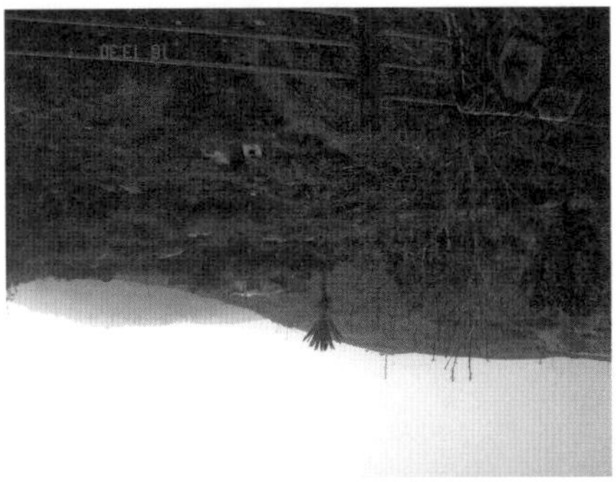
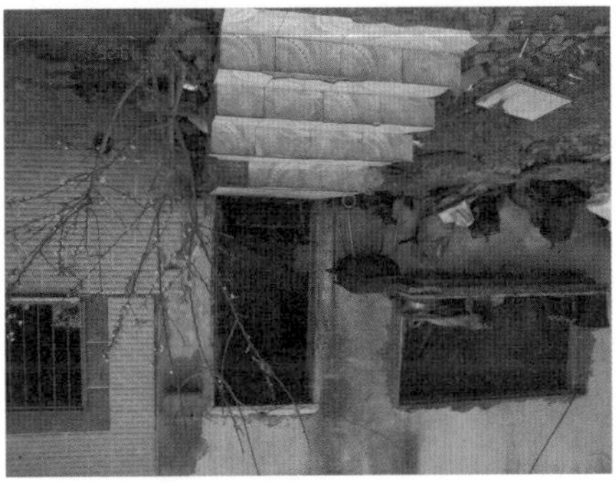
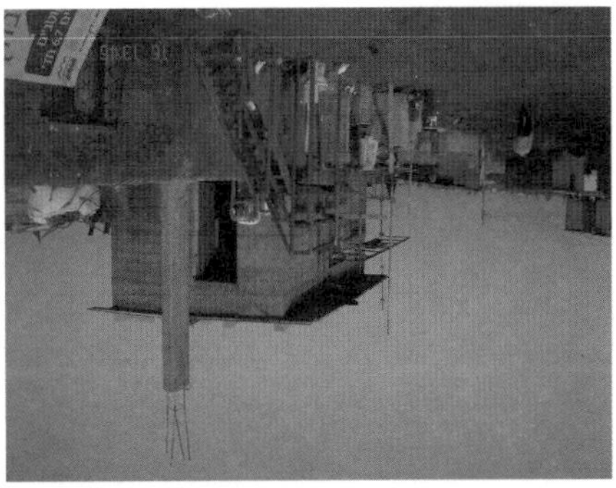
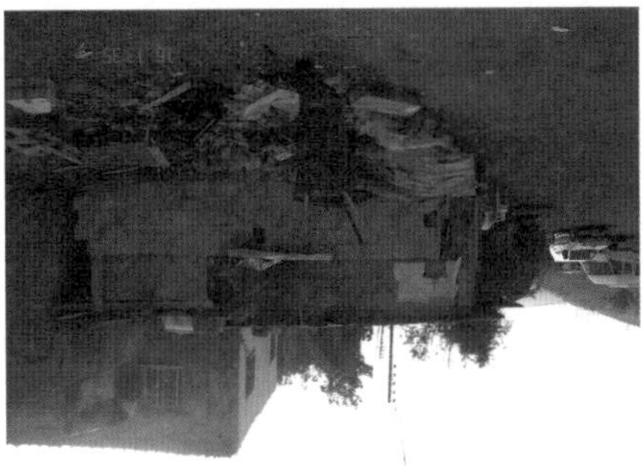
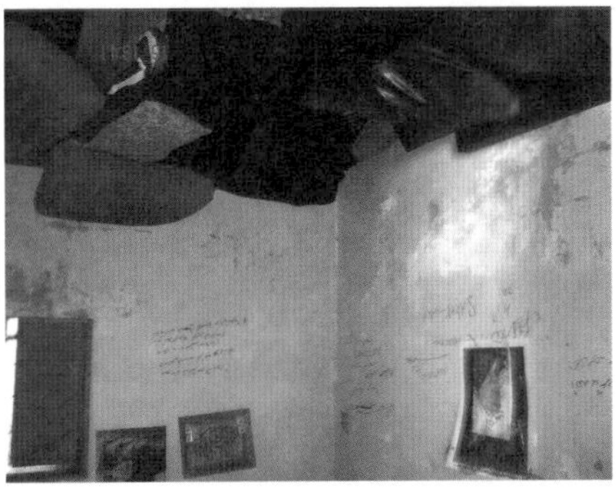

Galit Seliktar, born in 1970 in Jaffa, Israel, has published poems, short stories and comics in prominent literary and cultural magazines in Israel, France, the United States and England. She is the recipient of poetry grants in Israel and Germany. Forthcoming is *In One Thousand Days*, Galit's poem collection, which will be published in Israel by Helicon Poetry Society. Galit leads creative and memoir writing workshops and resides in Princeton, New Jersey, with her husband On Barak and their daughter Tamuz.

Gilad Seliktar, born in 1977 in Rehovot, Israel, is an illustrator and comics artist. His works regularly appear in Israel's leading daily newspapers and magazines, as well as in books and anthologies around the world. Gilad is the author of the graphic novel *Who Are You Anyway* (2005), the black comedy series *Mongol's Demons* (ATRABILE, 2009) and the co-author of the miniseries *The Biographer* (2007, with writer Ohad Tzofi). He is currently working on a remake of *Who Are You Anyway* which will be published in France by Editions çà et là. Gilad lives in Israel with his wife Adi and their dog Keshet, and teaches comics and illustration at **Bezalel Academy of Art and Design** in Jerusalem.

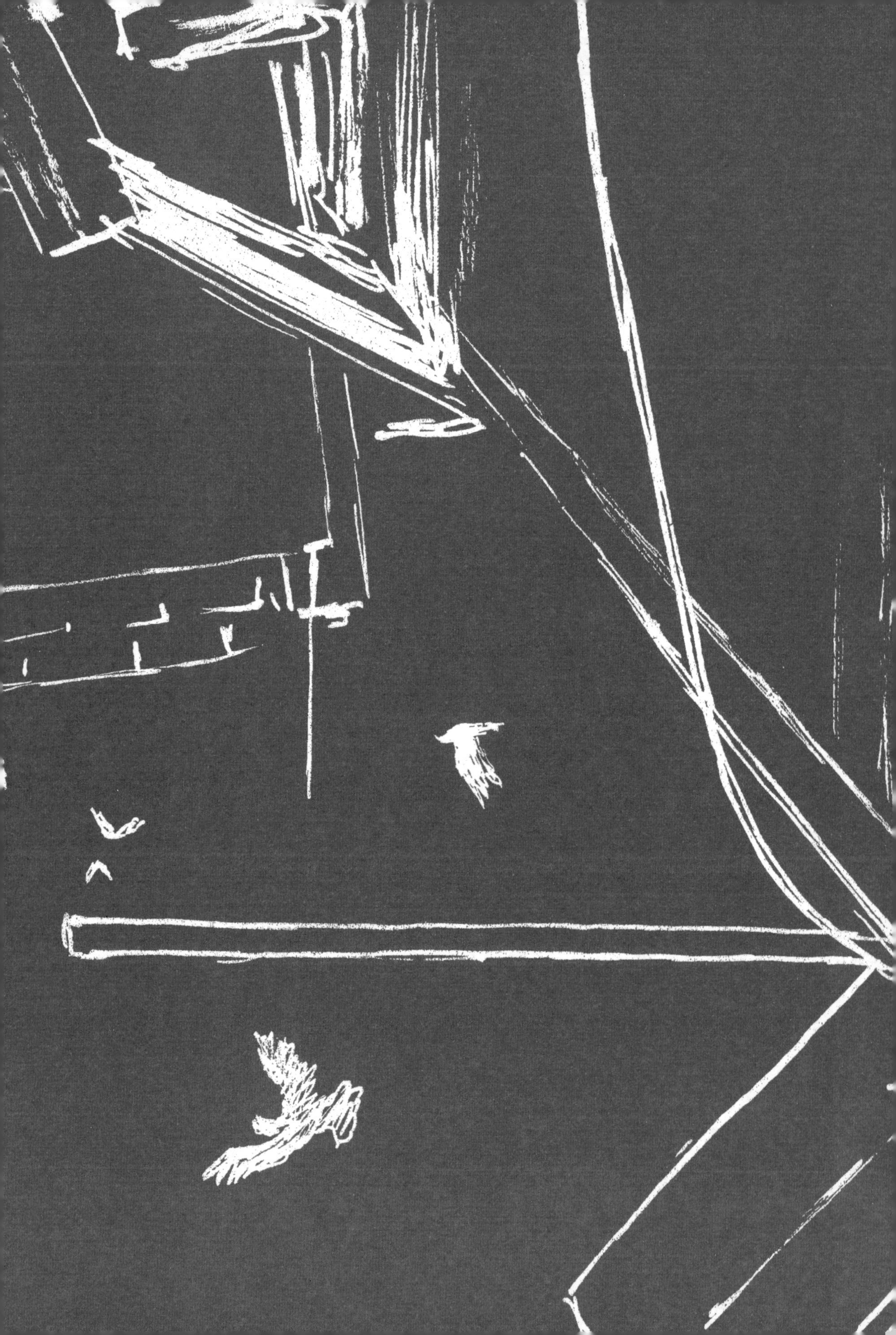